OMAN'S FOREIGN POLICY

OMAN'S FOREIGN POLICY

Foundation and Practice

MAJID AL-KHALILI

PRAEGER SECURITY INTERNATIONAL
Westport, Connecticut • London

Library of Congress Cataloging-in-Publication Data

Al-Khalili, Majid.
    Oman's foreign policy : foundation and practice / by Majid Al-Khalili.
      p. cm.
    Includes bibliographical references and index.
    ISBN 978-0-313-35224-9 (hardback : alk. paper) — ISBN 978-0-313-35225-6 (ebook)
  1. Oman—Foreign relations. 2. Oman—History. I. Title.
    DS247.O65A4 2009
    327.5353—dc22   2009006527

British Library Cataloguing in Publication Data is available.

Library of Congress Catalog Card Number: 2009006527
ISBN: 978-0-313-35224-9

First published in 2009

Praeger Security International, 88 Post Road West, Westport, CT 06881
An imprint of Greenwood Publishing Group, Inc.
www.praeger.com

Printed in the United States of America

∞

The paper used in this book complies with the
Permanent Paper Standard issued by the National
Information Standards Organization (Z39.48–1984).

10 9 8 7 6 5 4 3 2 1

I humbly dedicate this book to my parents

Contents

Acknowledgments

I could not have produced this work without the help of many people. I thank Professor Onuf for his kindness, encouragement, and personal attention; Professor MacDonald for his seemingly limitless patience and infectious positive attitude; and most especially, Professor Mesbahi for being my mentor and guide over the course of my studies—he was generous with his time and insights, and for these, as well as the countless discussions that have greatly expanded my knowledge, I am eternally grateful. I also thank Professor Olson for his constructive criticism

I am particularly happy to thank Jane MacDonald for proofreading my work; the Dissertation Year Fellowship, without which this research would not have been possible; and all my friends and colleagues in the Department of International Relations at Florida International University.

I would not, however, have been able to complete this book had I not been invited to the Middle East Center at the University of Oxford. I had the privilege of researching at that institute while at the same time traveling back and forth to the British Public Records Office investigating original materials. The generous support I received from both institutions made this work possible. The staff members at the Library of Congress were also of immense help, and I am grateful for their professionalism.

Good friends also have encouraged and supported me in my efforts these last few years. Thank you, Alla Mirzoyan—if not for your intelligent and practical advice, this work would never have progressed as quickly as it has. I am inspired by your strength, energy, and positive attitude. Thank you, Alex Barder, for sufficiently diverting my attention away from the difficult task at hand with your interesting discussions of political theory. Thank you, Fabian Romero, for prodding me along with your quick wit and good humor. Your solid advice, too, has served me well. Thank you, Serge Akl, for challenging all of my assumptions during those long hours at the blue tables. I am especially happy to thank Andy Correa and the Correa family for suffering my numerous visits to their home. Indeed, the Correas' house became my second home, where I could always expect a warm welcome, a good meal, and good company that bore with me when I incessantly talked about my work. I am deeply indebted to Andy's pragmatic advice, encouragement, and strong belief in the value of this work. Thank you, Cecilia Novella, for your gentle and patient companionship. Thank you, Fernanda Soto, for all the happy times and for your encouragement. Thank you, Ronald, Uri, and Emily, for the coffee breaks. Finally, thank you, Darwish Kaiyal, for being my friend.

Introduction

The Persian Gulf region has been one of the most sensitive and tumultuous areas in international politics in the last three decades. Indeed, this is not unexpected, given the strategic importance of the area, its rich resources, the graveness of the Arab-Israeli conflict, and the tensions of three Gulf wars. A wealth of literature has arisen on Arab governments and politics, ideology and state building, political evolution and intellectual trends that is instantly recognizable. However, as Korany and Dessouki point out in *The Foreign Policy of Arab States*,[1] literature on the foreign policy of Arab states is notably lacking. Hinnebusch and Ehteshami reach a similar conclusion in their *Foreign Policies of the Middle East States*.[2] If this inopia exists for such major regional states such as Egypt, Syria, and Saudi Arabia, the dearth of studies on Oman's foreign policy can hardly be surprising.

British expatriates have dominated the literature on Oman,[3] and their writings are fascinating testaments to the complexities of Oman's history. They offer valuable insights. Nonetheless, they remain the products of participant-authors, especially British soldiers serving Sultan Said during his campaign to quell the Imamate challenge of the 1950s and to resolve the 1965–1975 war in Dhofar. This literature, however, is less about Oman than it is about its military operations and the intricacies of counterinsurgency.[4]

John Peterson's *Oman in the Twentieth Century*[5] and John Wilkinson's *The Imamate Tradition of Oman*[6] arguably constitute the most important works on Oman. Both, however, only touch on Oman's foreign policy, and even Calvin Allen's *Oman: The Modernization of the Sultanate*[7] allocates only ten pages to Muscat's external relations. Carol Riphenburg's *Oman: Political Development in a Changing World*[8] devotes a chapter to Oman's foreign policy but relies exclusively on secondary sources, especially Anthony Cordesman[9] and Joseph Kechichian.[10]

Dissertations are not helpful either. They tend to focus on 1) Oman's history in Africa,[11] 2) the political economy of the Sultanate,[12] and 3) British and American involvement in Oman.[13]

One exception is Kechichian's study on the Sultanate's foreign policy *Oman and the World: The Emergence of an Independent Foreign Policy*,[14] which chronicles the Sultanate's external relations between 1970 and 1995. Kechichian recounts Oman's major challenges: 1) facing the insurgency in Dhofar, 2) relating to the Gulf Cooperation Council, 3) reacting to the Soviet invasion of Afghanistan, 4) avoiding sides in the Iran-Iraq war, and 5) positioning itself in the Arab-Israeli conflict. His conclusion emphasizes that Oman has practiced an unusually independent foreign policy.

Despite its value, Kechichian's study cannot avoid the shortcomings symptomatic of the literature on Oman: the almost total absence of analysis of the foreign policy of the period of Sultan Said (the father of the present Sultan and ruler of Oman from the 1930s until his overthrow in 1970). Interestingly, it appears that the 1930–1970 period shaped Omani foreign policy more than it is generally appreciated.

In sum, we see little substantial treatment of Oman's foreign policy in the early or formative period (1930–1970) and even less—literally nothing—on its foreign policy after 1996. Therefore, the purpose of this research is not only to revisit and reanalyze the foreign policy of the Sultanate of Oman from early twentieth century through the mid-1990s, but also to extend the account through 2004.

APPROACH TO ANALYSIS

This study examines published materials on Oman and includes the literature of various academic disciplines, such as international relations, history, geography, sociology, and diplomatic history. English and Arabic sources have been consulted in this research.

The unique contribution of this research lies in the extensive use of primary sources, including archival materials collected by the author at the British Public Records Office, the Middle East Center at the University of Oxford, and the Library of Congress. Significantly for the reader, the archival references will be footnoted, indicating the title, the year, and, when possible, the author of the source.

1 ⸻⸻⸻⸻⸻⸻⸻⸻⸻⸻

The Legacy of History

THE GEOGRAPHY OF OMAN

The history of Oman has been shaped by three recurrent themes: the tribal world, the history of the Ibadi imamate, and the struggle between inhabitants of Oman and foreigners over control of Oman's coastal provinces. The name of the modern state until the reign of Sultan Qaboos, the Sultanate of Muscat and Oman, calls attention to these three themes.[1] Equally important in shaping Oman's history is the geography of the region. The modern state is bordered by the Republic of Yemen and Saudi Arabia on its western boundaries and in the north by the United Arab Emirates, while its shores overlook the Persian Gulf, the Gulf of Oman and the Arabian Sea. Oman is almost an island. The vast desert of the Rub al-Khali, or Empty Quarter, separates it from the rest of the Arabian Peninsula. It is no wonder that the country has long looked outward to the Indian Ocean, South Asia, and East Africa, while it has simultaneously looked inward to the Arab world. The "seaborne influence of trade and overseas expansion has traditionally competed with the landborne influences of tribalism (a consequence of Arab immigration) and Islam (culmination in the imamate structure)."[2] Partly because of the geography of Oman, two traditions have evolved. The first tradition is that of the "interior" and is commonly described as inward looking and governed in accordance with Ibadi Islam. The second tradition is that of Muscat, which sees Oman as a "commercial, maritime power, whose merchants traded from one end of the monsoon world to the other, from China to the Sofala coast in East Africa, at least as far back as the eighth century A.D., and which periodically developed an overseas empire."[3] This expansion left the state with an exclave of territory in Gawadur on the Pakistani Makran coast until 1958, and an East African community centered on Zanzibar that was ruled by the Dynasty of Al-Bu Said until the rebellion of 1964.[4]

"Oman" did not always mean the same geographic region as it currently encompasses.[5] The Dhofar region became part of Oman only under Sultan Said in 1829. Conversely, the Arabian Gulf coast of geographical Oman, formerly called Peninsular Oman, Trucial Oman, or the Trucial Coast, has gradually disengaged itself from political affiliation with the rest of Oman. In 1971, it became the independent federation of the United Arab Emirates.[6] The British political resident at the Gulf from 1953 to 1958 recorded in his book *Footnotes in the Sand* that

> the nomenclature is confusing. In my time the state was referred to as 'Muscat' in all ordinary usage. 'Oman' was generally used for the interior. In order to emphasize the sovereignty of the Sultan over the whole area, the more formal term came to be 'Muscat and Oman'. Now 'Oman' has been adopted as the name of the whole state. Confusion is increased by the occasional use of the term 'Trucial Oman' in earlier records to cover the area of the Trucial States, now known as the United Arab Emirates.[7]

Defining the geographical boundaries of Oman is made even more difficult by the references made to the Sultan of "Muscat and Oman" as opposed to the "Imamate of Oman." Writing about the Imamate territories and boundaries throughout much of the twentieth century, a British expert on the region commented that the boundaries of the Imamate simply cannot be defined with exactitude, because of the absence of agreements with adjacent states indicating the extent of national territories.[8] The name Oman, just like most names of geographical regions, may be used in numerous ways, depending upon who is using it and the context in which it occurs. By and large, the name Oman is customarily applied "to the whole of the great bulge of the Arabian Peninsula between the Trucial Coast on the Persian Gulf and that part of the southern coast of Arabia running from Ras al-Hadd to the vicinity of the island of Masirah."[9] This usage is evidenced in the application by Westerners of the name Gulf of Oman to the arm of the Arabian Sea on which the city of Muscat is located. In eastern Arabia itself, however, most of the inhabitants use the name Oman only to refer to the interior of the bulge. As such, Muscat lies outside Oman, and so does Batinah, the region northwest of Muscat between the mountains and the sea. Accordingly, Oman begins at the mountains of the Hajar, the chain that sweeps down along a course roughly parallel to the outer edge of the bulge.[10]

Generally, Imamate authority extended to what has been termed Oman proper, the boundaries of which are formed by the Jabel al-Akhdar (Green Mountain) massif of the Hajar Range in the east and the Rub al-Khali desert in the west. To the north, Oman proper gives way to al-Dhahirah province somewhat south of Ibri; to the south, Oman proper extends to al-Sharqiya province and the Wahibah Sands. The domains of the Sultan on the other hand are composed of 1) the district of Muscat and Matrah, 2) the long stretch of coast called the Batinah between the Western Hajar and the sea, 3) the northern peninsula known as Rus al-Jibal, 4) territories in the vicinity of Ras al-Hadd, and 5) the region of Dhofar to the east of Hadhramaut.[11]

Within the domain of the Imamate's authority, the area of the interior, traditionally referred to as Oman, lies in the

> uneroded limestone plateau of the Jabal [this is the Jabel Al-Akhdar, or the Green
> Mountain] ... the ultimate bastion of the Omani fortress ... but it is the villages of
> the Ghadaf, Jauf and 'Sumail Gap' which are the real heartland of Oman and the spe-
> cific area to which the name Oman tends to apply.[12]

The economy of this area was determined and developed in pre-Islamic times by Persian settlers who, in the tradition of Persia and Central Asia, used tunnels, or qanats, for irrigation. The Persian population was initially challenged by the immigration of various Arab tribes into Oman in the pre-Sassanid times of the second century AD. With the rise of Islam, the Persian ruling class was evicted from Oman. Power transferred to the Arabs. Within a few years, however, the Caliphs abandoned direct administration of Oman. For much of the ensuing 150 years, Oman was left to the Julands, who had ruled before the rise of Islam.[13]

The Persian settlers' introduction of qanat tunnels helped create a "village" life, rather than a strictly nomadic one. As a result, Oman evolved differently from many of the other Arab Gulf states. To understand the difference, two terms must be explained: Bedu and Hadar. The first refers to the Bedouin, who are the nomads of the desert. The second refers to the settled population, or town dwellers. In Oman, the Hadar culture became dominant, while in Gulf societies, norms and customs were mainly acquired through the Bedu culture. The political history of Oman and the rest of Eastern Arabia attest to this difference. Arab Gulf states became distinct political entities in relatively recent times, while the acknowledgment of a legitimate central authority in Oman has long been an established tradition. As Peterson asserts,

> While the culture of the Gulf largely emanates from the desert, Omani culture has
> grown out of a long history of continuous cultivation, predating the arrival of the
> Arab tribes and complemented by the country's ancient traditions as a secure fastness
> for the Ibadi sect of Islam against a wide range of both Islamic and European
> invaders.[14]

OMAN AND IBADISM

The roots of Ibadi Islam, the most significant force in Omani politics, emerged in Iraq's Basra. There the foundations of a "national" concept that would eventually take hold in Oman developed. Al-Basra was the center for the Arabs of the Persian Gulf during Islam's Empire of the East. One of the most important tribes to settle in Basra was the Azd Arabs from central Oman. Omani Azds were granted a section of Basra, where they could settle and attend to their needs and those of subsequent Omani migrants. By the end of Muawiyah's reign, the Azd of Basra became one of the most formidable groups in the eastern Caliphate. Under their general, Muhallab bin Abi Sufrah, the Azd extended the power of Islam to Khursan and fought the Khawariji (those who seceded from the true path), whose heresy is universally acknowledged among all surviving Islamic sects.[15]

The Khawarij had three main sects: the Azariqa, the Suriya, and the Ibadia. The first two were fanatic groups that declared that those who did not join them were polytheists and therefore deserved death. Conversely, the Ibadia were respected members of the Basra community—many were wealthy and powerful merchants—who did not share Khawarij fanaticism. They were known as "the quietists" (qaadah).[16] These affluent merchants of Basra were reported to have "organized trading expeditions to China ... penetrated all the Muslim lands, however distant they might be."[17] They also trained missionaries called Hamalat Al-ilm, "the carriers of knowledge," to spread their teachings.[18]

Ironically, the Ibadis, who see themselves as "a moderate sect of Islam,"[19] have been accused of being Khawarij, but for them the term is synonymous with extremism, an epithet reserved for sects like the Wahhabis of Saudi Arabia.[20] As a result, Ibadi scholars take great pains to distance themselves from the Khawarij. Of the three Khawarij groups, only the Ibadia have survived. They formed small groups in Libya, Tunisia, Algeria, and Tanzania; only in Oman did they attain a majority of the population.

The only position that the Ibadia shares with the Khawariji is that Uthman, the third Caliphate of Islam, has failed the Muslim community. From this fundamental issue "stems the idea that the powers and duties of the leader of the community (Imam al-Muslimin) are prescribed by the Prophet through the Koran and the Sunnah (to which may be added Ijma in Oman). If the leader 'breaks this Islamic constitution, then it is the duty of the Islamic community actively to disassociate itself from him (barah), and he looses their support (wilayah).'"[21] Therefore, the Ibadia would not recognize any hereditary right to the tribe of the prophet Mohammed (Quraish), or the Prophet's descendents from his daughter Fatima, to the leadership of Islam (the Caliphate). The leadership of the Muslim community, they argued, belonged to the most qualified among the community, in accordance with the prophet's teachings. The leader, or the Imam, is elected by members of the community composed of the Uluma (religious scholars), and the notables of the community. His candidacy must be submitted for the people's approval.

Such a community must have a leader, an Imam. This principle was developed by the chief 'alim' of "Abd al-Malik b. Humayd's Imamate (207–26/823–41), Musa b. 'Ali (177?–230/793–844), as follows: 'No army is raised, no banner held, no fighting men commanded, no legal punishments (hudud) ordered, no judgment (hukm) given, except through the Imam. The Imam is an obligation (Farida) as shown by the consensus of the umma, muhajrun and ansar [i.e. the members of the original Muslim community].'[22]

As to the relationship between Ibadia and the rest of Islam, there were four possible paths that allowed the community to exist under any circumstances. Under Zuhur, the community could have an open manifestation of the Imamate. In Difa, the community is militarily defensive and has a restricted Imamate. Under Shira, the community sells itself "in God's cause" and openly opposes tyranny. On the fourth path, the community may not

> even be able to constitute itself as an imama under an imam at all. In that case there is a whole further range of situations concerning concealment (kitman), deriving from the principle of taqiya (prudence given rise to dissimilation) involving compromise with non-constitutional rulers (jababira).[23]

Ibadi Muslims often point that while they are interested in and read the literature of other sects of Islam,

> Non-Ibadis hardly ever look at Ibadi literature. Descriptions of Ibadism in the work of medieval Sunni scholars like Ibn Hazm are full of inaccuracies. Modern scholarship on Ibadism has been scant, and has tended to focus on its political dimensions.[24]

Early Islamic historians say very little about the Ibadia. Initially, the Ibadia did not engage in open revolt as the Khawarij did. Rather they tried to gain the support of the people for their convictions. They also solicited support from some of the orthodox Caliphs by means of treaties.[25] The founder of Ibadism, Abdullah bin Ibada, exchanged letters with the Umayyad Caliph Abd Al-Malik (685–705), whom he wished to convert to his doctrine.[26]

This conciliatory attitude, however, eventually came to an end. Iraq's governor at the time, Al-Hajaj, did not like the growing zealotry of the Ibadia community in Basra, nor did he like their close ties to the Muhallabs (the Muhallabs were strongly allied to the Omani Azd tribe, and many of them were Ibadia). Al-Hajaj began exiling many of the Ibadia to Oman. Included in the group was their intellectual leader Gaber bin Zaid, an Azd tribe member from Nizwa, which would become the capital of the Imamate in Oman.[27] His arrival, as well as that of many other important scholars, greatly enhanced Ibadi influence in Oman. Oman eventually became a center for dissent against the Umayyads. This forced Al-Hajaj to send an ill-fated expedition to Oman in 697. A second expedition, however, successfully defeated the tribal alliances under the Julandas, who then fled to East Africa. Dissention continued nevertheless, and after the death of Al-Hajaj, the Muhallabis regained control over Iraq and the Julandas regained control of Oman.[28] In 748, an Omani chief named Talib Al-Haq led the conquest of Medina. It took the Umayyads only a few months to regain Medina, but shortly thereafter, they were overthrown by the Abbasids, who moved the capital of the Caliphate to Baghdad.[29]

Although it is not clear when the Ibadi set up their own Imamate in Oman, the evidence suggests it was shortly after the fall of the Umayyads in 750 AD.[30] Like the Umayyads before them, the new power in Baghdad was intolerant of an independent Imamate in Oman outside Baghdad's control. The history of the Imamate struggle against the Abbasids over the control of Oman is beyond the scope of this work, but Omani texts bitterly denounce the Abbasid invasion, led by Muhammad bin Nur, who systematically devastated Oman and sent the Imam's head back to Baghdad as a gift. The harsh method employed by bin Nur, called Bin Bur (wasteland) in Omani chronicles of the period, left Oman bitterly opposed to Abbasid rule. In 896 AD, Bin Bur left Oman and assigned control of it to his governor in Nizwa. The governor was eventually ousted.[31] No less than ten successive attacks were carried out against Oman in the span of 200 years. Each invasion attempted to destroy the Ibadi community, which refused to acknowledge the Caliphate or pay taxes. All invasions, no matter how successful initially, were eventually defeated.[32]

The First Imamate, which reached its zenith in the ninth century AD, has captured the imagination and has become the ideal for future Ibadi political aspirations in Oman. Although the rule of the Yaariba imams in the seventeenth century rivals and perhaps surpasses it in both wealth and political muscle, the First Imamate still represents, in Ibadi imaginations, the nearest approximation to a just and legitimate polity. The modern revival of the Ibadi Imamate, during the eighteenth century (under Abu Nabhan Jaid Al-Kharusi (1734/5–1822); Said bin Khalfan Al-Khalili (1868–1871) and, eventually, Salim bin Rashid al-Kharusi (1913–20) and Muhammad bin Abd Allah al-Khalili Alkharusi al-Yahmadi al-Azdi (1920–54)) "was profoundly influenced by the model of the First Imamate."[33]

Although the institution of the Imamate should have been anything but dynastic, there have in fact been five dynasties in Oman: the Julandas, the Yahmad-Khruse (and their descendents, the Kharus and the Khalilis), the Nabahina (who called themselves kings), the Yaariba, and the Al-Busaid (who eventually became hereditary sultans, rather than imams).[34] The establishment of an Omani "state" (whether imamate or kingship) followed a similar historical cycle: elected imams were

> succeeded by secular dynasties, which were overthrown by familial squabbling and groundswells of religious indignation. This pattern was the natural culmination of the centrifugal tendencies of the tribal system and the democratic ideals inherent in the Ibadi faith.[35]

Both the tribal nature of Omani society and the significant restraints of the Ibadi "state" served to undermine the future well being of the imamate institution. While the Imam's residence represents the focal point in the Ibadi community, physical power remains vested in the hands of the leaders of the community. The Imam has no recourse to a standing army independent of what the "faithful" would provide. A standing army under the authority of an individual may easily degenerate to despotic power. As such, military force can be raised only through the local tribes, whose duty is to respond to the Imam's call in times of crisis.[36] The Ibadi archetypal state, as such, fulfilled the basic requirements for a national political authority without threatening the existing tribal concern for autonomy. The imamate in effect served as a super-tribe for the entire country, and the selection of Nizwa as its capital simply reflected its strategic location in the midst of the Arab tribal heartland.[37]

An imam is an elected leader of the community; he is the embodiment of a religious and temporal leader of the community. As such, the election was the function of both the "uluma" (religious scholars) and the tribal leaders. Indeed, without the support of either group, it is doubtful whether an imam could effectively rule. In Oman the two broad tribal confederations are those of the Hinawi and the Ghafiri. Both tribes must support the imam in order for him to be recognized as a national leader rather than just the representative of a particular group. Primary identification with the tribe or with one's kin and tribal self-containment (which fosters fierce independence) created a decentralized, centrifugal system. Peterson called it a "complex and interlocking network of alliances [which] caused many local disputes to expand and embrace more than just the initial tribes involved."[38] Even when an overwhelming tribal allegiance to the imam had been achieved, the imam served more as the mediator of a loose political organization than as its ruler. The imam needed a thorough knowledge of tribal politics and political acumen to maintain the well-being of the polity in the face of various tribal interests and even intrigues. Although Ibadi religious tenets had legitimized the role of the imam as the head of the community, they also restricted his powers through the lack of any military force.[39] The availability of troops to quell domestic or external threats depended upon the imam's ability to rally the tribes to a cause. As Wilkinson critically attests,

> It is easy to see that the Ibadi politico-religious ideology is an impractical basis for the permanent development of a state. It automatically develops a cycle which encompasses its own downfall. As the country is united so does its wealth and prosperity increase and the religious ideal weaken; the leadership becomes the prerogative of a single group degenerates into temporal power (Saltanah). There ensues a struggle for power in which tribal 'asabiyah is brought into play and every potential weakness in the country exploited until full-scale civil war is the outcome. The situation is usually resolved by one or more of the parties calling in an outside power, normally with disastrous results for the Omanis in general. This is the story of the First Imamate, of the Nabahinah, of the Yaariba and of the Al Bu Said.[40]

THE ARRIVAL OF THE PORTUGUESE (1507–1650)

In 1507, the Portuguese, under the command of Albuquerque, sacked and forced into submission the entire Omani coast: Ras al-Hadd, Qalhat, Quryat, Muscat, Suhar, and Khur Fakkan. For the ensuing thirty-two years the Portuguese forces maintained effective control of the area. During that period they faced numerous revolts, at Quryat and Suhar in 1522, at Muscat and Qalhat in

1526, and at Bahrain in 1529; however, their first serious challenge came in 1624 with the election of a new imam, Nasser bin Murshid Al-Yaaribi.[41] Nasser suppressed a number of revolts throughout the country and then gradually dislodged the Portuguese from the coast. He captured Suhar in 1643.[42]

Nasser's successor, Sultan bin Said Al-Yaaribi (1649–1679), captured Muscat in 1650 and attacked Portuguese strong holds in East Africa. From 1652 onward, the Portuguese began losing all their ports in East Africa. Mombassa, their last stronghold, surrendered to the Yaariba in 1665. Portuguese possessions in India and elsewhere also suffered Yaaribi attacks: Bombay in 1661, Diu in November 1668 and January 1676, Bassein in 1764, and Kung (Persia) in 1670. When the Portuguese attempted to regain control of Mombassa in 1678, their fleet was scattered by the arrival of Omani ships.[43] Two successive imams, Balarab bin Sultan (1679–1692) and Saif bin Sultan (1692–1711), continued the expansion of Oman's authority throughout the east African coast. By the end of the seventeenth century, the term empire was used to describe Oman's possessions, which extended from "East Africa, with Pemba, Zanzibar, Patta, and Kilwa all governed by the Yaaribah governor at Mombassa, to Bahrain, which was occupied in 1700."[44]

Oman also defended Persia from the Yaaribi. Imam Balarab bin Sultan "demanded, inter alia, of the Shah (without even the courtesy of a formal address) exactly the same privileges as the old European power had enjoyed, that is half of the customs: in exchange the Omanis would station twenty ships to defend the Persian coast."[45] Imam Sultan bin Saif II (1711–1719) attacked and captured Qisham, Larka, and Bahrain, though he was repulsed at Hormuz. After failing to convince European powers to limit the expansion of the Yaariba, Nadir Shah, who assumed control over Persia after the fall of the Safavids, created the nucleus of a navy, which he used to invade Oman. This was relatively easy because of rivalries that erupted among the Yaariba. One of the contenders for the office of the imamate, Saif bin Sultan II, around 1737–1738, requested the support of Nader Shah against his rivals. The Persians thus entered Oman to aid Saif but eventually carried out an open invasion of the country from their base at Julfar in 1743. Repulsing the Persian attack was left to the founder of a new dynasty, Ahmad Al-Busaidi.[46]

THE RISE OF THE SULTANATE: AHMAD BIN SAID AL-BU SAID (1744–1783)

Ahmad Al-Busaidi was the governor of Suhar under the Yaariba before he became the Imam of Oman in 1744 and the founder of a new dynasty. He was responsible for defeating the Persians at a battle in Sohar. Al-Busaidi was a man of considerable administrative skills and an active merchant who encouraged his subjects to trade outside Oman. In 1776, he allied himself with the Ottoman Turks against the Persians and sent an Omani fleet to help the Turks break Karim Khan Zand's blockade on Basra. In return, the Ottomans waived taxes on

Omani merchants involved in the profitable coffee trade between Yemen and Iraq.[47] Ahmad's actions in Basra also brought him good relations with the British, who had moved their factories from Bushire to Basra in 1763. By 1773 the East India Company had an Omani representative in Muscat.[48] Ahmad's leadership rested more on his mercantile resources, personal influence, and wealth than on the traditional tribal support and territorial conquest. The Al-Busaid "sought no religious sanction for their authority; they were content to rely on the prestige of their house and the military force they commanded, and, in later days, on the support lent them by their allies the British."[49] Ahmad's successors in the Al-Busaid dynasty would follow in his footsteps by directing their considerable skills to enterprises outside Oman: trade with India and East Africa and conquests in the Gulf. Eventually they shed the title of imam. Only Ahmad's immediate successor, who ruled very briefly, proclaimed himself an imam. Others instead preferred the title sayyid (lord), which did not indicate descent from the Prophet's family. After 1861, the title sultan was used, a title that was first applied by Europeans to address the rulers of Oman. Oman's history was beginning to witness a significant shift away from the world of the interior to Muscat as the center of political and commercial power.[50]

IMAM SULTAN BIN AHMAD (1792–1804)

Sultan was without a doubt a worthy successor to the founder of the Al-Busaid dynasty. He devoted his reign to overseas expansion and to consolidation of Muscat's power in the southern Gulf. Muscat's authority expanded over Gawadur on the Marakan coast and Chabar on the Persian coast. By 1798, after a short military campaign, Sultan obtained the customs authority for Bandar Abbas and the islands of Hormuz, Qisham, Hanjam, and Minab. This opened the door for trade with the markets of southern Persia, where control over the Strait of Hormuz was secured and followed by obtaining the profitable salt deposits of Hormuz.[51]

Sultan's reign, however, was beset by various external threats that continued to plague Muscat well after his death. The Utub, who occupied Bahrain in 1783, were considered rival merchants who traded directly with India and bypassed both Muscat and Bandar Abbas. The first campaign against the Utub was carried out in 1799, after which they promised to pay a transit tax and a tribute equal to half the amount that they had previously paid to Persia.

Once Sultan withdrew to Muscat, however, the Utub formed a strong alliance with the powerful Wahhabi leadership, which would continue to pose a threat to Oman for centuries to come. The Wahhabis' first excursion into Oman involved the attack and the occupation of the Buraimi oasis in 1799. They formed an alliance with the Qawasim in Ras-Al-Khaima. Muscat's commercial interests were now under a serious threat. Faced with Saudi occupation of the Buraimi oasis, Sultan gathered his forces and marched to Buraimi to expel the Saudis. The defeat forced Sultan to pay a tribute to the Saudi emir and to allow

a Saudi agent to reside in Muscat itself. Sultan attempted to limit Saudi influence by allying himself with the Sherifs of Mecca in 1803, but the alliance did
not bear any significant results. The Saudi threat, however, was neutralized
temporarily by the death of their leader Emir Faisal later that year.[52] Rather
than wait for the Saudi threat to materialize again, the Imam attempted to forge
another alliance with a different force in the region. When the Pasha of Baghdad refused to pay the custom charges levied on Omani imports to Baghdad,
Imam Sultan sailed to Basra's port in 1804 and threatened reprisals. Unexpectedly, the Pasha and the Imam both agreed to commit Ottoman and Muscat
forces to a joint attack against the Saudis. This venture never materialized,
since Sultan was attacked on his return to Oman and lost his life.[53]

It was also during Sultan's reign that Oman became embroiled in British and
French schemes over the control of the western Indian Ocean. Bonaparte had
already invaded Egypt in 1798, and his letters to Muscat and to India's Tipu Sultan caused the British concern. Muscat had already enjoyed relations with France
through the slave trade on the island of Mauritius. To counter possible French
designs on Muscat, the British dispatched their diplomats to Imam Sultan. He in
turn promised his friendship to England, especially after the East India Company
agreed to purchase more salt. Additional treaties followed between Oman and
Great Britain in 1798 and 1800. These agreements were "unlike the treaties Britain signed with the Gulf Sheikhs later in the nineteenth century[;] they were neither imposed by force nor did they turn Oman into a protectorate."[54] Despite the
treaties between both countries, Imam Sultan refused to allow the British a factory
in Muscat. His successor, Sayyid Bader, cemented Muscat's alliance with Britain
through a joint attack of Qawasim bases.[55] However, as Bhacker asserts,

> Ultimately Britain managed to achieve its goals at little coast to itself because the
> Albusaidi rulers of the second half of the nineteenth century found themselves totally
> powerless to assert their own legitimate rights. The roots of this impotence can be
> traced back to the time of Sultan b Ahmad who, as a result of the Wahhabi threat to
> his dominions and the Qasimi/Utabi challenge to Muscat's commerce, felt compelled
> to sign the 1798 Treaty with Britain, overawed as he was at the time by the unrelent-
> ing march of the British military machine as it rolled through India acquiring more
> and more territories and triumphing over all those who resisted its advance, notable
> among whom were the French and the ruler of Mysore, both former commercial
> allies of Oman.[56]

SULTAN SAID BIN SULTAN (1806–1856)

Sultan Said was barely 17 years of age when he seized power from Sayyid
Badir. The main threats to his leadership came from Saudi Arabia, the Qawasim
of Ras Al-Khaimah, and the Utub of Bahrain. The Saudi threat was temporarily
neutralized when Egypt's Mohammed Ali invaded the peninsula in 1811.[57]

After various attempts to subjugate both Ras-Al-Khaimah and Bahrain, Sultan Said turned to England for aid. England eventually took control of the defeated Trucial Coast (1819). The

> treaty agreement that followed led to the establishment of the Trucial system and with it the divorce of Trucial and Sultanate Oman. From now, on Julfar was independent and under British control. Soon the Gulf itself became an extension of the British-Indian domain, and Oman was totally excluded from it politically.[58]

Furthermore, the British refused to assist Sultan Said against the Utub of Bahrain. They allowed the latter to join the Trucial system and warned the Sultan against future attacks.[59] The British also exerted enormous pressure on the Sultan to suspend the highly profitable slave trade coming from the Sultan's African colonies. The Sultan concluded the first antislavery treaty with the British government, acting through the East India Company, in 1822.[60] In 1839, Said concluded another treaty of commerce with Great Britain according to the terms of which "'the subjects of Her Britannic Majesty shall … have full liberty to enter, reside in, trade with and pass with their merchandize through all parts of the dominions of His Highness the Sultan of Muscat."[61] The French also signed a treaty with Sultan Said in 1807. A treaty of commerce followed in 1844, which essentially granted the French the same "freedom of movement throughout the territories of the Sultan of Muscat that had been granted in 1839 to the British."[62] A treaty with the United States was signed in 1833, which granted U.S. citizens

> liberty to enter all the Ports of His Majesty and stated that those citizens "resorting to the Ports of the Sultan for the purpose of trade, shall have leave to land, and reside in the said ports." In addition, the treaty provided that the President of the United States "may appoint Consuls to reside in the Ports of the Sultan where the principal commerce shall be carried on."[63]

By 1829, Sultan Said added Dhofar, part of the Sultanate's geographical territory, to Oman's domain and he also controlled the Swahili coast (Tanzania and Kenya). (East Africa had already come under Oman's influence through the Yaariba and was the only place left for the Sultan to expand after the British involvement in the Gulf.) Sultan Said decided to live in Zanzibar. In fact, after 1832, the Sultan was almost permanently absent from Muscat, preferring to attend to his domains in Africa. Muscat's affairs, and in turn those of Oman, were left in the hands of a governor, while the port's financial administration was left to Indian agents.[64]

THE DEATH OF SULTAN SAID AND THE RETURN OF THE IMAMATE

After the death of Sultan Said, his dominions were divided between two of his sons through the British-mediated Canning Award. Thuwani bin Said was to rule Muscat, while his brother, Majid bin Said, presided over Zanzibar. As such, both Zanzibar and Muscat became two separate and independent sultanates. The Sultanate of Zanzibar was much wealthier than Muscat, and it was agreed that Muscat would receive an annual payment of 40,000 Maria Theresa dollars. Thuwaini's reign lasted from 1856 to 1866 and was followed by that of Salim's bin Thuwani. Salim's reign, however, was immediately challenged by the new forces of the Imamate under the leadership of Imam Azan bin Qais Al-Busaidi. By 1869, Azan captured both Muscat and the Buraimi. His Imamate however, lasted only from 1868 to 1871. The Sultanate arose again under Sultan Turki bin Said, who reigned from 1871 to 1888. His reign was continuously challenged by both his nephew, ex-Sultan Salim bin Thuwani, and the Imamate forces that continued to attack Muscat. British involvement was paramount in safeguarding Muscat against future attacks by the forces of the interior. The British declared publicly in 1866 that "their determination to afford Sayyid Turki active support in case of attacks on Muscat had the salutary effect of maintaining peace during the remainder of his life."[65]

The reign of Sultan Faisal bin Turki (1888–1913) witnessed the most flagrant aggression against Muscat's sovereignty as a byproduct of British and French schemes in Muscat. First the Sultan agreed to a French proposal to open a coaling station at Muscat and to fly the French flag on his fleet. Then, the British ordered him to board a British flagship and witness the bombardment of Muscat unless he withdrew his agreement with France. Worse yet, he was forced in 1899 to renounce his previous agreement with the French in a public speech. Faisal's rule "lapsed into oblivion. He died in October 1913 as the British reestablished their influence in Oman, the reconstituted imamate threatened the authority of the ruler in Muscat, and the government lay in shambles."[66]

Salem Al-Kharusi was elected Imam in 1913. He first occupied Nizwa and then moved against Muscat. Sultan Faisal died in October of that year and was succeeded by his son Taimur, who reigned from 1913 to 1931. The British had to land troops in Muscat to guard it against the Imamate forces and continued to do so for the next 5 years. Burdened with extensive debts and continuous rebellions, Sultan Taimur attempted to abdicate. When England refused his requests, he began to spend as much time as possible in Dhofar and abandoned the administration of Muscat to a council of ministers under a British advisor.[67]

In 1920, the relationship between Muscat and the Imamate of Mohammad Al-Khalili (1920–1954) was governed by the so-called Treaty of Sib. By 1932, a new leader, Said bin Taimur (Sultan Said), had become the Sultan of Muscat. His internal and external policies are the focus of this work and formed the foundation of Oman's foreign and domestic relations for the next seventy-five years.

The Reign of Sultan Said

REVISITING THE REIGN OF SULTAN SAID

The period of the reign of Sultan Said (between his ascension in 1932 and his overthrow in 1970) was undoubtedly one of the most important periods in the modern history of the Sultanate. The tumultuous events that led to the establishment of the modern state of the Sultanate of Oman, if untangled, can give some important indicators about the foundations of Oman's foreign policy and its specific directions.

To execute this chapter effectively, four avenues of research will be used. First, it is necessary to make the most of scarce data about the ruler's decisions, pronouncements, and actions for the duration of his reign. Subsequently, an extensive use of the archives is imperative in order to provide insight into the motives of all actors involved, whether in London, Riyadh, Muscat, or Abu-Dhabi. This chapter will be repeatedly punctuated by various statements—as well as memos, reviews, and notes—quoted from the archives, providing the reader with a carefully constructed record of the historical genesis of Muscat's most important challenges during the reign of Said. Third, an examination of the major strategic problems facing Muscat, as well as Sultan Said's actions and statements, highlights his course of action and the attendant considerations that affected his choices.

Finally, an examination and assessment of the most salient events of the reign of Sultan Said and a clarification of the literature are essential. Conventional wisdom has depicted Sultan Said as the classic tyrant who compensates for his administrative incompetence with brutal authority. He is portrayed this way without adequate explanations or analysis.

The spectrum of accusations thrown at Sultan Said by the conventional wisdom ranges from a hostile attitude toward education, leading to the underdevelopment of the country, to hoarding the country's wealth in his personal Swiss bank accounts,[1] and further, to outright complicity in British imperialism. Indeed, the "evidence" most often given for the latter includes 1) the sale of Gawadur, 2) his attempt to unite the country under Muscat's authority, 3) the lease of Masirah to the British Royal Air Force, and 4) the Buraimi Oasis dispute.

No leader in the modern history of the Arab Gulf states has been more vilified than Sultan Said. One of his harshest critics claims that Sultan Said was "one of the nastiest rulers the world has seen for a long time."[2] Such views typify the conventional wisdom repeatedly observed by the writings on Oman, albeit sometimes with less directness.[3] There are few sympathetic narratives.[4]

Confusingly, some of the Sultan's critics have contradicted their own accounts. In an article published by Peterson in *Middle East Policy*,[5] the author comments on Sultan Said's isolation, observing that "Even when Oman finally joined the ranks of oil producers, Sultan Said had no interest in joining either OPEC or OAPEC. His sole concession to membership in international bodies was a successful application to WHO."[6] In the endnotes of an earlier work, however, Peterson presents a different account of the same subject. There was

> an abortive attempt to join the Food and Agricultural Organization (FAO) in the late 1940's and another attempt in 1962 to join the World Health Organization (WHO): Ismail bin Khalili al-Rasasi was even sent to Geneva as an observer but Arab League lobbying prevented Omani membership … Another abortive attempt initiative came in 1967 when Said announced that he was sending an application for membership to OPEC but nothing seems have come of it.[7]

Petty and incomprehensible behavior is often cited by various sources as examples of Sultan Said's tyranny: the Sultan attempted to "shut the country by among other things, banning sunglasses and severely restricting education and foreign travel"[8] and "kept from the populations whole series of objects, including medicines, radios, spectacles, trousers, cigarettes and books."[9] This is repeated by Wikan[10] and by Graz,[11] who added that under specific circumstances, even shoes were forbidden. Subsequently we are told that such behavior can only be explained by some form of mental illness.[12]

What is absent from these stories is the original source. For example, there is no reference to the source of the following passage: "According to one story he [the Sultan] used to make them [slaves] swim in the swimming pool constructed in front of his palace in Salalah while he shot pellets from a tun at the fish."[13] Neither does the author claim that such information was obtained firsthand by his or her own investigations. When claims made by Miller and others (for example, regarding the banning of glasses and radios) were investigated, they were traced back to a surprising source: *Pravda*, the Soviet central propaganda mouthpiece. After a visit by special correspondent A. Vasiliev on the 29th of September 1969 to the "liberated" areas of Dhofar (please note that the author is only writing on a specific and rather small area of the country), he reported

> that the inhabitants of this town were forbidden from wearing shoes, spectacles, listening to the radio, or flying in aeroplanes … We entered liberated villages under the

thunder of welcomes for the Soviet Union ... The most dangerous [captured enemies] were taken out to the town of Muscat and thrown in to the pie [*sic*] of horrible prison of Jut Galal ... Here people are made fun of for the amusement of the prison warders, eyes are gouged out, people are kept years without light, others have poisonous snakes thrown at them, still others are left to the mercies of hungry rats.[14]

The British embassy in Moscow did not fail to take notice:

You may be surprised to learn that Pravda of 29 September devoted almost half a page to a long report from the 'liberated regions' of Oman ... Such accounts of liberation struggles are of course standard fare for the Pravda-reader. In this case however, the diet was improved by the addition both of some fascinating statistics (30% of the population of Salalah are slaves), and of some light relief (the sultan rarely moved from his Salalah palace even before 1966, preferring the delights of his harem and pornographic films) ... It does also seem odd that Pravda should have referred throughout to the 'Persian Gulf'; one might have expected more attention to Arab sensibilities in an article specifically about 'Arab liberation'.[15]

Under closer scrutiny, reports such as *Pravda*'s prove to be dubious at best. They represent, for the most part, a superficial description of the past state of affairs. The Sultan himself wore spectacles and sunglasses, and, as a glance at the book, *Old Oman*,[16] would show, so did many of his subjects. Radios, contrary to the conventional wisdom, were not forbidden and were surprisingly common and popular. A writer in the early 1940s estimated that there were 50–100 sets in the Muscat-Matrah area, and in the 1950s, tribal sheikhs visiting the capital avidly sought the new battery-operated portables as gifts. While it is true that Sultan Said placed restrictions on automobiles ownership, he did not forbid them. Permission from the Sultan was required for the importation of any vehicle other than saloon cars and short-wheelbase Land Rovers. These restrictions were security measures, an attempt to prevent continual smuggling of arms and mines by saboteurs during the unrest of the 1950s and 1960s; trucks and larger Land Rovers were, therefore, controlled but not forbidden (except those deemed security risks).[17] The following is a passage from the record of a meeting between Sultan Said and Her Majesty's Government (HMG) representative which may shed some light on Sultan Said's personal views:

As regards the restrictions on personal liberty, he preferred to call them regulations and there was much misunderstanding about them. A large number of them e.g the regulations about the form of dress, reflected the traditional Omani way of life ... Many of his people, especially those in the mountains, were very conservative and suspicious of foreigners and innovations; and rapid changes, especially any changes affecting religious matters, would arose their hostility and upset the unity and the balance of the country.[18]

Observers of Persian Gulf states, past and present, would note that some of the restrictions mentioned above are not exclusive to Oman, yet curiously, journalists, as well as scholars, have singled out Sultan Said as an object of reproach.

Alternatively, those who worked closely with Sultan Said attest to his moderation and reveal a remarkably different image. Their testimony, however, is absent from most of the literature. Wendell Phillips observed that the Sultan (in contrast to the extravagances of the ruling families of other Gulf states) "owned no Cadillacs, airplanes, or yachts, prefers to drive desert jeeps and trucks himself."[19] Townsend, described Sultan Said as "a most frugal man [who] lived a simple life."[20] McLeod Innes wrote of Sultan Said as "a ruler who was never a tyrant, a man of great charm, great dignity, and great integrity, whom I was proud to serve."[21]

To develop a proper perspective, it will be necessary to return to the reign of Sultan Said. A memo, dated 17 July 1958, introduces Sultan Said to Britain's prime minister upon a proposed visit to London:

> The Sultan of Muscat and Oman, an independent monarch, Sayyid Said bin Taimur, was born in 1910 and succeeded his father on the latter's abdication in 1932. The Sultan was educated in Baghdad and India and speaks excellent though slow English. He is a dignified person, inclined to be retiring, reserved and formal. He has a genuinely deep feeling for his relations with the British Crown and H.M government. He is normally addressed as 'Your Highness'. He is very shrewd ruler and able negotiator, who runs his country almost single-handed. He does not consider himself, nor is he, the same kind of person as other Arab rulers.[22]

A key to understanding Sultan's Said's reign lies in the political and financial situation of his father's government. The reign of Sultan Taimur bin Faisal was besieged by a resurgence of the Imamate forces that culminated in the Imamate of Salim bin Rashid Al-Kharusi (1913–1920) and Muhammad b. Abdullah Al-Khalili (1920–1954). The state's finances had collapsed. Only two years after his graduation from secondary school in Mayo College (1922–1927), Said returned home to head a Council of Ministers set up by his father at the "advice" of the British. At issue was the growing financial crisis that kept Muscat either bankrupt or on the verge of bankruptcy for approximately seventy-five years. That situation needed immediate attention:

> apart from some rather erratic exports of dates and fish, the Treasury relied almost entirely on customs receipts, the Zanzibar subsidy and, later, the oil concession rental. The amount was pitifully small; in 1931, according to the Sultan, the total budget was only about 50,000.[23]

By assuming presidency of the Council of Ministers, Said was, in essence, de facto Sultan. In 1930, one of his first acts as head of the Council of Ministers was to dismiss his father's finance minister, Bertram Thomas. By July 1931, he had appointed himself Minister of Finance and had balanced the budget. He maintained budget surpluses despite a prolonged drought in Oman and a worldwide depression.[24] Throughout his reign, Said maintained a simple fiscal philosophy: do not spend what you do not have.[25]

In November 1931, Sultan Taimur requested that the British accept his abdication with the ascension of his son as Sultan, citing medical reasons.[26] The British, however, refused to accept the abdication until January 1932. In his early twenties, Sultan Said had inherited a government that lacked sufficient resources for early success. His own strong determination to restore fiscal soundness became his paramount goal and was essential for political unification under Muscat's authority.

The young Sultan asserted his authority with respect to the British from the earliest periods of his reign. In August of 1937, he embarked on a visit to Europe and the United States.[27] London's political resident thought that he at least should have been informed of the trip. In a letter addressed to the Sultan, the political resident expressed surprise that Bin Taimur did not follow the customary practice of making his travel arrangements as well as contacts with foreign powers through HMG.[28] In an elaborate and dignified answer, the Sultan stated that:

> There is no doubt that We realize what are the Treaty Relations that exist between Us and the British Government. We do not think that Our writing directly to the President of the U.S.A.[29] would make a breach of the provisions of the Treaty. Further, as you are aware, there are Treaties between Us and the Government of the U.S.A. and France and We have to write to them directly on certain occasions when necessity calls for it … But should We have any such communications in the future and We consider that it is Our interests to send them through His Majesty's Government We would be pleased to do so, in view of the advantages that this will give to Us. Otherwise We shall continue to act in accordance with the old procedure which is usual to Our Government, and shall not in the least inconvenience His Majesty's Government and their officials.[30]

In July 1932, the Sultan visited India[31] on a three-month tour, and this time the political resident expressed no "surprise." The earlier reaction was due to British concerns about "subversive anti-British propaganda being conducted by the Italian Government in various parts of Arabia."[32] As the British ambassador to the United States commented, "If, for example, the Sultan should make a trip to Europe and should either desire or be induced to visit Rome, he felt certain that his Government would be seriously concerned."[33]

Said's domestic and foreign policy in essence revolved around two objectives: the restoration of Muscat's complete authority over the areas administered by the Imamate and the elimination of the debts accrued by the previous administrations. The fiscal weakness of the country had allowed undue influences on the government. This fact is clearly illustrated by a conversation between Sultan Said and a member of the British government:

> When he had succeeded his father in 1932 the income of the Sultanate was 50,000 a year. For many years he had no resources with which to effect improvements and he

had always been determined, as he still was, not to borrow as this would put his country under the influence of his creditors. It was for the lack of resources not lack of will that his country had remained backward, and in many respects still was so. However he had for long been maturing plans, which he had committed to notebooks, for the development of his country when resources became available. Since 1958 H.M.G. had made certain grants for which he was extremely grateful; these had made modest improvements possible. Now with the prospect of oil revenues he planned to embark on his wider plans ... He wished to live comfortably but not luxuriously.[34]

Wendell Phillips corroborates Sultan Said's concern in the late 1950s. The Sultan's view was that "certain conditions in Oman inherited from the past are not really my fault, and if I do not have the funds to change these conditions where change is desired, it is still not my fault; if however, I do have the means and do not improve my people and my country then I should be ashamed."[35]

The literature depicted the Sultan as a passive agent in the face of dramatic events. The death of Imam Al-Khalili in May 1954 initiated the first phase of the removal of the Imamate as a significant force in Omani politics. As early as the 1930s, and certainly during and after World War II, Sultan Said was already contemplating the extension of Muscat's authority over the territories controlled by the Imamate. In the late 1920s and throughout the 1930s, the British Royal Air Force endeavored to open up the air route from Britain to India and to the territories of the Far East.[36] When the threat of yet another war became clear at the end of 1930s, the importance of air routes and military bases became even more crucial to London. Sultan Said supported the allies against the Axis powers; he consented to creating three bases[37] on the Sultanate's territories and to opening his ports and harbors for the British Navy.[38] He clearly saw that British interests and his own would coincide in this matter. First, at that time, Muscat could not afford the development of extensive modern landing fields (fields that could by used by a future Omani air force). Second, the payments for the use of these facilities provided much needed revenue. Most important, however, is the fact that

> exploration parties looking for suitable sites gradually extended the influence of the Sultanate over some of the remote areas which had been lost during the reign of his father, Saiyid Taimur. Almost from the moment of his accession Saiyid had had to face a serious rebellion of the tribes. Provided the exploration parties did not venture into positively hostile areas, Saiyid Said gave them both permission and support to carry out their task. In this way he steadily extended his zone of control, especially along the coastal areas beyond Ras el Hadd.[39]

Sultan Said's effort to extend his authority over Imamate-controlled areas was already bearing fruit by the mid 1930s. He settled various tribal disputes within Imamate territories and improved relations with tribal leaders often through gifts. As Bierschenk comments,

> This policy to outbuy the Imam, who was unable to compete with it financially, was remarkably, successful. Between 1937 and 1939, the Sultan of Muscat was visited by

the two leading Sheikhs of the Eastern Province (al-sharqiya), Ali Abdullah al-Hamuda of the Bani Bu Ali and Isa Salih al-Harthi, leader of the Hinawi faction of the Omani tribes, Sheikh Ahmad Muhammad, the son-in law of the Imam, as well as by the leading men of the Dharihirah tribes. They all left Muscat showered with gifts and arms.[40]

By 1945, the Sultan's rising stature among the tribes of the interior, combined with the advanced age of Imam Al-Khalili,[41] set the stage for the Sultan to request British support to extend his authority to the areas administered by the Imamate. Sultan Said was well aware, however, that he could not move into the interior as long as the Imam lived.[42] Undoubtedly, he was testing British commitment when and if the opportunity materialized. Specifically, Sultan Said sought British assurances of air support by the Royal Air Force when the time was ripe.[43] The disappointing answer came on 12 June 1946, at a meeting at the India Office in London. Both the Foreign Office and the War Office "were reluctant to support the use of air power for operations against recalcitrant tribesmen, particularly in an independent state, because of its effect on world opinion, even though it was at the request of the Ruler."[44] Probably Sultan Said had earlier recognized that British help might not materialize. Within three months of the end of the war he had requested that British relinquish the facilities in accordance with the agreement of 1939. In 1946, both the French and the British Governments drafted agreements for landing sites in long-haul routes to the Far East. The Sultan's response, dated September 1947, was a firm refusal, at least as far as the French are concerned:

> As far as we can make out the matter has been clarified but just to make it more clear and to avoid any misunderstanding we should like to point out that it is understood that the French Military Aircrafts shall not fly over or land in our territories as they have not got the right to do so.[45]

The reunification of Oman under Muscat was propelled further by renewed postwar interest in oil exploration. Richard Bird, a representative of the Iraq Petroleum Company, which had concession rights in Oman at the time, had entered Oman in 1948 as far as Ibri (an area under the control of the Imam) without Sultan Said's consent. Said was understandably furious and rightfully concerned that London might begin to regard Oman's interior as composed of congeries of independent tribal leaders. The incident serves to "indicate both the thinness of his effective control in some parts of the country and his early recognition that boundaries and effective rule were essential tests of sovereignty for international purposes."[46] In addition, any oil reservoirs in Oman were most likely either in or adjacent to the interior of the country.

From its inception to the end of the 1940s, Sultan Said's reign had been a period of asserting authority and independence from London's long shadow. The unification of the country under Muscat's control was near. During the 1950s, however, internal and external crises appeared (such as the Buraimi

Oasis dispute and the Imamate challenge of 1957) that were sources of long-term discord for the country, enduring into the reign of his son Sultan Qaboos (in 1970).

THE 1950s CRISIS

The Buraimi Oasis dispute and the Imamate challenge of 1957 were linked from their very beginning, in varying degrees, to the absence of internationally defined borders in southeastern Arabia and to the Saudi exploitation of this juris-dictional lacuna. The genesis of the two disputes is dissimilar.[47] In the 1930s, the British government, acting on behalf of Oman and the Trucial Sheikhs, attempted to negotiate agreed boundaries with the newly united kingdom of Saudi Arabia. Though never settled, the Saudis essentially felt that their claim over more territories was justifiable. Buraimi[48] was part of those territories.

Al-Buraimi is a strategically[49] located oasis in the interior of eastern Arabia and a juncture of the major routes to the Persian Gulf (through the town of Abu Dhabi), the Gulf of Oman (via al-Wadi al-Jazzi) and the al-Dhahirah province of Oman. It is composed of nine villages, three controlled by the Sheikh of Abu-Dhabi and six by the Sultan of Oman. The Saudi attempts to dominate the oasis can be traced to the early 1800s when Sheikh Muhammad bin Abd al-Wahhab incited the Najdis to conquer the area. In 1819, the Sultan of Oman expelled the Najdis from the oasis. They returned in 1830, only to be subse-quently expelled by Imam Azan bin Qais in 1869.

In 1949, after protests that a party of American oilmen had traveled within Abu Dhabi territory without the authorization of the Sheikh, the Saudis put for-ward a claim of much to the territory of the Sheikdoms, including Buraimi. The British rejected the claim, but they did agree to discuss the matter further with Riyadh. Nonetheless, results materialized. In August 1952 a Saudi force seized Hamsa, one of the Omani villages of Buraimi. Subsequently, Riyadh sent a message to Imam Al-Khalili announcing that the authorities in Saudi Arabia had felt compelled to appoint a Saudi representative given the repeated requests by Saudi subjects in Oman. Furthermore, the message called on the Imam to join forces with the Saudis to expel the "foreign" influences in Oman; this was coupled with an offer of a large, cash "gift," which the Imam declined.[50]

The Saudi attempts to divide and conquer had failed. In fact, both the Sultan and the Imam had recognized the impending danger, and immediately had begun to raise the forces necessary to expel the Saudis from Buraimi.[51] For Sul-tan Said, this provided a golden opportunity to unite Muscat with the interior. The Sultan sent the Imam 100 camels, ammunition, rifles, and money to facili-tate sending his own militia from the interior to Buraimi. Omani tribes from various regions responded to the call; merchants in Muscat supplied the entire expedition with the needed foodstuffs and ammunition. By 7 October 1952, an assembled force of 8,000 tribesmen assembled at Suhar. The entire expedition, however, came to a standstill on 18 October and eventually disbanded.[52] Under heavy pressure from the United States, the British government directed Leslie Chauncey, the British consul in Muscat, to advise Sultan Said to forego the expedition. British and U.S. governments assured Sultan Said that a diplomatic solution could be reached. Sultan Said demanded that Chauncey "hand him the message in full view of his army and remain at his side while he read it to them, so that they would understand that the British Government, not the Sultan, was responsible for this cowardly withdrawal."[53]

Sultan Said's prestige and standing among the tribes suffered tremendously. From this event came the future accusations of Said's subservience to British interests. Meanwhile, the Buraimi dispute was transformed from what was essentially a local dispute into a significant crisis involving the United States and Saudi Arabia on one hand and Great Britain, Muscat, and the Trucial Sheikdoms on the other. Acceding to U.S. pressure, London agreed to accept arbitration with Saudi Arabia in Geneva in September 1955. The Saudis, however, had no intention of abiding by the "stand still agreement."[54] On behalf of the Sultan of Oman and Abu Dhabi, British forces eventually moved in and forced the Saudis out of Buraimi. In Washington, the news was not well received to say the least. In London, the Foreign Office was

'thrown into rage' on receiving messages from the Americans, one saying that we should go back to arbitration on Buraimi otherwise the Saudis 'will be very annoyed' and might take us to the Security Council; the other 'practically ordering us' to call off the impending move by the Sultan of Muscat to reassert his authority in the interior of Oman generally.[55]

And it is with the latter "impending move" that we must concern ourselves with at the moment.

From the beginning of Said's reign, Imam Al-Khalili's "nation-wide reputation for integrity and piety had been a considerable stabilizing influence in the country."[56] In May 1954, with the death of Al-Khalili, a "good deal of the fire went out of the Imamate movement."[57] His successor, Ghalib bin Ali al-Hinai, had served first as a judge then as an assistant under Al-Khalili. A 1982 interview with Sheikh Ahmed Muhammad al-Harthi, a participant in the election for the new Imam, gives a sense of the events surrounding the election of Ghalib. The notables who gathered at Nizwa upon the death of Al-Khalili were divided into three parties. A minority of those present called for resumption of the status quo, with limited contact with the outside world. Another faction (not party to the selection process) called for the interior to be under the Sultan's rule. The third faction favored the acceptance of military and financial aid so that interior Oman, recognized by the Arab league and the United Nations, might become a separate nation.[58] The third faction would win the day.

In the summer of 1954, the new Imam worked hard to assert his authority. In a bold move, Imam's Ghalib's dynamic younger brother, Sheikh Talib bin Ali, seized the town of Ibri when the inhabitants seemed to be hesitant to acknowledge Ghalib's election as Imam.[59] A more sinister reason behind this act was the importance of Ibri to the Imamate as an essential station to maintain direct contact with the Saudi outpost at Al-Buraimi.[60] In October 1954, Sultan Said responded by sending a detachment of his forces, reoccupying Ibri without opposition.[61] Henceforth, the relationship between Muscat and Nizwa—the Imamate's capital—deteriorated to the point of no return.

Sultan Said may have tolerated Imam Ghalib's move into Ibri, had it not been for the momentous action that ensued. On 25 November 1954, the Imam forwarded via his brother, Talib bin Ali, a request for full membership to the Arab League for the "Kingdom of Oman."[62] The Imamate sought to capitalize on the surge of Arab nationalism and thus identify its struggle with a broader appeal that had far more resonance in the Arab world than the Imamate cause.[63] The application was infused with Islamic connotations emphasizing that Oman was an independent state, governed by Islamic law, or sharia.[64] As the issue lingered in the Arab League, and then in the United Nations, the Imamate cause became closely identified with Arab nationalism and the various forms of anticolonialism.

The Imamate's application for membership in the Arab League was a clear demonstration that Said's schemes for a gradual reintegration of Oman under Muscat's authority were not working. A second indicator occurred in September 1955 when the news reached Muscat that an Egyptian intelligence major arrived in Nizwa via Saudi Arabia in order to organize the Imamate forces.[65] There is a question as to why the Sultan failed to take a firm action against Nizwa for more than a year. For Landen, this was to be expected since for him, Said was "more a spectator than initiator of events."[66] Joyce shares the same assessment, assuring us that "Sultan Said did not like to make decisions."[67] After all, the Sultan was out of the country on a trip spanning Baghdad, Bahrain, and London for more than a month in the summer of 1955.

On the other hand, the lack of a firmer, more immediate approach by Sultan Said to the events could be justified by the high risks associated with failure in the new environment. If anything, Sultan Said showed political acumen by allowing time for a careful planning and efficient execution of his plans. No sultan had entered the Imamate's capital Nizwa in over a century. To enter Nizwa with military force and the possibility of bloodshed would antagonize the local population, including Muscat's supporters. A premature attack on Nizwa, given the meager forces at the Sultan's disposal and the likelihood that the Imamate forces were well equipped through Saudi, might fail, with untold consequences for Muscat. Said's trip to London becomes of key importance. London was the only ally likely to provide the necessary political and military aid. Indeed, London encouraged Sultan Said to eliminate Ghalib's threat throughout 1954. Said was thankful for the verbal support, but he preferred words to be followed with substantial military aid.

The record shows that in addition to visiting and dining with the Queen of England, the Sultan had several meetings at Whitehall. The discussions centered on the possible elimination of the Imamate as a political force. Was British support certain in a possible showdown with the Imamate? If so, to what extent would the British involve themselves? The Sultan was informed that any assistance provided would be limited and that it would likely involve some air support and fewer than ten technical advisors in the field.[68] Timpe argues that London's unwillingness to offer more substantial aid was a manifestation of a British desire for the Sultan to fail: an opportunity for the British to demonstrate their importance. The Sultan was well aware of Britain's importance, however, as his journey to London at this time indicates. Far more probable is that Britain forestalled involvement to mitigate the effects of prior clashes with the United States (remember the Buraimi dispute).

In September 1955, the Buraimi arbitration talks between Britain (acting on behalf of Abu Dhabi) and the Sultanate broke up in Geneva after the resignation of the British delegate, Sir Reader Bullard. According to British sources, Saudi bribes of the members of the Tribunal had by now convinced HMG that a diplomatic solution was not at hand. Sultan Said's opinion had been vindicated: He had been convinced from the beginning that the Saudis were bargaining in bad faith. The Sultan had thought that their primary objective was to instigate uprisings throughout the interior of Oman with calls for independence while actually seeking Saudi suzerainty over the interior of Oman.[69]

On 26 October 1955, Trucial Oman Scouts "escorted" Saudi forces out of the oasis. This seemed to end the dispute over Buraimi, or, as Halliday and the majority of the literature asserted, after 1955 "the Buraimi dispute was dormant: Muscat administered three villages, and Abu Dhabi six. The Saudis did not accept the outcome, but decided to leave matters as they stood."[70] In reality, however, the Buraimi dispute continued to be of primary importance to various regional states and a source of serious discord between London and Washington.

Once the Saudis were removed from the area, Sultan Said began his advance against the Imamate forces with remarkable swiftness and success. Rustaq, which was an important area for the Imamate and was being defended by Sheikh Talib bin Ali (the Imam's brother), was captured in four days without casualties (Sheikh Talib departed to Saudi Arabia). Nizwa, the Imamate's capital, fell on 15 December 1955, with only one shot being fired. Sultan Said departed from his residence at Salalah on the Indian Ocean and drove across deserts and mountains to enter Nizwa triumphantly on 24 December 1955.[71] Imam Ghalib abdicated and returned to his native village Sait, while other prominent tribal leaders followed suit. This was undoubtedly an important day for Sultan Said. His long efforts to assimilate the interior had been accomplished. He was the first sultan to visit the interior in over a century.[72] To conclude the victory, the Sultan organized a royal trip of his new domains: Adam, Nizwa, Ibri, Buraimi, Suhar, and the Batinah coast. While 4,000 tribesmen gathered on the grounds of the famous Nizwa fortress, a representative of the Sultan (with the Sultan standing beside him) read a speech. He had come to Nizwa to unite the country and stop the shedding of Muslim blood, he assured the gatherings. He promised amnesty to all those who accepted his rule: "the past will not be brought up again."[73] The Sultan did not make any

> radical changes in the social and religious life in the tribes of Central Oman after this operation. Nor did he replace existing leaders by his own nominees. The only persons who were still un-reconciled were the Imam's brother, Talib, who sought sanctuary in Saudi Arabia and one or two ambitious hangers-on who went to Egypt.[74]

F. C. L. Chauncy, the British Consul-General, wrote the following:

> I am impressed with the detailed knowledge of his country and amazing sense of judgment and timing which the Sultan has shown and his courage in adversity and the resilience and staying power which have enabled him to achieve this personal triumph … Experienced, his views are always sound, and even if they do not sometimes accord with our own, they are invariably worth consulting. He can … act very quickly and resolutely in case of need and procrastination is usually only encountered when he is in fact testing a proposal or staving off something in which he genuinely had no faith.[75]

Unfortunately for Sultan Said and the country, this triumph was short lived, and a fresh rebellion ensued.[76] While in Riyadh, Saudi Arabia, Talib and his supporters established a "government in exile" and an "Imamate Office" in Cairo. Establishing the "Imamate Office" in Cairo would take advantage of the spirit of Arab nationalism promulgated by Nasser. Saudi Arabia provided refuge, money, while Radio Cairo was the "platform from which they could simultaneously project both the impression of independence and the claim of having been abused by the Sultan and his "foreign allies."[77] On 14 June 1957, Talib bin Ali led a new group, called the Oman Revolutionary Movement, into Batinah and eventually to the interior of the country. Talib went to visit his brother, the former Imam who was allowed to retire with the promise of good behavior, in the village of Sait (in central Oman).[78] The area was under siege by the Sultan's regiment, but they were soon outnumbered and had to withdraw. Talib's forces had recaptured the former Imamate capital.[79] According to a secret memo sent to the Foreign Office,

> the military reverse was due to bad leadership; technical failures of mortars and antique guns to destroy the fort; refusal of tribal auxiliaries to face automatic fire; the lack of local intelligence leading to ambush at Nizwa of the forces withdrawing from Sait; and collapse of morale following this due to the inexperience of the men and the lack of seasoned N.C.O.'s.[80]

The message that came from Muscat to the Foreign office in London reveals the level of desperation and the centrality of Buraimi to the parties concerned:

> In view of the disaster which has overtaken the Sultan in Central Oman, I think we should now allow for the possibility of … movement from Saudi Arabia aimed at taking Buraimi and so linking-up with the ex-imam's supporters in Central Oman.

I recommend, therefore, that very urgent thought be given to protecting Buraimi which is now, more than before, a key point. This is to my mind more important than Central Oman which must be regarded for the time being as definitely lost to the Sultan. We must hold Buraimi securely to be able to reach Fahud which is now the center of the Sultan's forces.[81]

The actions of Muscat, Riyadh, or the Sheikdoms were largely going to be determined by the degree of support received from either Washington or London. A quick review of Britain's position on the Middle East is necessary to fully appreciate the implications on Muscat's possible course of action.

In the 1950s, the United Kingdom was the dominant power in the Middle East and wished to remain so for the foreseeable future. The United Kingdom's reliance on cheap oil to stabilize an otherwise weakening economy necessitated the ability to project authority and power within the region. More importantly, however, many in London believed that Britain's position as a great power throughout the world relied heavily on their continued influence in the Middle East. To that end, the Suez Canal alone boasted 80,000 British troops; Aden had numerous naval facilities; air squadrons flew over Iraq; and finally, a string of protectorates dotted the Persian Gulf. Regional interference in Omani politics came not only from Saudi Arabia (as in the case of Buraimi) but also from Egypt under its rising star, Nasser, and Iran under Prime Minster Mossadeq.[82]

Given the United States' global commitments, Washington had limited resources to commit to the Middle East. This gave the British room to maneuver in the region—an assumption that proved to be subsequently disastrous and possibly contributed to the Suez crisis. Yet for London to retain its supremacy in the Middle East and in order to avoid major disagreements, there had to be a mutual respect and understanding between its and Washington's sphere of influence. To that end, Prime Minister Churchill visited President-elect Dwight D. Eisenhower in January 1953. Eisenhower did not share Churchill's enthusiasm. In his diary he recorded that "Churchill was old-fashioned and feeble, and surely due for retirement." "Anglo-American unity," Eisenhower wrote, "was nothing but a ploy to maintain British influence in the Middle East; the re-creation of the wartime alliance was inappropriate now, and of little value."[83]

While the United Kingdom perceived King Saud's behavior over Buraimi as reckless and sustainable only with Washington's support,[84] Dulles had nothing but scathing remarks about the British and French presence in the Middle East, and described both in a trip to the Middle East on 6 September 1953 as "millstones around our neck."[85]

Whether the Buraimi dispute had a direct result in undermining the Anglo-American alliance and could have eventually led to the rupture of the Atlantic Alliance during the Suez crisis is beyond the scope of this research. However, one can confidently claim that the Buraimi dispute had far more repercussions upon the alliance than both powers expected. After the Suez crisis, Dulles explained to a reporter that the recent chains of events in the Middle East had very largely stemmed from the British action in the Buraimi Oasis. If the effects could be reversed and an Anglo-Saudi agreement secured King Saud could be detached from Egypt,[86] possibly join the Baghdad Pact, and the United States might be able to do likewise.[87]

The British prime minister of the period during the Suez Crisis, Anthony Eden, wrote in his memoirs: "During the Suez crisis, I learnt that the United States[88] Government had regarded our action during the autumn of 1955 in furthering the reoccupation of Buraimi by the Sultan of Muscat and the Sheikh of Abu Dhabi as an act of aggression."[89] Eden continued to maintain that his actions over the Suez were justified, as a short Cabinet paper written by him indicates. More importantly for our purposes, he pointed out that "it may be that the United States attitude to us in the Middle East dates from our refusal to give up Buraimi."[90]

Certainly as early as 1953, the Eisenhower administration was already under pressure from Riyadh to do something about "British aggression." The following excerpt from a declassified memorandum of conversation between United States Secretary of State John Foster Dulles and Crown Prince Saud bin Abdul Aziz on 18 May 1953 is instructive:

> The Crown Prince claimed that the US had deserted the Saudis in their dispute with the UK over Buraimi, that UK actions constituted aggression against Saudi Arabia, and that President Truman had stated that any aggression against Saudi Arabia would be of concern to the US. Secy. of State Dulles replied that the US had tried to use its influence with the UK to bring about a peaceful solution, and the UK had expressed its desire for neutral arbitration; in any case the US could not promise to go to war with the UK over Buraimi. "Mr. Dulles asked Prince Saud to tell him frankly whether it was in the interest of America and Saudi Arabia that America engage in war with Britain? The Crown Prince replied by asking whether it was in the interest of America that the British take aggressive action against Saudi Arabia."[91]

Buraimi was obviously of key importance to Saudi Arabia, for even when Eisenhower sent a letter of condolence on the death of the founder of the kingdom, King Bin Saud, the new King Saud Al-Saud saw this as an opportunity to bring up the Buraimi dispute. In his reply, he expressed his appreciation for the efforts of the United States in the Buraimi dispute but also expressed his "disappointment that these efforts [had] not been more successful."[92]

In Muscat, the political situation was escalating dangerously, with Talib's successful foothold in the interior and eventual occupation of Nizwa in July 1957.[93] Sultan Said's hard work and plans to unify the country under Muscat and to limit Muscat's dependence on Great Britain—by relieving the country of its debts—were unraveling. Not only did Muscat lack the resources to match Talib, who was receiving generous aid from the Saudis, but also Britain, Muscat's oldest and closest ally, had just emerged from the disastrous Suez crisis. Prime Minister Harold Macmillan wrote in his memoirs that after 1956, "to embark single-handed upon a further military enterprise, even of a modest character, seemed at first to some of my colleagues hazardous and even foolhardy."[94]

In addition, London was being hounded from almost every quarter in the Middle East by the rising tides of Arab nationalism and anti-imperialism. In the Gulf region, Saudi Arabia had already cut diplomatic relations, allegedly in protest over the Suez crisis debacle. In other words, London had to be considerably more cautious and tactful in its actions with the new rebellion. Also, Washington had no sympathy for London's pleadings. Indeed, when Crown Prince Abdullah of Iraq asked Dulles what he "thought the real attitude of King Saud was toward Iraq and the Baghdad Pact," Dulles replied "that one of the great hurdles to overcome was the rather belligerent attitude of the British along the Arabian Sea, particularly in relation to Oman."[95]

Meanwhile, Sultan Said recognized that he clearly lacked the forces necessary to dislodge the rebels from the interior of Oman. He had no alternative but to request British aid, which although forthcoming, was weak and hesitant.[96] On 16 July 1957, the Sultan wrote to the British Consul General in Muscat requesting assistance:

> You have full knowledge of the situation which has now developed as Nezwa and I feel that time has now come when I must request the maximum military and air support which our friend Her Britannic Majesty's Government can give in these circumstances, as on those past occasions which have so cemented our friendship and for which I bear lasting gratitude.[97]

Although the British were hesitant to provide aid, the initial results were promising. Nizwa fell to the Sultan on 11 August 1957; however, the leaders of the Immamte forces and their supporters managed to depart to the Jabel Akhdar (Green Mountain). Al-Akhdar is a

> sheer limestone massif between forty and fifty miles in length and twenty miles wide, with a fertile plateau at six thousand feet and peaks rising to nearly ten thousand feet at the summits; the approaches to the mountain led through narrow ravines which could be held by a few determined marksmen against an army.[98]

Dislodging the Imamate forces was obviously going to be an arduous task. As Philips contends,

> throughout the rest of 1957 and the long months until June 1958, the military operations consisted of small groups of fighters going up one track to another and returning to base after twenty-four to forty-eight hours. On the Sultan's side there were no deaths and only four men were wounded.[99]

According to David Smiley, the Commander of the Sultan's Armed Forces (SAF), this grim situation was only improved when a

British mission led by Julian Amery visited Muscat in January, 1958, and in the following July, during the Sultan's visit to the UK, there was published an Exchange of
Letters between HMG and the Sultan which covered the provision of assistance in
the expansion and reorganization of the Sultan's Armed Forces and in financing a
civil development program.[100]

Joyce contends, however, that

> although Whitehall agreed to provide subsidies that would permit him to improve the
> quality of his army, to establish an air force, and to begin a development program,
> for almost three months, from May to July 1958, the Sultan remained in London,
> removed from events in his country.[101]

This assessment is neither fair nor valid. The above line of argument ignores the
fact that this may have been Sultan Said's method of pressuring Whitehall to act.
By remaining in London, Sultan Said was at the center of the events of his country,
not at the periphery. He recognized that without substantial British aid, the interior
might be lost with or without his presence. He also recognized, as Joyce herself
points out, that Whitehall depended on him to secure "an interest vital to our own
position in the Gulf, that is the control of the interior."[102] She adds that the Sultan
was considered an "outstanding negotiator, cool and careful."[103] It seems more
probable that Sultan Said was vying for time while requesting more aid. Ever since
the "Agreement," great progress had been made in reorganizing and reequipping
the Sultan's forces. Records from the British Army indicate that they were "still not
sufficiently trained to carry out unassisted the difficult though small-scale military
operations involved in an occupation of the Jebel."[104]

A top-secret document from the Ministry of Defense indicates that by 12
August 1958, the Imamate forces were still a force to contend with and actually
were gaining new ground:

> The situation in Oman has become serious for three main reasons.
>
> (a) The limited harassing action we have been allowed to take has proved inef-
>   fective against the rebels.
> (b) The blockade of the Jebel Akhdar with the troops available has been one in
>   name and does not appear to have seriously interfered with the supply of
>   arms to the rebels. Indeed so good is the supply that Talib has been able to
>   step up his operations to include 81 M.M. mortaring of SAF camps and the
>   use of heavier mines.
> (c) The political situation amongst the tribes on and near to the Jebel Akhdar is
>   deteriorating. Recent reports show that this deterioration is spreading. For
>   these reasons it is clear that this situation cannot be allowed to continue but
>   must be settled now and that nothing less than a full scale operation will
>   bring this about.
>
> Now, however, the rebel forces with Saudi Arabian small support have been built up
> and contain in addition to small arms, a plentiful supply of mines, mortars, and possi-
> bly heavy machine guns.[105]

Despite knowing perfectly well that the Saudis were behind the supply of weapons, London never acknowledged it publicly, because it feared the consequences of upsetting the Saudis or, more importantly, their Washington backers as the ensuing secret telegram distributed to the commonwealth on 19 July 1957 indicates:

> You may now inform Commonwealth authorities that this revolt against authority of the Sultan had broken out in Central Oman; and that Sultan has appealed to United Kingdom Government for help, which will be given as necessary though the precise forms it will take have not yet been decided ... You may add that we have ample evidence that revolt has been inspired and fomented by Egyptians and Saudis and sustained by arms smuggled from outside, but that in any publicity which becomes necessary we shall do our utmost to avoid making accusations with King Saud. This may be difficult as the press will no doubt get hold of the facts ... you should not give the impression that this incident provides ground for international concern. It should be represented as a minor outbreak of local trouble, with which we are dealing on routine precautionary lines.[106]

It is rather remarkable that while lives were being lost in Oman (British as well as Omani) due to continued supplies of weapons (especially mines) from Saudi, London's reaction was so low-key. Smiley reports that by the end of 1958, the British began to

> have casualties, sometimes fatal, from the heavy American mines, although fortunately its bulk and weight made it harder to smuggle. The ideal answer, of course, would have been for us to stop the mines at source, in other words to persuade the Americans either to stop supplying them to the Saudi Army or to exercise some control over their use. I know we tried, but the Americans were brutally unsympathetic. Their reply was that they supplied the mines to Saudi Arabia under their military Aid Program, and it was not their concern how the Saudis chose to employ them.[107]

Riyadh, on the other hand, continued to deny that it was the source of the arms. A top secret document from the Department of State records that King Saud was alleging that the "arms Ghalib and his followers have now were brought there by the Government of India by agreement between Nasser and Nehru concluded through Krishna Menon."[108] Washington certainly had other concerns more important than British "sensibilities," as the following record indicates:

> Since the Oman rebellion began, I have seen Mr. Dulles three times. Throughout, he has been studious enough to avoid anything which could be construed as interference or comment. But that does not mean that the United States Government are not deeply concerned. They are alarmed on two main counts. First they are worried lest their recent efforts to win King Saud away form Nasser will be prejudiced. Secondly, they are always anxious when force is threatened or used by others than themselves. They argue that no one can tell where such things may lead from small beginnings and they calculate that, in the last resort, they are the only power on the Western

front who can carry any ultimate involvement to a final conclusion. These worries are now beginning to find their way into the American Press.

—I do not, of course, suggest that the Americans are on balance wise.[109]

The press started covering the story, as expressed in an editorial of the *New York Times* dated 6 August 1957, under the headline "Mediterranean Balance Sheet." The editorial stated that

as the revolt is fed with arms smuggled from or through Saudi Arabia, this intervention threatens to bring Britain into conflict with King Saud who sides with the United States against Nasser on the Communist issue, but could now be forced back into Nasser's arms.

Great Britain attempted to placate the United States' concern over Saudi Arabia, by proposing a joint U.S.-U.K. assessment of the Persian Gulf. The response from the State Department states was a courteous refusal:

In our view, UK-Saudi Arabian relations remain the key to improving US-UK understanding on Persian Gulf problems ... The basic differences [arise] from our respective approaches to these problems ... These approaches are unlikely to be modified by a joint assessment in the absence of an indication of UK willingness to take the necessary steps to reestablish relations with Saudi Arabia on a satisfactory basis.[110]

Whatever the source of the weapons at the disposal of the Imamate forces, clearly for the Sultanate and the British troops, the mines were of the greatest threat. According to P.S. Allfree, the mines were "an imperial headache ... At the height of the plague, we lost two and sometimes three trucks blown up in one day. We had no wealth of lorries and certainly none to spare, so this was developing for us into something like the U-boat blockade was to Britain."[111] In addition, Oman's infamous heat was taking its toll on the Sultan's forces. In Nizwa, the temperature reached 125° Fahrenheit in the shade and limited British troop's operations until the "cooler weather began in October. As a matter of fact, of the fifty British troops attached to me, forty-five had to be flown out to hospital suffering from heat exhaustion and two more died of it."[112] Things began to change for the Sultan's forces by November 1958 when British troops from the Special Air Service (SAS) arrived. They were "the coolest and most frightening body of professional killers I have ever seen."[113] After identifying possible routes onto the plateau, the first incursions into the plateau began in December but faced fierce resistance. They had to call for further SAS reinforcements to carry out the final assault in January 1959. By February 1959, the Al-Akhdar was under the Sultan's forces, but the main leaders of the rebellion again managed to escape to Saudi Arabia.

The Suez crisis was a debacle, yet soon after Britain was prepared to get involved in Oman. The question is why. What would Britain have to gain by supporting the Sultan? Was it oil, as many claimed?[114] Or was it the

long-standing friendship between the two countries? Should British involvement in Omani affairs be taken for granted? And finally, and most importantly,
what is Oman's role in all of this?

To attempt to answer these questions, it is necessary to return to January
1958. According to David Smiley, the Commander of the SAF, the armed conflict between the Imamate forces and the Sultan's forces in Oman was essentially at a standstill. The Sultanate forces began to gain the upper hand only
after an exchange of letters between HMG and Sultan Said during his visit to
England in July 1958.[115] An important agreement, the 1958 Agreement, was
signed and is reproduced here:

> In pursuance of the common interests of Your Highness and Her Majesty's Government
> in furthering the progress of the Sultanate of Muscat and Oman, Her Majesty's Govern-
> ment in the United Kingdom have agreed to extend assistance towards the strengthening
> of Your Highness's Army. Her Majesty's Government will also, at Your Highness's
> request, make available regular officers on secondment from the British Army, who
> will, while serving in the Sultanate, form an integral part of your Highness's armed
> forces. The terms and conditions of service of these seconded British officers have been
> agreed with Your Highness. Her Majesty's Government will also provide training facili-
> ties for members of Your Highness's armed forces and will make advice available on
> training and other matters as may be required by Your Highness.
>
> Her Majesty's Government will also assist Your Highness in the establishment of
> an Air Force as an integral part of Your Highness's armed forces, and they will make
> available personnel to this Air Force.
>
> Your Highness has approved the conclusion of an agreement for the extension of
> the present arrangements regarding civil aviation and the use by the Royal Air Force
> of the airfields at Salalah and Masirah.
>
> We also discussed the economic and development problems of the Sultanate and
> Her Majesty's Government agreed to assist Your Highness in carrying out a civil de-
> velopment programme which will include the improvement of roads, medical and
> educational facilities and an agricultural programme.[116]

Much of this agreement reiterates British support to Sultan Said, with the
exception of one part, where Said purportedly approved the conclusion "of an
agreement for the extension of the present arrangements regarding civil aviation
and the use by the Royal Air Force of the airfields at Salalah and Masirah."
This is in stark contrast to a secret document that elaborated on the same
"agreement":

> As your Excellency is aware His Highness the Sultan of Muscat and Oman paid a
> private visit to this country from the 26th of May to the 27th of July, and during this
> time conducted negotiations with Her Majesty's Government.
>
> 2. In these negotiations Her Majesty's Government pursued four main objectives.
> These were, to confirm the arrangement provisionally agreed as the result of
> Mr Julian Amery's mission to Muscat in January concerning the reorganization of
> the military and civil administration of the Sultanate; secondly, to complete the

details of the extension, to which the Sultan had agreed in principle in January, of facilities for the Royal Air Force at Masirah and Salalah; thirdly, to persuade the Sultan to agree for a satisfactory settlement with the Government of Pakistan and Gwadur; and finally, to discuss with the Sultan the improvement of his relations with Saudi Arabia. The first three of these objectives were achieved, but no progress was made with the fourth.[117]

BRITISH OBJECTIVES AND MUSCAT'S POLICIES

In this document Saudi Arabia and Pakistan are at the forefront, coupled with the hope for a completion for an extension for the Royal Air Force facilities at Masirah. However, the exact nature of British interests and objectives in supporting Sultan Said are still not evident; for that we need to look at a confidential British document describing British Objectives in Muscat on 17 July 1958:

- In supporting the Sultan as part of our general policy in the Persian Gulf we wish to strengthen him enough to avert any renewed necessity for open intervention by British forces.
- We wish to retain the R.A.F. facilities in Masirah and Salalah which are granted to us by the Sultan.
- We need to protect the oil interests of the British-managed Iraq Petroleum Company, a subsidiary of which holds the concession for the promising oil areas in Central Oman.
- We must encourage the Sultan to compose his differences with his neighbors, particularly Saudi Arabia and Pakistan, since these differences are an embarrassment in our own relations with these countries.[118]

Because of Britain's importance to Muscat, and because no serious study of Muscat's foreign policy during this period can be conducted without taking into account Britain's interests and objectives, an analysis of these objectives and the details of Said's response to each follows.

1. In supporting the Sultan as part of our general policy in the Persian Gulf we wish to strengthen him enough to avert any renewed necessity for open intervention by British forces.

British involvement in Omani politics is centuries old. Neither Muscat nor London wanted an intimate involvement in Oman's internal affairs. Sultan Said strove throughout his life to keep close relations with London—as long as he could control them to his own advantage. He understood that seeking Britain's help against the Imamate supporters would only give more credence to the accusations made either internally or externally of his subservience to British "imperialism" at the expense of his "Arab brothers," but he had no choice. He lacked the necessary resources in sufficiently trained men and military hardware, and he faced a rebellion that, although small in numbers, was better equipped and supported by two of the most significant players in Arab politics at the time, Egypt and Saudi Arabia. Sultan Said had to turn to London or risk the creation of a full-fledged state that might eventually swallow Muscat itself.

As for London, the timing of Sultan Said's request for aid, shortly after the Suez crisis and during its tension with the United States over Buraimi, could not have been worse. British credibility and prestige had to be maintained. The British dilemma was to assert its credibility among the regional allies and avoid the appearance of aggression against another Arab nation, as Nasser and Saudi Arabia had made it seem. The 1958 Agreement between Muscat and London was more or less an attempt to provide that delicate balance, as the following document from the Foreign Office to Washington clearly indicates.

As you also know we have tried to avoid giving the Sultan the kind of help which can be represented as a large-scale British military intervention in Arab Affairs. On the other hand, if we do not bring this matter to a successful determination, the friendly elements in the Arab world will think that we have no longer the power to give an effective help. I have already had an enquiry from a visiting Sheikh from Kuwait as to whether we are still capable of giving effective help to those whom we have promised to support. ... One possibility was to mount a large-scale operation with British troops to clear the mountain once and for all. We have decided against that because it is precisely the kind of operation which would be grist to Nasser's propaganda mill.[119]

In fact, the official Foreign Office view was very much opposed to military operations in Oman, arguing that the operation might be "stopped in the United Nations before it got under way and that in any case it would cause a great public outcry ... The Foreign Office have the very definite impression that the Sultan has realized that he cannot expect us to go on pulling his chestnuts out of the fire."[120] The Prime Minister concurred, as recorded in minutes dated 28 August 1957: "The war seems to be beginning again ... We can stand a lot more of this, in the hope of getting the rebels. But the ungrateful Sultan should be told he cannot order our air about at will."[121] Yet again, Whitehall realized that "whatever the theoretical legal position, we are regarded in the Gulf and indeed generally as protecting Muscat and failure to do so would have repercussions elsewhere." A British representative in Dubai reported that the "Oman affair" was harming Britain's reputation in the Trucial States, "the more so perhaps because it has not yet succeeded in finishing off the rebellion."[122]

London could have disengaged itself from the 1958 Agreement because of the frustration coming from Whitehall, directed at Sultan Said, as indicated in the following record:

Record of Conversation Between the Minster of State and his Highness the Sultan of Muscat and Oman.

Mr. Profumo said that at this point he would like to go back to the Secretary of State's warning that, if another crisis broke out, the kind of risks which we had been willing to run in 1957 would make it impossible for us to assist the Sultan in the same way as we had done last time. The object of our help last time was to put the

Sultan in a position to defend himself without recourse to outside assistance. We could not, however, go on pouring out arms, money and men to provide a makeshift military solutions to a problem which was essentially political and economic …

The Sultan said that one important point not mentioned by Mr. Profumo had been the fact that the rebels were being helped from outside his country. The Sultan was not up against the rebels only but also against Saudi Arabia and Cairo. What was going on was being forced on the Sultan by other people, and largely because the Sultan himself was being accused of friendship with the British.[123]

However, possible alternatives were simply unfeasible:

4. There are alternative courses to the proposed increased program:
    (a) Some form of disengagement.
    (b) To continue our aid only to the extent of the program decided in 1958 at an annual cost of 80,000.
    (c) To give a guarantee of protection to the Sultan, enabling us to dispense with expansion of his forces.

All these courses have disadvantages … Briefly, the Foreign Secretary concludes that disengagement would be dishonorable and imperil our material interests in the Gulf; that to peg the subsidy at about 800,000 a year would be ineffective; and that a guarantee would make British military intervention, with all its undesirable consequences, almost inevitable in the event of any serious threat to the Sultan's position. Thus, he concludes that there is virtually no choice but to meet the increases coast that is now seen to be necessary for the kind of assistance agreed in 1958.[124]

The British required a balancing act among several goals: supporting Muscat, acting in Britain's best interests, living up to its responsibilities to the Arab Gulf states (many of which were not full fledged states yet) without undermining its relations with Saudi Arabia, and, importantly, guarding the Persian Gulf against Nasser. Arab and non-Arab capitals felt the brunt of Nasser's pressure to limit, if not end, British presence. The following lengthy cable illustrates the spirit of the times:

The Iraqi press and public were slow to begin to take an interest in the Omani rebellion. Once they had done so the reactions were uniformly critical of Her Majesty's Government and often hostile … As I have reported … the Iraq Government at first hoped that the whole affair would be over before they were compelled by events to take a stand; at that stage their only concern was to ensure that nothing was said publicly to suggest that we were using our staging post facilities at Habbaniya to assist our military effort so that they could no be accused by the other Arab countries of assisting imperialism against their "brother Arabs" … in the end they found themselves obliged to commit themselves, and at this point, despite their correct understanding of the statue of the Sultan, they do not appear to have doubted that the right course was to stand with the other Arabs in disregard of what they knew to be the right cause. This was because the initiative in pressing for action in the Security

Council was taken by the Saudi representative and they feared that any hesitation would throw King Saud back into the arms of Nasser at this critical Juncture. The Foreign Ministry were extremely distressed at having to support a view of the status of Oman with which they did not believe, but Ministers were inclined to take the line: "Surely you would prefer that we should sign an objectionable letter attacking you about this unimportant affair that that we should risk damaging our *rapprochement* with Saudi Arabia which we, urged on by you, have so laboriously achieved." The Government was undoubtedly right in thinking that they would have incurred unpopularity if they had not gone along with the other Arabs in attacking the United Kingdom. From the start they allowed the press, which is feeling its oats under the new administration, to follow the line put out by the Egyptians and "The Voice of the Arabs." Once this has happened they could not have put the machine into reverse without strong and unpopular measures. So the Omani rebels became "heroic Arab nationalists" struggling to be free; the British were "aggressors" and, because of exaggerated reports of the fighting, "bloodthirsty imperialists." The rebels became accepted as the protagonists of a progressive modern force and the Sultan as the representative of a reactionary servility to imperialism ... I think we must draw from this affair two conclusions. First the use of British forces in Oman or in the Persian Gulf in the future would inevitably tend to range the Iraqi press, public opinion and Government against us, in varying degrees, but more strongly than on the present occasion. We could not hope that reactions will be slow or so restrained, and the effect upon our relations with the Iraq may well be serious.[125]

The following cable was sent from a British representative in Tehran on 27 July 1957:

I had already spoken to the Minster of Foreign Affairs after dinner on July 24. I did again formally and in full this morning to Political Director general. Their reactions were to the same effect, viz: fear of a "Second Suez" ... I am afraid that this situation, unless quickly liquidated, will prove very awkward for us here. It is raising again all the old Suez bogies—anti-colonialism, Moslem solidarity, dislike of violence, alleged contempt of the United Nations, etc.[126]

The Foreign Office in Amman tried to use its good relations with King Hussein to remind King Saud that "we remain anxious for the restoration of the old friendship between our two countries and that we for our part do not desire that the Oman episode should delay this process. We are anxious to play the matter down and we hope that there is a corresponding desire on King Saud's part not to turn present events into an issue of Arabs against the West."[127] At the same time, London persistently tried to convince Sultan Said to mend fences with King Saud of Saudi Arabia, pointing out,

In the face of the Egyptian and Communist threat in Arabia it was particularly important to find some way of improving relations between the Sultan and the Saudi Government. The Sultan's view was that relations should first be restored between the United Kingdom and Saudi Arabia, after which it might be easier to establish more friendly relations between the Sultanate and Saudi Arabia. Indeed, he thought it would be positively dangerous to have an apparent détente at present since this would merely increase the opportunities open to the Saudis for the penetration of Oman. The Sultan withdrew the agreement which he had given in January to the suggestion that he might meet King Saud in certain circumstances. He did not consider that there were any problems other than Buraimi which could be usefully discussed with the Saudis, since Buraimi was the key to everything else.[128]

MUSCAT BETWEEN THE ARAB LEAGUE AND THE UNITED NATIONS

Although the actual war in Central Oman was over by January 1959, the political battle moved to the halls of the Arab League and the United Nations, where it remained for more than a decade. In December 1954, an obscure entity called the Imamate contacted Arab League authorities. The council was uncertain how to proceed. Ironically, it called on Saudi Arabia and Yemen to provide advice on the matter.[129] Apparently the Imamate was very much a mystery to the Arab League authorities, so much so that at one point during the early meetings dealing with the question of Oman's membership application, several distinguished members of the Arab League "adjourned to the library in a futile attempt to locate the 'state' in question on the map ... a 'state' without government, without boundaries and without recognition as a state by any other state."[130] The council of the Arab League needed time to investigate and postponed action on the pending application. Finally, on 14 October 1955, the Arab League reached a resolution on the pending membership in a manner that illustrated its lack of desire to face the issue.[131]

> The Council decided to request those member Arab states, who have not yet expressed their views on the question, to formulate their point of view regarding this [question], to the Council of the Arab league at its next session, so it may take a decision regarding the admission of the imamate to the League.[132]

Six months later, another resolution, dated 22 October 1956, recommended the following:

> 1-Continued efforts by the Member States should ensue until the Imamate of Oman recovers its rights and liberty.
> 2-Member States should instruct their delegates to the United Nations to address the present hardships of the Imamate at the forthcoming session of the General Assembly.[133]

The findings are significant, for they illustrate that the Imamate failed to gain recognition as a nation and consequently as a member of the Arab League. Because some of the League member states treated the issue as an internal problem of Oman, they preferred to refer it to the United Nations rather than deal with it themselves.[134] Thus, on 13 April 1957, the "Question of Oman" was raised in the United Nations by the representatives of several permanent Arab states (Egypt, Iraq,[135] Jordan, Lebanon, Libya, Morocco, Saudi Arabia, Sudan, Syria, and Yemen), who called on the President of the Security Council to convene so they could consider

> the armed aggression by the United Kingdom of Great Britain and Northern Ireland against the independence, sovereignty and the territorial integrity of the Imamate of Oman. In addition, the letter accused London of subjecting the people of Oman to armed aggression, which had taken the form of "full-scale war, involving the use of modern destructive weapons—such as rockets, bombers, Venom jets, armored cars, heavy mortar and machine guns—and military operations by British sea, air, and ground forces."[136]

This happened again on 15 August 1957. The Security Council received a cable from an Arab member of the United Nations requesting that they "convene an urgent meeting" to deal with the question of Oman and consider the "extreme gravity of the situation in that part of the Arab world." A letter dated 22 November indicated the role of Saudi Arabia and the importance of Buraimi and added that the United Kingdom, as a "prelude to the conquest of Oman, had seized the Saudi oasis of Buraimi."[137]

The agenda failed to obtain the affirmative votes of seven members and was not adopted. The question of Oman was subsequently considered at three sessions of the General Assembly.[138] Although Prime Minister Macmillan requested that the United States vote against inscription, President Eisenhower replied that "we can recognize that the common goals which we have cannot always be best achieved by our necessarily always taking a uniform public position."[139] The United Kingdom delegation to the United Nations reported that the Security Council debate on inscription was as follows: "Against inscription: the United Kingdom, France, Australia, Cuba, and Colombia; for inscription: the Soviet Union, Iraq, Sweden and the Philippines; abstentions:[140] the United States. The representative of China did not exercise his vote. The item therefore failed."[141] The permanent representatives of the Arab states, however, did succeed, on 29 September 1960, in placing the question of Oman on the agenda. Between 1960 and 1963, the "question of Oman was considered by the Special Political Committee, although none of its recommended resolutions were adopted by the Assembly."[142]

The heart of the matter, and the confusion over the question of Oman, was clearly articulated by the representative of Chile over a number of issues: Why did the Sultan not send a representative to the Assembly to defend his case? Did Oman and Muscat constitute a single state or two separate entities? Was the principle of self-determination at issue or was it a matter of the dismemberment of a sovereign state? Was the Treaty of Sib an international treaty between two sovereign independent states or was it only an agreement between the government of the Sultan and Omani tribal chiefs concerning internal matters? What was the present situation in Oman? Was there oppression? Were the inhabitants fighting foreign troops or did peace exist?[143]

The Secretary General created a fact-finding mission to clarify issues and look into the events reported in a letter dated 7 March 1963 by the head of the office of the Imamate of Oman in Cairo. The letter reported "horrible massacres committed by the colonial forces against the innocent citizens."[144] The mission headed by de Ribbing, Swedish ambassador to Spain, visited Oman from 25 May to 9 June 1963. Members of the mission had absolute freedom to go wherever they pleased, including the so-called stronghold of the Imamate forces, in Jabel Al-Akhdar. They were able to meet with about twenty government officials, interview eighty-six representatives, and explain the purpose of the visit to approximately twelve hundred people assembled at meetings. Attempts were made by many Arab delegates of the General Assembly to validate alleged statements by those interviewed about continued fighting; however, many meetings occurred without the presence of a government official, and mission members were "unable to hear one single shot in the most remote area of the country, or to detect a single sign of the excitement usually generated by a fight."[145] Disappointed with the report, the Arab states "backed by a comfortable Afro-Asian, anti-colonial majority, convinced the Assembly to establish another committee (the Ad Hoc Committee) to emphasize the case of the rebels. Subsequently, another committee of twenty-four was established but was denied entry into Oman."[146]

By 8 January 1965, the Ad Hoc Committee submitted its findings, and again the report was inconclusive. The committee expressed the belief that the question of Oman is a "serious international problem, requiring the special attention of the General Assembly; that it derived from imperialistic policies and foreign intervention in Muscat and Oman."[147] Having attributed the unrest and suffering of the people to this problem, the committee, therefore, believed that "all parties concerned should enter into negotiations to settle the question without prejudice to the positions taken by either side and should refrain from any action that might impede peaceful settlement."[148] The question of Oman remained open well after Sultan Qaboos' accession to the throne in 1970.

> The Arab countries request the inclusion of the item in the agenda because it is a colonial issue; Great Britain objects on the ground that it is an internal question; meanwhile a majority is easily gathered to vote for inclusion. The debates have the same themes: accusations and counter accusations, assertions and denials. The upshot is a committee of a sort coming out with a report reaffirming as ever the right of the people of Oman to self-determination.[149]

The single most important aspect of these debates for our purposes is the debates over the meaning of the Treaty of Sib, or the Agreement of Sib, which was signed at the village of al-Seeb by the tribal leaders of Oman's "interior" and the Sultanate on 25 September 1920. Through the mediation of R. E. L. Wingate, the document ushered in thirty-five years of peace. Under its terms, Imamate representatives pledged to 1) live in peace with the Sultanate; 2) not restrict trade and travel with the coast; 3) return fugitives from justice, and 4) honor claims of coastal merchants. The Sultanate, in turn, agreed to 1) charge no more than 5 percent duty on exports from the interior to the coast; 2) impose no restrictions on entry to and exit from coastal towns; 3) return fugitives from interior justice; and 4) not interfere with the tribes' internal affairs. "Despite its controversial nature, no authentic text of this agreement was presented to that body; it has been invoked by numerous delegations."[150] Sultan Said refused the British request to publish the agreement, claiming that the publication of the text,[151] "even with the statement that the agreement is dead, will open the door for argument."[152]

In his memoirs, the main architect of the Agreement, Sir Ronald Wingate, describes the difficulty of the initial negotiations:

> This was fatal, and I knew that I could not possibly agree to it on behalf of the Sultan, for this would mean that the Sultan acknowledged another ruler, and a ruler who was already an elected spiritual leader and an admitted temporal representative of the tribes. From such an acknowledgment it was only one step further for the spiritual leadership and temporal representation of the tribes to develop into a claim for the spiritual and temporal leadership of all Oman. The word Imam was omitted from the body of the document, which simply read as a conditions arranged between the Sultan's Government and Isa bin Salih as representing the Omani.[153]

On the signing of the Agreement, Sir Ronald observes:

> It was signed by me on behalf of the Sultan, with his full authority, and granted to the tribal leaders of Oman, all of whom signed individually, the right of self government, or non-interference by the Sultan in their internal affairs, in return for peace and for the payment of the customary dues at the ports in the territories controlled by the Sultan. The question of sovereignty was never mentioned. Had it been, there would have been no agreement. It recognized the facts of the situation, a situation which was not a new one, but had been a source of controversy and conflict for three quarters of a century. For in Arabia allegiance is tribal, and the tribe had no defined boundaries. Yet the existence of a Coastal Sultanate, a tribal confederation, and a religious leader, who would claim through election the temporal allegiance of the tribes, had, up till then, made impossible a modus vivendi where, by agreement, the coast and the interior each looked after its own affairs, while remaining in friendly contact.[154]

Supporters of the Imamate argued that the Agreement established an independent "Imamate of Oman," as opposed to the "Sultanate of Muscat." Thus, British aid and involvement in Oman from 1957 to 1959 were attempts to aid the Sultanate of Muscat to subjugate an independent Imamate of Oman.

Furthermore, if the question of legitimacy were raised at all, it would be directed to the Sultanate of Muscat, which was itself only two hundred years old, and which since 1891 could be considered to be a British protectorate or vassal.[155] Equally important was the fact of Britain's interference in Oman's affairs (the reference here is to both Muscat and Nizwa) was immoral and contrary to United Kingdom obligations under the United Nations (UN) Charter.[156] This last point seems to contradict the earlier contention that the Sultanate of Oman (Muscat) was a protectorate of Britain, and if that were the case, then the British would have been obliged to aid it.

The response from Muscat via the British representative at the UN was as follows. First, the

> sovereignty of the Sultans over the whole of Muscat and Oman has long been recognized internationally, e.g., by international treaties concluded with them, for example, by Great Britain in 1891 and again in 1951; by the United States in 1833 and 1958; France in 1846 and by India in 1953.[157]

An Arab scholar writing in 1975 supports the British contention that the Sib Agreement did grant Nizwa an internal independent character of its own, under which Nizwa reserved full authority in terms of administration, taxes, and "laws." As exemplified in the provisions concerning the extradition of criminals, however,

> there is nothing in the treaty which shows that the Sultan by signing it had in fact intended to relinquish his sovereignty over Oman, although he did not expressly assert it. There does not seem any reference in the treaty to the independence of Oman or to the government of the Imam. Instead, the reference is being made to the people of Oman.[158]

Finally, Sultan Said questioned whether the Imamate had lived up to its proper Ibadi election, thereby casting doubts on Ghalib's legitimacy.[159]

The question of Oman's legal status as a possible protectorate was important to British policy makers independent of the proceedings in the United Nations or the Arab League. Parliamentary questions were raised back in London: By what right was London intervening in Oman? Was there any obligation to assist the Sultan in maintaining internal security? If not, what was Britain's legal position in regard to military intervention?[160] If the Sultanate were legally considered a protectorate, Secretary of State for Foreign Affairs Selwyn Lloyd would not have had to stand in front of the British parliament justifying British military presence in Muscat. The Parliament was wary of a "second Suez," so British aid to Sultan Said had to be justified to a skeptical audience.

On 29 July 1957, Secretary Lloyd read a statement to the Parliament that the

> decision of Her Majesty's Government to give help to the Sultan was made for two reasons. First, it was at the request of a friendly ruler who had always relied on us to

help him resist aggression or subversion. Secondly, there is the direct British interest involved and I have no need to stress to the House the importance of the Persian Gulf.[161]

Lloyd then went on to indicate British obligations and interests in the Gulf:

In the gulf, we have certain formal and implicit obligations to the rulers of sheikh-doms under our protection to protect them against attack. This is generally understood throughout the area and it has always been assumed that Her Majesty's Government would honor her obligations.[162] The difference between a formal obligation of a long standing relationship of friendship[163] is not readily apparent to the local rulers and people. If we were to fail in one area it would begin to be assumed elsewhere that per-haps the anti-British propaganda of our enemies had some basis to it and that Her Majesty's Government were no longer willing or able to help her friends.[164]

The Imamate upheaval had been confined to a small though important area and the greater part of Omani tribes did not lend support to the former Imam. If they had, "it would have been impossible for the Sultan (British or no British) to hold the rebels in the Jabel Akhdar area, and they, for their part, would never have remained in their refuge had they been able to command tribal support in Oman."[165]

2. We wish to retain the R.A.F. facilities in Masirah and Salalah which are granted to us by the Sultan.

Masirah is "a large island, measuring some 40 miles (65 km) in length and up to 10 miles (16 km) in width. It lies 10 miles off the south-eastern coast of the Sultanate."[166] In 1930, British Lt. Col. M. C. Lake, the political officer from the Residency at Aden, had landed on the island to evaluate whether the island was suitable for the construction of a landing-ground for aircrafts as part of a potential development of air routes from the United Kingdom to India. On the outbreak of World War II, Sultan Said offered a general authorization to the Royal Air Force to use all air facilities available in the Sultanate, including Masirah. These facilities were in turn requested by the United States Army Air Corps in 1942, along with permission to construct various buildings for mainte-nance and personnel. The Sultan granted these requests with the understanding that some conditions had to be observed: stone buildings were to revert to the Sultanate intact, and all American personnel were to accept and abide by the local rules.[167]

For decades London had been satisfied with what was an ad hoc arrangement with Sultan Said concerning Masirah. The request had been made on the basis of a need and in turn approval had been granted. The importance of the island for London had been military in nature, as the following secret memo indicates:

It was agreed with Mr. Parsons that the question of phasing out our dependence on Masirah should also be raised. Masirah has been such a sacred cow with the Ministry of Defense that this suggestion may come as something of a shock to some quarters of the MOD. Presentation of the idea may be important and since the implications of giving up Masirah go wider than Arabia Department's responsibility.[168]

Between 1957 and 1959, as Muscat struggled with the Imamate force, all would change. One of the conditions for granting support to Sultan Said was the continuous use of Masirah by the British Royal Air Force, according to the Agreement of 1958. Whitehall now wanted a 99-year lease for Masirah with the possibility of an extension. This was a significant departure from the previous ad hoc arrangements.

> As your Excellency is aware His Highness the Sultan of Muscat and Oman paid a private visit to this country from the 26th of May to the 27th of July, and during this time conducted negotiations with Her Majesty's Government.
> 5. The Sultan handled the negotiations on Royal Air Force facilities entirely on his own, and most capably. He succeeded in his object of keeping the arrangements as closely as possible to the existing arrangements. He also made it clear that he intended to exact the maximum rental which the market would bear, and in the end he obtained a total of 17,000 compared with the previous 6,000 a year (15,000 a year for the facilities at Masirah, and 2,000 a year for those at Salalah). These figures were acceptable to Her Majesty's Government, but it is doubtful whether the total could have been restricted to a reasonable sum if the British delegation had started with a higher opening bid that the 8,000 which was offered. The Sultan expressed some concern during the exchanges over Masirah about the possible consequences for the Sultanate of the use by Her Majesty's Government of the facilities there which he thought might involve his country in a major war. In the end, however, he accepted Mr. Amery's explanations of the uses to which the leased area would be put, and understood that in legislating for a period of 99 years it was difficult to be very precise.[169]

The available literature on Oman either makes a passing mention of Masirah, or describes the importance of the island solely in the context of the post-1970 period. It neglects to mention that London sought a 99-year lease of Masirah. In other instances, Masirah is mentioned for the mere purpose of depicting Sultan Said as a subservient agent of British imperialism.[170] However, Masirah was a key component of the 1958 agreement, and the simple fact that Whitehall was looking for a 99-year lease in contrast to the usual short ad hoc arrangements signifies the introduction of important new variables that should be investigated. Equally important is the clause stating that the 99-year lease had proved to be a contentious point between London and Sultan Said. For the latter point, the following record, dated 18 August 1960, between Sultan Said and Her Majesty's Government representative is clear:

> Mr. Walmsley showed to the Sultan the original record of the meeting between the Sultan and Mr. Julian Amery, prepared by Mr. Amery and presented to the Foreign Secretary, containing the sentence "on the question of the jurisdiction the Sultan said he had come round to the view that Her Majesty's Government should have the full

jurisdiction over the British Service personnel in the leased area for the full duration of the lease."

The Sultan said that he did not recall having used the words "for the full duration of the lease." The record had not been cleared with him at the time of the visit to London in 1958, and he had not signed any document which committed him on this subject. So far as he was concerned the position was that Her Majesty's Government had jurisdiction in the leased area of Masirah on the basis of exchange of Letters of 1951 and the further Exchange of Letters of 1955. When the time came for him to deal with the 1951 Exchange of letters, which was due to expire on December 31, 1961, the question of jurisdiction in Massirah would of course be dealt with at the same time.[171]

When the subject was raised once again on 24 August 1960, the Sultan remained unconvinced:

Mr. Heath ... Her Majesty's Government had been working on the assumption that jurisdiction in the leased area was assured for 99 years ... The Sultan said that he had not signed anything relating to the surrender of jurisdiction for 99 years. He had discussed jurisdiction in 1958 with Mr. Julian Amery but he did not remember saying about 99-year period.[172]

(Unfortunately, due to the present inaccessibility of the archives, I am unable to verify which of the claims proved accurate; however, Masirah did revert to Oman in 1977.) Differences of interpretation aside, the questions remain: Why did London request a lease at that particular juncture, and why is the island a significant part of the 1958 agreement?

Masirah had an importance for the British Defense Department that other British government agencies, such as the Arabian Department, did not quite understand. London's 1971 Foreign Office review of long-term policy in the Persian Gulf maintained that "support of UK forces stationed in Hong Kong, Malaysia and Singapore depends upon the continued availability of the CENTO air route or, if necessary, its less desirable alternatives ... Integrity of the CENTO route rests upon continued security of tenure in Cyprus, Masirah and Gan and of the overflying rights over Turkey and Iran."[173]

An earlier, perhaps more accurate assessment of the importance of Masirah was made in the review of 1959. It stated that "strategically, Masirah island is important, though not essential as a stepping stone to the far east. Masirah is essential so long as we have to conduct military operations on any scale within the Gulf itself."[174] This is not to claim that Masirah is not important as a staging post or as a stepping stone to either the far East or South-East Asia, but rather to demonstrate the primary importance of Masirah: to protect British interests within the Gulf itself.

3. We need to protect the oil interests of the British-managed Iraq Petroleum Company, a subsidiary of which holds the concession for the promising oil areas in Central Oman.

The 1958 document uses the word "promising" to describe the discovery of oil, yet as early as 1925 and as late as 1956, the results of oil exploration in Oman had been disappointing. Most of the oil companies had refocused their energies on Kuwait and Saudi Arabia. Admittedly, oil was found in 1957; however, its viscosity made it too expensive to utilize.[175] By contrast, oil was found almost immediately in Bahrain, and in Kuwait, oil fields were developed so quickly that by 1953 Kuwait became the largest oil producer in the Gulf. In short, although the agreement points to protecting "promising" Omani oil fields as a key component of British objectives in Oman in 1958, in reality Omani oil played a minor role. London's desire to lease Masirah for 99 years was an effort to secure oil interests in the rest of the Persian Gulf, especially in Kuwait. When Secretary Lloyd had to justify London's involvement in Oman in July 1957, he had concluded that Her Majesty's Government was bound to help a friendly ruler like Sultan Said, saying, "there is the direct British interest involved and I have no need to stress to the House the importance of the Persian Gulf."[176] A memo from 1960 called The Future Policy Report was circulated to various Ministers attesting to Britain's oil interests:

> While we have at present no alternative to maintaining our political obligations to the Persian Gulf Rulers, and particularly to the Ruler of Kuwait, it should be the object of our policy over the next ten years to create a situation in which they can be terminated without undue damage to the security of our oil supplies and the general political stability of the area.[177]

In the same secret memo, the Foreign Secretary describes specific British objectives in the Persian Gulf and divides them into three categories: 1) Economic: access to oil produced in the Persian Gulf states (the oil and the sterling balances of Kuwait are particularly important); 2) Political: treaty obligations and defense of the area against the spread of Russian influence; 3) Strategic: maintenance of rights over Masirah.[178]

Masirah was important as a staging post to protect Kuwait.[179] The significance of Kuwaiti oil to the British economy is further demonstrated in the record of a discussion between Sir Roger Stevens of the Foreign Office and Mr. Lewis Jones of the United States State Department:

> Mr. Lewis Jones said he had heard that H.M.G. were rethinking the British role in the Persian Gulf … Sir Roger Stevens said that there was no specific "rethinking process" going on … everything turned on Kuwait: nothing else was of really vital importance, and indeed our other positions in the Gulf and even Aden itself were maintained ultimately in order to secure Kuwait.[180]

On 27 July 1960 a minute submitted to the British Prime Minister clarifies the role of Oman with regards to Britain's oil interests:

> In general terms, however, there is no doubt that the stability of Muscat and our strategic rights in the Sultan's territory are important for preserving the position of the

United Kingdom in the Persian Gulf area as a whole, including Kuwait. In this context there are very valuable commercial and financial interests at stake ... So far our most important oil interests are centered round Kuwait. But there are prospects of development further South in the Gulf area and in the East Aden Protectorate. If these were to materialize, Oman would play an even more important part in their protection.[181]

So while protecting the possible finds of commercially viable oil in Oman may have been one of Britain's stated interests, it was not the main driving force behind British involvement in the 1950s. It was only when oil in commercial quantities was finally discovered in Oman in 1964 that Oman's relative importance became elevated. The following memo was sent from the British Prime Minister in the summer of 1964:

> The Press reports that oil has been discovered, possibly on large scale, in Oman suggests that covetous eyes may soon be turned to this area afresh. Would it be a good thing if the Official Defense Committee had a look at our arrangements for safeguarding our interests in Oman and preventing any attempt at a "take-over," whether by overt means or by subversion?[182]
> 4. We must encourage the Sultan to compose his differences with his neighbors, particularly Saudi Arabia and Pakistan, since these differences are an embarrassment in our own relations with these countries.

In July 1958, the date of the British objectives, the world had just witnessed the brutal overthrow of the Hashemite Kingdom of Iraq. In 1955, the Iraqi government and Turkey had concluded a most important agreement that would lead to the short-lived arrangement in 1958 known as the Baghdad Pact (and which also included Iran, Britain, and Pakistan). These events, together with the merging of Egypt and Syria the same year, ended all illusions that a key Arab country would be tied to the Western camp. As Nasser's successful bid to draw more Arab countries away from the West gained ground, the British encountered mounting pressure to support more vigorously those who regarded themselves the "true" friends of Her Majesty's Government. In this instance, both Islamabad and Riyadh considered themselves to be allies of HMG, at least as far as containing Nasser was concerned. Both countries also had claims on Oman's territory. Saudi Arabia's claim involved the Buraimi oasis. Pakistan was aggressively pursuing an old claim on Gawadur. Islamabad argued that Gawadur must be returned to Pakistan, since members of the Baghdad Pact were attempting to draw King Saud away from his previously close relations with Egypt's Nasser. Pakistan's Foreign Minster Firoz Khan Noon "warned that it would be impossible for Pakistan to support the sultan unless finally the Omani ruler agreed to relinquish Gawadur."[183]

Gawadur is an enclave on the Makran coast of Pakistan that had been part of the Sultanate from the late eighteenth century until its sale to Pakistan in 1958. A description of Gawadur in 1945 indicates that

> it had a population of 52 Omanis and 6830 Baluchis who were Muscat subjects, 400 Khojas, followers of the Agha Khan, 120 Hindus and some 371 others who were

British subjects, making the total of about 7773 in all. Of these, 5975 lived in the town of Gawadur.[184]

As early as 1948, Islamabad had approached Sultan Said through the appointed British political resident in the Persian Gulf, Sir Rubert Hay, to look into Sultan Said's position should Pakistan wish to negotiate for Gawadur. The Sultan had answered that he "could not willingly part with any of his dominions."[185] Islamabad raised the issue again in 1949 when Sultan Said visited Pakistan. However, the Sultan was not interested, and Pakistan's appeals for intervention to Whitehall fell on unsympathetic ears. By 1954, Islamabad, through London, offered to lease the area in perpetuity. The lease draft that was agreed upon by both Islamabad and London was presented to the Sultan in January 1955 via the political resident in the Persian Gulf, Sir Bernard Burrows. Once again, Sultan Said rejected the offer while indicating that he might be willing to negotiate, but only with London's participation.[186] Why was the Sultan suddenly willing to negotiate? Was he serious about these negotiations or was he vying for time?

The so-called draft lease reached Sultan Said in January 1955. By this time, the first Imamate forces had already taken over the interior, and more importantly, the Imamate leadership had approached the Arab League for membership. London's assistance was imperative, and Whitehall knew that Sultan Said would be hard pressed to resist mounting British pressure. London, argued Whitehall, was taking the brunt of anti-British propaganda from the Arab world for defending Sultan Said.[187] Pakistan might have taken this opportunity to follow suit and lash out at Muscat and London if Gawadur was not relinquished. The Sultan, argued Whitehall, was obliged to London "to purchase such support as is possible for our efforts to represent his cause abroad."[188] For the Sultan, a clear rejection of the offer, as in earlier times, was not prudent because of the importance of London's support to quell the rebellion. Thus, he opted for negotiations, while making the case that Muscat did not have the power to collect the rent from Pakistan if and when the Pakistani government stopped the payments. London's participation in the agreement would be vital to ensure the observance of all conditions agreed upon by all the concerned parties. Without British participation, Said argued, he would be forced to reject Pakistan's offer. Furthermore, Said was well aware of Whitehall's position against a third party bargaining between Muscat and Islamabad. In essence, the Sultan appeared to oblige British requests while repeatedly maintaining his earlier assertion: he "could not willingly part with any of his dominions."[189]

The pressure to sell Gawadur did not subside. Writing in 1957, Sir Bernard seemed to be among the few who continued to stress the importance of selling Gawadur to Pakistan, while showing some sympathy for Sultan Said:

> We are asking him to take a gamble with an important part of his patrimony in circumstances in which many of the determining factors are unknown, such as the presence of oil both in Muscat and in Gawadur, the future general policy of Pakistan.[190]

It is puzzling that Sir Bernard would mention the possibility of finding oil in Gawadur when he knew, or at least should have known, that hope of finding oil had been abandoned in Gawadur as early as 1939.[191] Sir Bernard's sympathy notwithstanding, by July 1958 Sultan Said had finally capitulated and agreed to sell Gawadur. Joyce claims that the Sultan's reluctant agreement came "not out of concern for Pakistan, but in order to help the British."[192] This is highly unlikely. If Said's desire was to please London, then he would have relinquished Gawadur in 1955 when the pressure first started mounting. Indeed, he could have relinquished Gawadur as early as the late 1940s, given his desire to rid Muscat of its crippling debts. Furthermore, Sultan Said was not a man likely to relinquish part of Muscat's territory to please London. If anything, throughout his life, he had attempted to regain Muscat's authority throughout Oman, rather than reduce Muscat's holdings, however distant. Even if he did want to please London, certainly there were many other ways London could have been pleased, not the least of which involved initiating contacts with Saudi Arabia. Sultan Said agreed to relinquish Gawadur for reasons that became clear in a conversation between Sultan Said and Britain's Secretary of State Julian Amery:

> The point he had in mind was that the position which the Sultan took up on Gwadur must inevitably affect Her Majesty's Government handling of the agreements on the matters, particularly with regard to their presentation in Parliament and elsewhere and in regard to timing. Pakistan's interest in Gwadur led them to very interested in the other matters. The Pakistanis knew that the Sultan was having discussions with Her Majesty's Government. Their pressure was mounting. If the Sultan did nothing about Gwadur, the Pakistanis might do something at any moment which would make the Sultan's position very difficult, and which Her Majesty's Government could not prevent.[193]

This meeting took place in June 1958 at the height of Imamate control of Al-Akhdar Mountain and a month before the July "Agreement" of 1958. The crux of the Secretary's comments to Sultan Said that "Pakistanis might do something at any moment which would make the Sultan's position very difficult, and which Her Majesty's Government could not prevent," is nothing short of a veiled threat. If and when Pakistan opted for a military solution and occupied Gawadur, HMG would be either unable or unwilling to restrain Islamabad. As such, Sultan Said would stand to lose both the territory and the possibility of renting or selling the enclave. Peterson's brief interpretation of the sale of Gawadur rests on the conclusion that the rebellion of 1957–1959 was simply beyond the financial capabilities of the Sultan, and thus he was forced to sell the enclave.[194] It is undeniably more realistic than Joyce's, but not entirely accurate either. Careful reading of a secret record from the Prime Minister's office may shed some light. The record summarizes the most salient points discussed and agreed upon by Sultan Said in a private visit to London between 25 May and 27 July 1958:

The Sultan stayed his hand on Gwadur until towards the end of the talks. He had been given to understand that Her Majesty's Government would not necessarily make a settlement on Gwadur a pre-condition of agreement on the subsidy. Nevertheless, care was taken to avoid completing the arrangement for the subsidy until the Sultan had both shown his willingness to transfer Gwadur and had indicated the probable size of his requirements for the rent of Masirah.[195]

A casual reading of the document seems to vindicate Peterson's conclusion, namely that the sale of Gawadur was due to the revenue needed to finance the campaigns against the Imamate forces. However, this is not the case. Whitehall was well aware that if the money gained from the sale of Gawadur was suffi-cient for Sultan Said's financial requirements to carry out the campaign against the Imamate forces, then threatening to withhold assistance until the sale of Gawadur was finalized was useless (since the finances needed for the campaign presumably would be already available from the sale of Gawadur). Realisti-cally, both the Sultan and Whitehall knew that the sale of Gawadur would not produce sufficient funding for the military campaign against the Imamate forces. To make the point, Said had insisted upon certain conditions for the sale: he demanded that the amount should be

3 million as compensation for loss of revenue and that he should have a lien on 10 per cent of any profits resulting from the discovery of oil for 25 years from the date of the commercial production. The Sultan also attached importance to the continued supply of recruits from Gawadur for his army.[196]

Comparing this with the amount of subsidies granted to Muscat, it becomes clear that the sale of Gawadur was not going to generate the necessary capital. Subsidies would be a necessity:

As regards the subsidy involved in the proposals for military reorganization and civil development in the Sultanate, the talks were delayed during the first weeks of the Sultan's stay when it became clear that the costs of the assistance which Her Maj-esty's Government had undertaken to give were considerably in excess of the esti-mates made at the time of Mr. Amery's mission ... In the event, after a major reduction in the building programme for the army as envisaged in January, the amount of the subsidy was agreed by Her majesty's Government at about $540,000 total capital and about $375,000 recurrent expenditure in a normal year, an increase of $176,000 and $4,000 respectively over the figures in January.[197]

Gawadur was not sold to finance the campaign; the amount was simply too small to accomplish the task at hand, especially since an exact estimate of the sale price would be difficult to ascertain. A steady and secure flow of subsidies clearly was more important than the one-time sum that the sale of Gawadur could provide. For all intents and purposes, the possibility that Pakistan would occupy Gawadur militarily and the Sultan's need for British support to suppress the Imamate's rebellion eventually forced Sultan Said to relinquish Gawadur. As late as November 1955, the Foreign Office reviewed the Gawadur issue.

> Unlike other gulf rulers, the Sultan of Muscat was an independent ruler. He did how-ever, lean heavily on British support and had steadfastly refused to negotiate with the Pakistanis except through London. Nevertheless, the Foreign Office was still unable to convince the Sultan to sell Gawadur. The Sultan professed "to fear posterity if he traded away his ancestral rights."[198]

If the Gawadur issue had been resolved to the satisfaction of some of the parties at least, Buraimi proved to be much more of a quandary for all parties concerned. A complex web of events and personalities became entangled with what seemed to be a wretched fight over a territory completely devoid of oil. The extent of diplomatic maneuvering, energy, and time spent on this issue, as evidenced in British Archives, let alone the archives in Riyadh, Muscat, and Abu Dhabi, is confounding. Was Buraimi only a means to an end? Was it the prestige of a nation state or that of a king and sultan?[199] What role did Muscat play? And was London ever an honest party?

By the late 1950s, the threat to Muscat from the interior had been shattered, yet it was by no means eliminated. Equally important was Muscat's struggle with a new and much more dangerous foe emanating from Southern Oman (Dhofar). Beginning in 1965, communist-inspired guerilla attacks were pro-ceeding with increasing success against Sultan Said. Moreover, London's deci-sion, under Harold Wilson (reflected in the "White Paper" document of 1967), to end nearly a century and a half of British dominance in the Gulf by 1971 raised eyebrows among the Gulf leaders who were mindful of external threats not only to their stability but to their very existence. The threats stemmed from the rising tide of pan-Arabism. Within the Arabian Peninsula, London had rec-ognized the weakness of the Trucial Principalities, as well as their importance to British interests, and had proposed a federation of nine: the seven Trucial States plus Qatar and Bahrain. Such a federation, London presumed, would cre-ate a more viable political and economic entity that would survive British de-parture at the end of 1971. Most Gulf rulers were anxious over the British decision and attempted to reverse it with whatever means they thought appro-priate at the time:

- The Political Resident said that the purpose of his visit to the Ruler was to inform the Ruler of H.M.G's decision on the offer made by Shaikh Zaid and other Gulf Rulers to contribute to the coast of maintaining British military forces in the Gulf. This offer had been made by Shaikh Zaid to the Minster of State during the latter's visit to Abu Dhabi on 9 January 1968 and more recently to the Political Resident by the Ruler of Bahrain, Qatar and Abu Dhabi. On this occasion the Ruler of Dubai had asked for an early reply form H.M.G to the offer.
- The official reply from H.M.G which the political Resident had been instructed to deliver to the four Rulers concerned was that while H.M.G were grateful to the

Rulers for their offer and appreciated the spirit in which it had been made they regretted that they could not accept the offer ... there was a financial reason for withdrawing H.M Forces from the Gulf but another reason was the decision not to maintain overseas forces in a global basis.[200]

Only two countries were missing from this group: Oman and Saudi Arabia. As far as Oman was concerned, British withdrawal[201] did not concern Muscat since London was not withdrawing its forces from Muscat. In addition, in light of Muscat's poverty, Sultan Said was in no position to offer financial incentives to London. The Saudis, on the other hand, were hostile to the proposed federation. They reasoned that the federation would never succeed, and worse yet, might open the door for "progressive" elements to penetrate this weak entity to the disadvantage of Riyadh. Two key factors led the Saudis to finally welcome the federation. First was Nasser's crushing defeat in 1967, coupled with the subsequent moderation of Egypt's regional foreign policy. Second was the opportunity this withdrawal presented to Riyadh to exert its hegemony over the region, especially in areas where it had failed in the past.[202] About no area was Riyadh more adamant than Buraimi.

When the question of the proposed federation was posed to Faisal, he made it clear that this federation must "not include Buraimi which was Saudi territory."[203] Saudi representatives had in fact made glaring threats against Sultan Said, and, as the following record indicates, against Sheikh Zaid of Abu Dhabi:

Pharon [King Faisal's advisor] then said that Zaid should have regarded to his long-term interest: it was obvious that the British would leave the Gulf in a few years time and Zaid would then have to face the Saudis alone and be in no position to resist should they then wish to assert sovereignty over Buraimi. The Saudis know this well and are prepared to wait these few years if necessary though they would like an amicable settlement earlier. For the King and Saudis this matter is entirely one of prestige: the Regime must be able to show to Saudi Arabia and the world that Saudi Arabia has regained her sovereignty over Buraimi ... they could not contemplate now letting it be seen by the people of SA and elsewhere that a country of SA position and strength had weakly had to concede their claim to a small place like Abu Dhabi.[204]

London, on the other hand, made it clear to Riyadh that Whitehall did not enjoy the amount of power over the Gulf rulers that Riyadh continuously alleged:

I told Pharaon that he really must not see the wicked hand of the British in every failure of a Gulf Ruler to accept Saudi proposals ... in a case like Buraimi, so long as Zayid maintained his position and had good arguments to support it we were bound by treaty to take his side; and in any case we could not, even if we wanted to, impose our advice upon him. The Saudis should realize that Gulf Rulers might sometimes find it convenient to say that, though they were willing to accept a Saudi suggestion, the British would not let them; but it was seldom true.[205]

The Saudis were obviously not impressed with the "alleged" autonomy of Gulf rulers, as the Saudi ambassador clearly articulated:

> I was talking to the Saudi Arabian Ambassador on the 13 February ... [he] brushed aside the suggestion that Zaid was in any way a free agent in this. It was the British Government who had called the tune over Buraimi ... Zaid had face to save, Britain had face to save; the Sultan had face to save and Saudi Arabia had face to save; the only way that this could be done would be for the four parties to administer the area under some sort of condominium.[206]

To claim that Gulf rulers had absolute control over the affair of Buraimi is a dubious conclusion, but to insinuate that "it was the British Government who called the tune over Buraimi," is equally improbable. Abu-Dhabi is a small place, but it was ruled by a shrewd man who understood perfectly well, maybe even more than the British themselves, King Faisal's strengths and limitations. He set out to meet the King and stayed in Riyadh from 12 April through 16 April 1967. Sheikh Zaid's words were, in the Bedouin tradition, even more obliging. He said that "King Faisal [*sic*] was his father and he the son King Faisal must tell his son what he wanted of him in way of help and co-operation ... urging him to speak as 'one who was great to one who was small, as one who was admired to his admirer.'"[207] These words were masking the simple fact that Zaid had recognized, as evident in his own words, that "he had two enemies, Nasser and Saudi Arabia."[208]

Nothing concrete came out of the visit except maybe for Zaid himself, who saw the visit as an opportunity to assess Riyadh's true intentions. London was pushing Zaid to be flexible (although what was meant by flexibility is not clear) with King Faisal and to look for a final solution. Sheikh Zaid's words were encouraging, according to London. This optimism was not well placed, for Zaid's own subtle, but clear, words undoubtedly indicated that Buraimi would not be relinquished: "It is possible to take blood from any part of a man's body, without killing him, except from his heart."[209] However, he kept informing London of his support for an amicable solution with Faisal, and his understanding (which he repeatedly communicated) that Faisal's dignity and prestige must be preserved in this matter, especially since the "continued failure to solve the problem was placing him in an increasingly humiliating position vis-à-vis the Arab League because his enemies were exploiting his apparent inability to stick up for Saudi Arabia's."[210] Zaid's own prudent assessment of Faisal and the situation, as he returned from his visit, explains it best:

> So far as the Saudi position was concerned, Zaid's considered that the visit had made two things quite clear:
>
> (a) that the Saudis, from the King Faisal downwards, were tired of the dispute and wanted to bury it for at least a time; but

(b)   they were greatly afraid of President Nasser and seriously worried about the
      situation inside Saudi Arabia. Indeed the Saudis seemed obsessed with their
      own domestic problems and had no real energy left for matters outside their
      borders.

Zaid accepted that the combination of these two points meant that King Faisal could
not be seen publicly to give up his claim, though Zaid believed that he would do
nothing to pursue it while circumstances remained as at present ... On the other
hand, Zaid said he was under no illusions about the long term ... and that he believed
that when the Saudis were relieved of their dear Nasser, they would inevitably raise
the Buraimi claim again unless they had been persuaded to drop it meanwhile.[211]

What was more urgent and more important in Sheikh Zaid's mind was where
the British stood in all of this, as the following memo illustrates:

The Ruler {Shikh Zaid} said that he agreed with all you had said; but he wished to
be assured on one point; HMG's position. It seemed that in these days whenever a
country got angry with HMG the latter gave into it. Now King Faisal was playing a
two-stringed lute, one string being HMG and the other Abu Dhabi. If both strings
were in tune King Faisal would be able to play a tune suitable for dancing. But if
they were not in tune the music would be bad and the dancers would be thrown out
of step. Moving away from his metaphor, Shaikh Zaid said that he knew his own policy and he though he knew HMG's ... Were HMG's and his policies the same?[212]

London's position on the Buraimi dispute vis-à-vis Muscat, Abu-Dhabi, and
Riyadh, coupled with the question of the federation and British policy in the
region, is accurately reported in this remarkably candid memo sent from the
British Embassy in Jedda on 25 June 1969. It is reproduced here almost in its
entirety due to its importance to this chapter:

As always, it is what the King wants that matters. My estimate at present is that he is
sincere in saying that he wants the Federation of the Nine to work and that although
he is depressed and anxious about the prospects for it, he does not have an alternative
option which he is consciously pursuing—except in the vague sense of believing that
Saudi Arabia will not tolerate a repetition of South Arabia in the Gulf and "will have
to act" if that is threatened. I believe that his support for the Federation derives from
his natural caution, from the advice he receives from people ... from his realisation
that if Saudi Arabia starts throwing her weight in the Gulf area, the beneficiaries may
be Saudi Arabia's enemies, and from his belief that he cannot afford to antagonize
the Iranians, or engage in competition with them—support for the Federation is a
way of getting others to keep their hands off ... [in reference to Buraimi] Here, I
think what counts is the question of face-honour, as Feisal calls it; jealousy and irrita-
tion at Zaid's prosperity and the way in which it has enabled him to out-smart the
Saudis; and similar frustration at the knowledge that H.M.G have out-smarted him by
15 years of fair words and stalling, which remains basically our policy on the Buraimi dispute ... I do not think, then, that we can really talk of a "Saudi policy" on
this issue ... the King is ruled by two conflicting principles: he *must* support the idea

of a U.A.E. because it meets all the right criteria of good statecraft and good Arabism; ... His head may tell him to give up the struggle; his pride will not let him. He racks his brains to think of something to do, but there is nothing. ... So what do we do? There is a case for saying we should do nothing; just keep calm and let him go on kicking. It is after all almost inconceivable that Saudi Arabia will invade Abu Dhabi either before or after we leave ... But if there is to be a solution, one side had to give way. We surely must rule out any idea of neutral zones or condominiums as suggested ... If it were possible that the offer of a piece of territory other than Buraimi—even access to the sea at Khor el Odaid—would satisfy Feisal, then I might recommend that we should seriously consider urging it on Zaid. But all evidence available at present suggests that this would not do the trick ... In spite of discouragements, we must therefore continue to press the suggestion which you will see was put forward by our side at all three meetings: that Feisal should offer, on condition that the U.A.E.[213] is established as a working institution, a birthday present of the withdrawal of his claims on the member states. This would more that save his honour: it would enhance it ... But not now, and not by us. Not now because the best time will be when the Bahrain issue is settled and it can be represented to Feisal that if an Iranian can be magnanimous to the new-born Union, how much more so should be its Arab uncle. And not by us, because a climb down by Feisal would represent the successful conclusion of fifteen years of British diplomacy—and he would know what we had done. Who then might persuade him? Not his own advisers: they do not have the stature. Perhaps the Shah? Perhaps the Rulers of Bahrain, Qatar and Dubai in a delegation of friendly mediator and the scene would be right—three rulers entreating their revered senior to make a generous gesture.[214]

If Riyadh agreed to meet and negotiate with Shaikh Zaid, it took a much harder line with Sultan Said, as a report from the British embassy in Saudi Arabia indicates:

I must state the obvious, namely that Faisal does not like the Sultan because the latter is sitting in what Faisal considers to be *his* territory ... Buraimi is Faisal's blind spot and it is even blinder in the case of the Sultan because it was from the Sultan's sector that we expelled the Saudis by force in 1955. Faisal was Foreign Minister at the time and this humiliation has rankled deeply ever since ... what Faisal is after is Buraimi. Perhaps, too, Faisal sees the Sultan as a major barrier to the assertion of Saudi sovereignty in South East Arabia.[215]

The situation in Muscat was no better; the Sultan's position regarding Riyadh seemed to have hardened over time:

The Sultan's thinking remains dominated by the Saudi aggression of the early fifties and the total duplicity they practiced in support of their policy of expansion, by the Saudi support of the cause of the Imam from 1956 until recently ... by the rebels have in the past been able to cross Saudi Arabia to enter Dhofar with arms ... We were in his eyes proved wrong to have restrained him from turning Turki out of Buraimi in 1952, to have believed in the possibility of an honest arbitration, and to have tried to persuade him to make concessions over the Buraimi rebels ... we are not therefore well placed to convince him that there has been a genuine change of heart on the part of the Saudis … By the same token I think that it is essential that James Craig and others in Jedda should peg away at educating the Saudis … about the common interest of the two countries in keeping out subversion and communist infiltration (exemplified by the Dhofari rebel who was killed inside the Sultanate, but near the P.R.S.Y. border on 24 June, and was found to be wearing a Mao Tse Tung badge and carrying a communist automatic). If the Saudis should come around to a real rethinking about Buraimi, so much the better, but I realize that this is unlikely to happen soon.[216]

THE DHOFAR REBELLION AND THE END OF SAID'S REIGN

Whether Buraimi was the King's "blind spot" or whether Sultan Said stood in the way of Saudi hegemonic ambitions remained a moot point. By the 1960s Muscat had to contend not only with Saudi support for the Imamate forces but also with a combination of communist- and nationalist-inspired rebels in southern Oman (the region of Dhofar). Riyadh continued to deny support for such groups, but both British and American archives of the period indicate that Saudi Arabia was supporting the Dhofari rebels.[217] What is surprising about Saudi support, as a confidential State Department assessment states, is that while the Saudi government continued to permit "arms believed to originate in Kuwait and Iraq to transit Saudi territory for Omani rebels and the Dhofar Liberation Front … the Saudis seem[ed] to be mistakenly looking at Dhofar exclusively in the context of their traditional dislike for the Sultan and overlooking the danger to themselves of a potentially hostile regime on their periphery."[218]

As the report indicates, even Kuwait (the word "even" is warranted here because such support was expected from a radical state like Iraq, but not from Kuwait, which had neither sympathy for the rebels nor a bone to pick with Sultan Said) supported the Imamate and had an Imamate office at its capital. Presumably the consolidation of Muscat's authority should be in Kuwait's best interest, argued the British Consulate in Muscat. This would be true since the more vulnerable his position, the greater would be the threat for the Saudis to

> grab Buraimi and for the Iranians to grab the southern side of the Gulf of Hormuz: and presumably one this which Kuwait can do without is the start of a practice whereby large powers in the Gulf grab territory from smaller neighbors … An essential prerequisite will be their ceasing to recognize the imam and, in general, their hampering rather than helping the activities in Kuwait of those of the Sultan's subjects who are working to overthrow him.[219]

Just when it seemed that Muscat was finally in control of the country and that the Imamate cause was defeated militarily, new and old dangers joined forces and put in motion a chain of events that eventually led to Sultan Said's abdication in 1970.

The cause of the Imamate may have begun as a defense of an Omani/Ibadi institution; it was, however, dead by the day they worked with Saudi Arabia and then became entangled with Pan-Arab causes. Halliday's assertion is that "the Imamist movement was incapable of leading a mass struggle against imperialism because of its own class interests and because it relied on a traditional tribal military system. It had failed and was discredited," and therefore, the task of leading and "freeing the people of Oman awaited a more determined revolutionary leadership."[220] Halliday, however, completely misses the mark. The whole notion of a "struggle against imperialist forces" is alien to the Imamate. Even the vocabulary must have sounded quite bizarre, if not altogether unintelligible. Indeed, the Imamate movement failed and was discredited because it abandoned its original social and religious base for a broad struggle against imperialism. The Imamate struggle had become, under Saudi aid and Egyptian rhetoric, an essential part of the Arab nationalist struggle, the fight for Arab socialism, or the struggle against the imperialist forces. In other words, the Imamate cause had lost its authenticity and simply degenerated into symbols and slogans of an entirely different cause.

While Arab nationalism is a complex phenomenon and a very modern one, the Imamate core was and remains fundamentally religious/tribal with deep roots that are essentially local. The language of an "Army of Liberation," with its nationalistic zeal, may have aroused the curiosity of some, but indifference was evidently the dominant mood. How could the cause of the Ibadi Imamate be enhanced by the portrayal of the Imamate

> to the world at large as an instrument of revolutionary nationalism; with the issuing of pronouncements in Cairo, Damascus, and Baghdad about a shared faith in Arab socialism; with public affirmation of solidarity with a weird miscellany of alien governments and causes; and with the soliciting of pecuniary aid in capitals as far as London and Peking.[221]

Furthermore, Riyadh had been historically hostile to the Imamate for various religious and not so religious reasons. Wahhabi antipathy toward Ibadia and their Imamate is centuries old.[222] Thus, for the Imamate to seek support from Riyadh must have been intolerable for many of the Ibadia religious and tribal leaders.

Ironically, even Beijing was enlisted to support the Imamate cause. Yet what also is surprising is the almost total absence of scholarly interest in China's role in supporting the Imamate. Very little is discussed by Peterson, Townsend, or Allen. Despite the fact that China's connection with Oman's "nationalist" movement was its first political involvement in the Arabian Peninsula,[223] initial contacts were through the Imamate office and the Chinese embassy in Cairo during the 1950s.[224] Although China's offer of military aid in 1957 was rejected by the Imamate, this did not end contact, which culminated in a visit by Sheikh Saleh bin Isa Al-Harthy, one of the main leaders of the Imamate, to

Beijing from 29 January to 20 February 1959. There he met Mao and Zhou.[225] It should be noted that from 1955 until the palace coup of 1970, China continued to "associate the former Sultan Said's rule with British imperialism and the oppression of the Omani people." China has "never denounced any other Arab head of state over such a long period and with such intensity."[226] In turn, the Imamate representative being interviewed in Cairo declared that

> as regards China, he affirmed the Omani people's full support to the just struggle of China to restore Taiwan; he also asked that the best wishes of the Omani people be conveyed to the Chinese government and people, thanking them for their support of the Omani struggle. He emphasized that he was in complete agreement with Chairman Mao Tse-tun's statement that "imperialists and all reactionaries are paper tigers."[227]

Rhetoric aside, the Imamate had been reluctant to accept military aid from Beijing. The record shows that as late as 1969, the Imamate movement, or at least its leadership, continued to resist assistance beyond political and moral support from South Yemen, the USSR, and China. A memo from the British Embassy at Beirut dated 5 March 1969 bears witness:

> he regarded the matter as now with urgency in that there were proposals for substantial aid from the PRSY, made, I understand, three or four months ago, which the Imam and his associates were under strong pressure to accept. They did not wish to do so because they were doubtful of the motives of the Adenes and in any case did not wish to become indebted to or involved with people of their ilk. Their young men, however, did not share these inhibitions, and they feared that, if no solution could be arrived at, their control over the Omani rebels would disappear.[228]

Imamate representatives were simply not willing to go as far as accepting military and logistical aid from avowed Marxists. However, we should not discount the possibility that such support was not offered by the date specified above. The representative may have been bluffing to pressure London to the negotiating table. After years of violent and not so violent resistance, the leaders may have recognized the futility of their struggle. According to Behbehani, China's support for the Imamate was essentially over by 1968. Behbehani concludes that the lack of Beijing's military aid to the Imamate forces was the product not only of the latter's reluctance but also of the simple reality that the Imam did not have either a regular or an irregular army. And it was not possible to send Omanis to be trained in China; most members of the "nationalist movement" were already being trained in Syria and Iraq.[229]

It seems more likely, however, that Beijing recognized that the Imamate was a spent military force, though it was still a political player outside Oman. More importantly, Beijing recognized that the newly founded Dhofar Liberation Front (DLF) that was dedicated to the "liberation" of the area of Dhofar from Sultan Said's rule was a much more attractive alternative than the Imamate movement.

The DLF was founded in 1962 and was composed of Dhofari insurgents and other exiles. Egypt allowed the group to open an office in its capital while Iraq provided military training and aid.[230] When the Independent People's Democratic Republic of Yemen was established in 1967, the DLF expanded its activities, since a more reliable supply of weapons and support was closer to home. The most daring act for the DLF came in April 1966, "when a group of Qara tribesmen loyal to the DLF but also serving in Said's bodyguard, the Dhofar Force, attempted to assassinate the Sultan."[231] The attempt failed, but it helped to isolate Sultan Said from the population. After the incident he hardly ventured out of his palace.[232] Indeed, Sultan Said's isolation was so complete that "rumors were rife inside as well as outside the country that he was actually dead and that the British ruled Oman in his name."[233]

It was no longer sufficient to liberate Dhofar from Sultan Said, however, as the movement adopted a much more militant Marxist ideology, calling itself the Popular Front for the Liberation of the Arabian Gulf (PFLOAG). By 1969, another group of malcontents and Omani exiles belonging to various leftist organizations formed the National Democratic Front for the Liberation of Oman and the Arabian Gulf (NDFLOAG) in Iraq.[234] The PFLOAG was ideologically akin to Beijing and South Yemen, better organized, and more committed to the overthrow of Sultan Said. As Behbehani asserts, from 1968 to 1972, China was the only foreign nation that gave military assistance to the PFLOAG.[235] As to why China was the choice of the DLF instead of the much more resourceful Soviet Union, the spokesman of the PFLOAG commented, "China at the time was championing 'world revolution through armed struggle'; the contact with the Chinese embassy in Cairo began after the June war during which Arab officials' feeling was one of disappointment at the lack of Soviet aid."[236] In contrast to the Soviet Union, which "sought to maintain government-to-government ties, China moved toward supporting the anti-Western imperialism struggle in South Yemen and the guerrilla war in Dhofar."[237] It should be noted that just as Imamate leadership was not disposed to accept military aid from South Yemen or from the "Marxists," the DLF also was not inclined to work with the "reactionary" Imamate movement. An Omani revolutionary speaking in 1971 made the following evaluation of the 1957–1959 uprising:

> The most important thing to say about Imam Ghalib's movement is that it represented a clash within the imperialist camp. It was a conflict between the Imam and Said bin Taimur, i.e. a conflict between an absolutist regime and a caricature of that obsolete regime, represented by the Imam himself. When we say that it is a conflict within the imperialist camp, we mean that behind Said bin Taimur and Imam Ghalib were Britain on the one hand and America and Saudi Arabia on the other.[238]

Probing China's interests in assisting the PFLOAG is beyond the scope of this chapter, but by the end of the 1950s the Sino-Soviet alliance was deteriorating rapidly, and Beijing began to regard the Persian Gulf and the Arabian Peninsula as "an area of Chinese-Soviet rivalry as well as a stage to wage a campaign against Western imperialism."[239] Surprisingly, however, the British political resident in Bahrain was not sure Peking was actively involved in supporting the PFLOAG as late as January 1969. He wrote of Soviet involvement in Dhofar that

> so far as can be judged from here, the Southern Yemen Government is not actively concerning itself with events in Dhofar, but is acquiescing in support being given to the Dhofari rebels from Southern Yemen territory. This support may be coming from Moscow, from Cairo and possibly from Peking (although presumably not all in concert).[240]

Whether the Imamate representatives were bluffing or not, the political resident in Bahrain had certainly concluded that the Imamate was a spent force. The following record, dated 3 September 1968, demonstrates it.

> I entirely agree with the line you took about the Imamate Movement and its office in Kuwait. I think it is broadly true that the Imam (ex-Imam to be pedantic) is a dead duck; his present prospects of starting a successful rebellion in the Sultanate are negligible. But the movement still has some capacity for mischief. The Imam and Talib remain dependent on Saudi hospitality, and periodically try to extract larger subsidies from the Saudis; they must try to present themselves as an effective military force as well as a unified political movement (of course they are neither).[241]

The sacrifice of authenticity in order to marshal the support of Pan-Arab nationalists did cost the Imamate its core supporters, or would-be supporters, yet it gained new converts who did not care about the Imamate per se but rather about the larger issues of the Arab world and the genuine desire to modernize the Sultanate. It was simply more acceptable than the alternative—a thoroughly Marxist insurgency. This, along with a new wave of insurgents in Dhofar, proved to be a challenge that Sultan Said was not able to overcome. The question is why? Why was there a significant discontent in all parts of the country that led to a serious rebellion in Southern Oman? Why had Sultan Said's diligence, patience, and prudence, which had served him well in prior decades, failed him now? Was he personally responsible for this gathering danger that he failed to contain? Or were the circumstances simply beyond his control, requiring totally different measures from those for which his temperament was made?

From 1958 till the day of his abdication, Sultan Said was to spend the entire decade at Salalah rather than at the capital, Muscat. Colonel Smiley recounts Said's explanation:

> 'You may wonder, Colonel Smiley,' he once observed in a rare mood of expansion, 'why I never show myself in Muscat. I will tell you why. If I go to Muscat I will be surrounded by supplicants, all asking me for money. I have no money to give them, and so they will go away discontented. Therefore it is better if I stay here in Salalah.'[242]

This should not be dismissed as a hollow justification. Tribal societies, like modern societies, do expect access to their leaders, albeit in a different fashion. And more importantly, the leader is expected to provide, within reason of course, for various members of tribes for whom the leader is responsible. This is not considered charity but a duty.

Also, Muscat was becoming increasingly less secure. A car belonging to the Minister of External Affairs had been bombed in 1958; the Minister of the Interior became the target of another explosion in 1959—he barely survived. By 1961, land-mine explosions directed against both civilian and military targets had become ever more sophisticated and deadly, as evidenced by the sinking of the British liner—the *Dara*—with more than 200 lives lost.[243]

Those who fought against the Sultan and those who provided the most convincing critique of his leadership rightfully pointed to the dismal state of development in the country. This was especially true at a time when other countries of the Arabian Peninsula were actively pursuing developmental projects and services for their populations with newly acquired oil wealth. However, the Sultan remained, for a good part of the 1960s, indefatigably opposed to any major developmental project. If development of the country was the catalyst that might have begun the process of defeating the various groups conspiring against Muscat, or at least limiting their potency, why was Sultan Said so reluctant to begin the process at once? Part of the answer lies in Said's frugality and restraint since the early 1930s:

> These 1930's virtues ... were his biggest mistake, because financial restraint became a way of life and an end in itself. Even the income from oil which could have met the expectations of his people was not spent because mentally Sultan Said could not attune to the new prosperity.[244]

For Sultan Said, falling into debt again, as had his predecessors, represented a loss of autonomy and was not an option that he was willing to undertake. He simply was not willing to allocate funds for projects if he did not have the absolute assurance that he would be able to sustain all of the future expenditures required. Such guarantees were simply not possible prior to 1968, when oil was finally being sold in commercial quantities. It seems that the "lessons the Sultan learned from his budget balancing exercises of the thirties and forties [had] been so deeply imprinted on his mind that he [found] it almost impossible to comprehend a situation where such exercises are a total irrelevance."[245] However, as Peterson rightly points out,

> Said's started his own capital development programme and a fairly ambitious one at that. The problem was that it was too slow to obtain results: development efforts had become obvious only by 1970, which was too late.[246]

The danger to the country from Sultan Said's "fiscal policies" at home, coupled with the isolation of Muscat in the region, had begun to compromise the territorial integrity of the country. In Dhofar, as time passed, the rebellion gained more ground and scored serious blows at the Sultan's expense. Nothing clearly indicates this fact more than a report submitted by Oldman, the Sultanate Defense Secretary, in which he states that

> in the longer term, if things go badly this autumn, we cannot rule out the possibility of the Sultan eventually being forced to abandon Dhofar. In that event it is difficult to predict what his reaction would be in the rest of Oman with the implications for the continued use of Masirah as a staging post.[247]

Most scholars, although aware of the threat to the Sultanate's territorial integrity, often speak only of Dhofar and overlook the danger to other regions (specifically to Al-Batinah and Al-Sharqiya), which, although not as obvious as that of Dhofar, was nonetheless just as real. The following paragraph is a part of a report by the British Consulate General touring Al-Batinah:

> The Batinah remains, therefore, relatively prosperous. It is, however, an artificial prosperity ... There is no other industry apart from fishing which is traditional and static. The only compensating feature is that some new date and lime gardens have been established by Omanis who have returned to settle on the Battinah after acquiring sufficient capital for this purpose outside the country ... Finally an intriguing thought remains with me after my tour. If the Batinah is so economically dependent on the Trucial States and the Sultan does nothing to arrest the trend, how long will it be before economic dependence will be transferred into political dependency?[248]

In another region, Al-Sharqiya, the danger of open rebellion may have been unlikely, due to the presence and influence of Sheikh Ahmad Al-Harthi, the leading Sheikh of the area. However, the discontent at what was essentially an economic problem might have escalated into a political one:

> Shaikh Ahmad recalled that he had been instrumental in unifying the country under the Sultan's rule ... Basically, Shaikh Ahmad's main complaint was that the Sultan's failure to provide employment opportunities had obliged the able bodied men to find work outside the country. This by itself did not matter so much since they sent money back to their families in the interior, but it was the new ideas they learned and their discontent when they paid brief visits to their home area which pointed to the real dangers. These were the evil influences especially communism.[249]

Sultan Said simply failed to see that time was not on his side, and he refused to deal with the Dhofari rebellion as a political problem, rather than merely a military campaign. The Sultan was not one to opt for a "heart and mind campaign," let alone envision a full strategy to counter the insurgents beyond military means:

> [The] Sultan still taking a depressingly hard line on the Dhofar problem. He was robustly determined not to be browbeaten by the rebels, whose movement he saw as

essentially rooted in South Yemen, and he claimed that he would do whatever was necessary to develop SAF so that it would overcome the rebels. He had shown no disposition to consider political methods for dealing with the rebellion.[250]

As far as the Sultan was concerned:

the Jebalies were rebels, brigands and outlaws, they had to be treated accordingly. No mercy should be, or would be, shown to them as this would be weakness and the jebalis would only be encouraged in believing that their present course was right.[251]

Within the region itself, various capitals continued to lend support to those opposing the Sultan by either providing military training and assistance, hosting the exiled leaders either of the imamate or of the Dhofari rebellion, lending diplomatic support, allowing the exiled leaders to establish offices at their capitals, or lending their various national news outlets to be the mouthpiece of the rebels. Iran remained an exception. It became quite clear that Tehran, unlike Riyadh, which shared Tehran's antipathy toward the Marxist influence in the region, was acutely aware that the success of the Dhofari rebellion might set in motion incalculable consequences for the region:

When I saw the Political Under-Secretary at the Foreign Minister [Iran's] on 7 march, he expressed great anxiety about reports of the present state of Muscat and Oman ... He said he felt HMG should do something soon to allay current discontent there ... He referred to the influence of Chinese Communists: and also said that he thought the existence of a future Union of Arab Emirates would be very precarious if Muscat were in hostile hands ... there is some danger that the Iranians would use any Anglo-Iranian dialogue as a vehicle for pinning on United Kingdom the responsibility for any threat to Gulf stability which might appear from Muscat and Oman in the post-1971 situation. Against this, however, it is very much in our general interest to convince the Iranians that we are hoping and trying to leave the Gulf in stable conditions and thus check any thoughts that may be emerging here that we are doing no more than brushing all the latent security problems under the carpet. And if we cannot do this it would at least be prudent to show the Iranians that we have assessed the situation and concluded (if we dare say this) that Oman is not likely to be a major threat in the immediate period after our withdrawal.[252]

The conclusion that "Oman is not likely to be a major threat in the immediate period" was certainly not true. London was well aware that Muscat was in serious danger, and even up to 1971 might have to abandon Dhofar. However, Whitehall kept the message to Tehran the same, as the following record indicates:

It seems to me that we must take this question in slow time and consider say two or three months hence whether we can say anything substantive to the Iranians, following our coming contacts with the Sultan. For the time being, I think that Denis Wright should continue to speak to the Iranians on current lines and feed them any publishable pieces of information to show that development is making progress. I would not advocate handing over a security assessment of the Sultanate at present.[253]

If a competent "security assessment of the Sultanate" were made, it would have vindicated Tehran's suspicion that Muscat, and along with it the rest of the Gulf, was in real danger.

The territorial integrity of the country was under a serious threat: 1) the strengthening threat of the Marxists/Arab-nationalists in Dhofar; 2) the continuing claim of the Imamate representatives debated at the United Nations for an independent state in the interior of Oman; and 3) the crippling emigration of capable men from both Al-Sharqiya and Al-Batinah, with the latter region moving ever closer economically to the future Sheikhdoms of the United Arab Emirates. The situation was exacerbated by Said's refusal to approach the Dhofar crisis as a political conflict rather than a purely military one; in addition, the ever-sluggish pace of development and the British presence were causes of intense propaganda. Said's son Qaboos realized that the situation could be tolerated no more. The entire country was either in active subversion or moving in that direction. On 12 June 1970 the Sultan's forces based at Izki were attacked by the NDFLOAG. The attack was repelled, and many of the attackers were either killed or captured. The audacity of the attack, combined with the information obtained from the prisoners about caches of Chinese arms in Matrah, Sur, and Muti, made a clear demonstration that a fundamental change in policy was required or the country could be lost.[254] Trouble spots in different parts of the Sultanate signified the wide presence of plotters, a competent organization, and a strong presence of sympathizers.[255]

To save the country, the future Sultan, Qaboos bin Said, had to act, and act he did:

When your predecessor engaged in general policy discussions with the Sultan in May Sayyid Said was polite but unyielding. Development in the sultanate would go at the pace he determined for it, and any attempt by ourselves to interfere in his internal affairs would be unwelcome. While he might rebuff us and other [sic] who wished to see the Sultanate survive, it became clear in June that elements hostile to his rule were intensifying their efforts to destroy it. A series of incidents in Oman revealed that a new organization, the National Democratic Front for the Liberation of Oman and the Arabian Gulf (NDFLOANG) had embarked upon a campaign of unrest and had picked as its main target the Sultan's armed forces. This proved to be the final piece of evidence required by the Sultan's only son to convince him that his father's policies had brought the Sultanate to the brink of despair. For several months he had disclosed his anxieties about the state of the country and, in particular, he feared what he described as the contamination of Dhofari minds by the Communists. From June onwards Sayyid Qaboos knew he had to act and supported by a small group of loyal followers in Salalah he initiated an almost bloodless palace coup on 23 July.[256]

Oman's Foreign Policy (1970–1989)

THE SULTANATE OF OMAN: OLD AND NEW CHALLENGES

The accession of Sultan Qaboos to the throne began a remarkable period in Oman's modern history. This period is known as a Renaissance for the Sultanate, and its achievements are fully documented and clearly demonstrated to any observer of Gulf affairs or to any visitors to the Sultanate. It is not only the incredible speed with which socioeconomic developments took place that is the object of this research but also the Sultanate's importance in regional and international foreign policy. The use of archives is paramount once again in revealing the challenges that Muscat had to face, and in documenting new subtleties that the literature on the Sultanate has often overlooked.

Rather than outlining the challenges the Sultanate faced at the outset of Sultan Qaboos' accession, two personal commentaries from the period will serve as an ideal conduit to understanding the Sultanate's seemingly insurmountable domestic and international challenges. First is the 1971 Annual Review:

> The steps then taken by the new Sultan to establish his rule were rapid, effective and decisive. His family pledged their loyalty to him, the citizens of Salalah, in scenes of great jubilation, showed where their feeling lay and messages of support poured in from all parts of the Sultanate. In a succession statement the Sultan expressed his growing anger and dismay at the inability of his father to use the country's wealth for the needs of the people. He promised to establish forceful and modern government, and to create as rapidly as possible a happier and more secure future for all … If this view reads like a modern fairy tale it is good that it should, since it is true. The handsome young Prince did drive out the wicked old King but whether Sayyid Qaboos will live happily ever after is the question that dominates the reminder of this review. There can be few countries less developed that the Sultanate. It had, until July, no communications, apart from two graded roads, only three primary schools, and one hospital … To start afresh, therefore, in the second-half of 1970 with a hostile neighbor to the west and with an increasingly uncertain future for the Gulf States

to the north, could only be a formidable and uncertain undertaking for the new regime ... By the end of 1971 the most severe test facing Government may be the decisions it takes on the best use of scarce financial resources, since Oman is by no means a wealthy country. The Budget for this year is currently estimated to be $43 million of which defense will take $21 million. The civil side of Government has still to demonstrate that it will have the ability to spend the $22 million it proposes to spend during the year, but, as the needs of the country become more apparent, the pressures on the regime to meet them will become more intense.[1]

Second is the impression of Oman by the British ambassador to Muscat:

The Dhofar rebellion drags on. The Sultanate might not survive for very long unless it achieves victory, negotiates a political settlement or effectively contains the rebels ...

Oman has in recent months applied for membership of the United Nations and the Arab League as well as for membership of some of the United Nation Specialized Agencies. They were admitted to WHO in May, despite the opposition of the People's Democratic Republic of Yemen (PDRY) and the abstention of Saudi Arabia. Oman has also attempted to break out of its former isolation by sending missions to the Arab capitals in June suggesting the establishment of diplomatic and only Morocco, Algeria and Tunisia have so far agreed. The Arab group at the United Nations have decided that Oman's application for the United Nations membership ought to be postponed until they have obtained membership of the Arab League and Tariq's idea of bypassing that body has thus not been successful. The basic difficulty, apart from the implacable opposition of PDRY, is the position of the former Imam Ghalib and the other former Omani rebels who have not already returned home. Tentative moves towards rapprochement so far made by the Sultan have been unsuccessful but he has not given up, though it is ironical that the Sultan is prepared to allow Ghalib to return with the title of Mufti and to offer Talib a Government post, which is exactly what Faisal of Saudi Arabia has recommended. There seems to be a blockage of communication somewhere. The Omanis are nonetheless suspicious that the Saudis wish to keep the Ghalib issue alive as a cover for their traditional ambition in Oman as well as in the Trucial States and Omani memories of former Wahhabi incursions remain bitter. If Oman is successful in gaining wider international acceptance the external pressure on the country from PDRY might be somewhat eased. However there is a danger that certain Arab countries may demand, as some of them already have, a lessening of British influence as a price for recognition and closer relations. Meantime this is the only Embassy in Muscat, though the Indians are likely to exchange diplomatic relations with Oman soon.[2]

These assessments indicate an unpromising future for the Sultanate, to say the least. The two major challenges facing Muscat, apart from a lack of socio-economic development, were the growing strength of the insurgency in Dhofar and the Imamate challenge. Conventional wisdom is correct in its analysis of the Dhofar insurgency as the primary danger to the survival of the Sultanate. The literature is incorrect in presuming that the Imamate cause had been crushed by the late 1950s. Comments are frequently made that the "question of Oman" remained in the halls of the United Nations, but immediately after the accession of Sultan Qaboos, the problem seemed to vanish. The following paragraph is an example of the standard interpretation of the period:

> Qaboos promptly set about the task of legitimizing his rule to a larger world. On 2 June 1971 ... Oman wrote to the Security Council applying for membership in the United Nations. As a result of this application, the Special Committee on the Situation with regard to the Implementation of the Declaration on the Granting of Independence to colonial Countries and Peoples dropped Oman from its list of countries under consideration. The committee's decision enhanced the credibility of Oman, which was duly admitted to the United Nations on 7 October 1971. Qaboos also joined the newly formed Arab League. These diplomatic moves made it very difficult for the insurgents to claim that he was a British puppet.[3]

Oman's admission to the United Nations is mentioned as a footnote. Its membership in the Arab League is treated with even less importance. Moreover, joining both institutions is treated as a "natural progression" of events after the accession of Sultan Qaboos. Nothing could have been further from the truth.

The Sultanate's membership in both institutions is an important moment in the country's history and deserves to be adequately investigated. These memberships were essential to a country as isolated as the Sultanate. In addition, the regime faced a determined insurgency while its very legitimacy was being debated at the UN. In reality, the likelihood that the Sultanate's membership in both institutions would be rejected was high. Furthermore, the real battle for Oman's membership to the United Nations lay in the halls of the Arab League and in the intricate labyrinths of regional politics. Muscat had viewed the Arab League as a stepping stone for its admission to the UN, but without that step, membership in the UN would have been highly unlikely. A secret memo from the British Consulate General in Muscat, dated 28 December 1970, asserts that the

> results of the recent General Assembly proceedings on Oman have only served to reinforce the point that, if the Sultanate aspires to membership of the United Nations and the Arab League next year something will have to be done about the continuing political influence in the Arab world of the Oman Rebel Movement [this is in reference to Sheikh Ghalib].[4]

Ghalib, in turn, had sent two petitions to the United Nations (UN) objecting to the Sultanate's possible membership to the UN:

> U Thant
> Secretary General
> United Nations Cairo, 10 June 1971
> New York
>
> The United Nations General Assembly has taken many successive decisions since 1961 to 1971 all these decisions condemn and ask for abolishing the British imperialism from Oman and giving the Omani people the right to decide his [sic] own fate by his [sic] own self but Britain has not carried out these decisions on the other side

she [*sic*] began to tell lies and disfigure facts Britain secretly asked her agent the Sultan of Muscat to ask for joining the United Nations the Omani people ask you to execute effectively the United Nations decisions before deciding anything concerning the Sultan applications to join the United Nations

Ghalib Bin Ali
Imam of Oman[5]

During the same month, the representative of the PDRY informed the United Nations that Oman could not be admitted to the UN before admission to the Arab League.

United Kingdom Mission To The United Nations
   845 Third Avenue, New York, N.Y. 10022
   17 June 1971:

Permanent Representative of the PDRY called on Francios de La Gorce on 11 June to describe to him the position of the Arab group on Oman. Ambassador Ismail told him that the decision was:

(a) Oman should not be admitted to the United Nations before admission to the Arab League.
(b) Before being admitted to the United Nations Oman must comply with the March Resolution of the Arab League, i.e. that a Fact Finding Mission of the Arab League should visit Oman in order to investigate the matters covered in the Report of the Committee of 24.[6]

The three key states that could have blocked Oman's admission to the Arab League were Saudi Arabia (which supported Ghalib), South Yemen, and Iraq (both of which were supporting the Popular Front for the Liberation of the Arabian Gulf [PFLOAG]). This is clearly spelled out in the following confidential record:

You will remember that at the March meetings of the Arab League Council the Secretary General was asked to make a fact finding trip to the Gulf and Oman and to report back, so that the Council could consider Oman's application for the membership at the September meeting. ... The Saudis, South Yemenis and the Iraqis could argue that without this preliminary step Oman's credentials could not be properly assessed, and could thus ask for consideration of Oman's application to be deferred again. The Hassouna mission may be quietly forgotten. If, however, two or more countries objected (e.g. because the question of the Imam Ghalib had not been settled by then) this would be enough to block Oman's membership for the time being.[7]

Although King Faisal was more willing to deal with Sultan Qaboos than with his late father, the question of Ghalib remained a stumbling block between the two states:

The Saudi Arabian Ambassador told me at lunch on 25 June that he had been very impressed by the Sultan who he thought was an extremely nice and well-intentioned young man. As we already know, he had had a long talk with him about all aspects of Saudi/Omani relations. He had told him that he did not think the problem of the Buraimi villages need be too difficult. It could either be left in abeyance or would be settled if the Abu Dhabi problem were settled. The major issue was that of Ghalib. He had advised the Sultan to write a letter to King Faisal abetting out what he was prepared to do for Ghalib.[8]

Sultan Qaboos was well aware of the urgency of Saudi demands in terms of its support of Ghalib. Here he saw some form of accommodation that both parties could accept without losing face. This is especially true given the fact that many Arab governments were not willing to support the Sultanate's membership without some form of accommodation with Ghalib, as the following record indicates:

> I told Sultan that we had heard that the Lebanese Government intended to support Oman membership of the Arab League but that the Lebanese also had stressed the importance of an accommodation with Ghalib. The Sultan assured me once again that he fully intended to take this matter up as soon as he got back to Muscat. The Sultan said he thought his contacts with the Saudi Ambassador in London and Shaikh Sa'ad of Kuwait had been useful … The Sultan told me that he understood that he was to be invited to the 2,500th anniversary celebrations of the Iranian monarchy and that he would probably accept. He asked me if I knew whether King Faisal would be going. I said he was certainly invited and would probably attend. The Sultan agreed that this might be a good opportunity for him to meet Faisal for the first time on mutual grounds, though obviously there would be little opportunity for any serious discussion.[9]

Finding an accommodation with Ghalib, however, was not necessarily an easy task. Skeet writes of an agreement reached in Beirut between Sheikh Ghalib and the Sultanate that eventually led to the Sultanate's membership to the Arab League.[10] Refuting this claim is a confidential record from the British Embassy asserting that "since the Beirut meeting the prospects for reconciliation between the Imamate exiles and the Sultan seem remoter than ever."[11] King Faisal's attitude to Oman, as the U.S. ambassador asserted, "will never be on a satisfactory footing until the problem of Ghalib can be overcome. He specifically mentioned the idea of Ghalib being given the title of Mufti."[12]

London, after receiving positive indications from Muscat, immediately took the opportunity to contact Washington, and appeal for its influence in Riyadh:

To immediate Washington Telegram number 1510 of 27 May

1. There have been several indications that Qaboos would agree to Ghalib having the title of Mufti provided he gives up all pretensions to the Imamate and agrees to live quietly in Oman.
2. We agree that the key to Saudi/Omani relations lies in a satisfactory solution to the question of Ghalib. We see no objection to Murphy asking members of

the King's party whether any progress has been made. The important thing seems to be for the Saudis to make informal and direct contact with the Sultan. Between them they should be able to settle the difficulties over Ghalib in Arab fashion …

3. Otherwise we suggest that the State Department should urge on the Saudis and if possible Faisal himself the importance of establishing friendly relations with Oman. They might point out that it looks astonishing to outside would that the UAR, Algeria, Jordan, Kuwait and others can sponsor Oman for membership of the WHO, while the Saudis abstain on the vote and PDRY and Albania vote against it.[13]

In this accommodation, Saudi Arabia, an archconservative, and PDRY found common ground in their rejection of Oman's membership to the Arab League. The Sultanate was admitted to the Arab League in late September 1971, and yet as late as 20 September 1971, the Sultanate's successful nomination could still have failed.

Shaikh Saud Alkhalili (Leader of the Delegation) had informed that sultan that in Cairo Omar Saqqaf had raised every possible objection to Oman's application to join the league … Saud said that apart form Saudi Arabia and PDRY every other Arab League member particularly Algeria and Syria supported Oman's admission … Adding that it was ironical to observe a country like Saudi Arabia uniting with PDRY in opposition to Oman's admission to the league.[14]

In Muscat, frustration at Riyadh's reluctance to support the Sultanate's membership to the Arab League was becoming apparent.[15]

During my discussion with the Sultan on 27 September I showed him Cairo Telegram No. 4 to Muscat (Not to all). He said that he still had hopes that the Arab League would reach a favourable decision on Oman's membership at their meetings on 29 September … His people had never expected that the discussion to be concluded before that date. He agreed that it would be a mistake to rush Oman's applications for membership of the United Nations until she had either joined the Arab League or assured herself of the active support of the Egyptians … The Sultan added that he did not know what more he could do to satisfy King Faisal about his intentions towards Ghalib. He was quite sure that the Arab League, all the Arab countries, and Ghalib himself knew that he was willing to welcome Ghalib back to Oman and appoint him Mufti … He was now willing to readmit every exile who was prepared to live at peace and renounce the idea of an independent Imamate and this included Suliman bin Himyar and Saleh bin Isa as well as Ghalib and Talib.[16]

It may seem odd that the above discussion is primarily concerned with the Saudi objection to the Sultanate's membership to the Arab League when Iraq and the PDRY were of the same opinion.[17] After all, both states had close relations with the Soviet Union, which was capable of vetoing[18] the Sultanate's membership to the United Nations regardless of the support of the Arab League. As such, both states should have received more attention in this narrative than hitherto articulated. Had it not been for the fact that neither Iraq nor the PDRY could effectively lobby either the Soviet Union or other Arab governments, that would have been the case. The ensuing memo from the British representative at the United Nations may shed some light on the matter.

United Kingdom Mission to the United Nations
845 Third Avenue, New York, N.Y.10022

3. … There are two main problems. First, the fact that Oman is not a member of the Arab League and second that the Oman question is still on the Assembly's agenda. He added that there were two aspects to the latter problem: the Imamate and the Liberation Front. Clearly nothing can be done about the latter (and consequently about the attitude of the PDRY) but this was not important. The main problem was to do something about the Imam. This would not only remove Saudi Arabia's difficulties but also those of a number of others, who would be able to argue that the settlement with the Imam had changed the situation and thus justified the dropping of the Oman question from the agenda and their supporting Oman's application for membership …

4. None of the Arabs to who I have spoken, including the Kuwaitis and the Saudis, seem to be prepared to comment at this stage. I have not yet had a chance to speak to Adnan Raouf (Iraq).

5. Meanwhile, according to the French, the Soviets Mission are taking the line that there is no hurry but that this is clearly a matter for the Arabs to decide.[19]

Two statements require explanation: The first concerns the PDRY's implacably negative position regarding the Sultanate's admission and the note that "this was not important"; second is the Soviets' attitude that it is "clearly for the Arabs to decide." The British representative would never have referred to the PDRY attitude toward the Sultanate's application to the Arab League as unimportant had he thought that the PDRY could lobby the Soviets to block membership. The representative may have recognized a few simple facts. First, it had been over a year since the demise of Egypt's Nasser. Since then, Cairo and Riyadh had quickly improved their relations. This is clearly demonstrated in Riyadh's role in the 1973 war. If two important states in the region were willing to support the Sultanate's applications to the Arab League, it certainly was not appropriate for the Soviets to block such a nomination for the sake of the PDRY. The Soviets had been successful in establishing diplomatic relations with Kuwait as early as 1963 and had sought to further relations with the rest of the Arab Gulf states.[20] Second, and perhaps more important, Moscow's attempts to improve its relations with Iran would have been hampered by blocking the Sultanate's admission to the United Nations, given that Muscat and Tehran seemed to be on good terms from the earliest periods of the new regime.[21]

The Sultanate's membership in the Arab League was without a doubt the ticket required for its admission to the United Nations. Even the Soviet "veto" was conditioned by the decision taken by that body.

United Kingdom Mission To The United Nations
845 Third Avenue, New York, N.Y. 10022

... Thirdly, it was pointed out by several speakers that the Soviets' veto would be available to prevent Oman's admission if the Arab League had not reached a favorable decision on the question before it was considered by the Security Council.

3. Among those who have given me an account of the meeting is Adnan Raouf (Iraq), who added that he had warned Baghdad as far back as January that an Omani applications might be forthcoming in the next few months and drawn attention to the problems which this would present both in the Arab context and from the point of view of the United Nations.[22]

How the Sultanate was admitted to the Arab League in the face of Saudi reluctance is clearly portrayed in the following record and explains the formula found to preserve King Faisal's prestige:

> When the Ambassador called on Dr. Hassan Sabri al-Khouly on 9 October al-Khouly gave him an account of Oman's admittance to the Arab League, for which he claimed a measure of credit.
>
> [Al-Khouly] had told King Feisal that it was clear that Oman was going to be admitted to the Arab League and that it was a matter of considerable surprise to many people in the Arab world to ding Saudi Arabia and the PDRY in the same camp opposing Omani admission ... al-Khouly suggested that if Saudi prestige required the king to maintain his opposition to the first session of the of the Arab League Council a solution could be found by not admitting Oman at the session but agreeing that it should be admitted a forthnight [sic] later. The King had acquiesced at this suggestion. Al-Khouly had therefore attended the Arab League Council and, when he found the majority to be in favour of admitting Oman there and then, he argued that the decision should be postponed for 15 days and that thereafter Oman should be admitted without further discussion. This caused a good deal of argument since many of the delegates wanted to know they had to be put off by unconvincing answers, though al-Khouly suggested that they had had a good idea of what was afoot.[23]

Riyadh, then, was of fundamental significance to the Sultanate's membership in both the Arab League in September 1971 and the United Nations in October 1971. The Sultan visited Riyadh in December 1971 for an important meeting with King Faisal. Kechichian claims that "although the visit to Riyadh was successful, it did not produce the expected level of support longed for by Sultan Qaboos. Without even a formal communiqué, this was a significant mark of recognition."[24] It is difficult to locate the standards that Kechichian used to judge the success of the Sultan's visit, but if part of the visit was the normalization of relations between the two states, and the final termination of the Imamate issue (which in itself represents a complete victory for the Sultanate), then the mission was a success. It would be no exaggeration to assert that the Sultan's visit to Saudi Arabia with its attendant consequences for the exiled Imam was the final death blow to the institution. Furthermore, Kechichian's claim that

His Majesty's visit did not receive a "formal communiqué, itself a significant mark of recognition," is inaccurate. The following record asserts:

> The following statement was issued by the Royal Court prior to the departure of the Sultan yesterday afternoon 14 December.
>
> ... the two leaders stressed the essential need for the steadfast adherence to the Islamic creed in order to face the violent currents blowing over the atmospheres of this region: And to make such a creed as a beacon for the illumination of their way in all their deeds to develop the area ... After his Majesty King Faisal listened to a statement by his Majesty Sultan Qaboos on the development of the situation in the sultanate of Oman: To the wise policy pursued by his Majesty the Sultan for the interest of his country: And to the sincere desire felt by His Majesty King Faisal from His Royal brother the Sultan to call upon all Omanis to return and to contribute to the progress and prosperity of Oman Sultanate [*sic*], the Kingdom of Saudi Arabia declares its recognition of the Sultan of Oman wishes her a full-scale success and the brotherly people of Oman progress and prosperity. The kingdom affirms its support for this Sultanate so long as she proceeds on the road which will enhance the prestige of Islam and unite the Arab ranks.[25]

A confidential note elaborating on the Sultan's visit, by a British representative,[26] accurately assessed the importance of the visit and the subtle political language contained in the joint statement issued above:

> This announcement issued in effect as a joint statement, is a bonus for Qaboos in return for his adherence to Faisal's prescription of Islam as the panacea for the troubles of the area and his invitation to all Omanis to return home (Which provides Faisal with the necessary face saver in respect of the Imam and his supporters—we do not know if Ghalib has accepted), Qaboos has gained formal recognition of Oman without mention of Boundaries by the Kingdom of Saudi Arabia (And promotion from Azimat (Highness) to Jalalate (Majesty).[27]

The statement issued by both leaders asserted the Islamic character of the region, but considering that various forms of Pan-Arabism were still a force to be reckoned with, the language becomes understandable. Faisal was a self-designated champion of maintaining the Islamic character of both the Arab and the Muslim world. Since the 1960s, when Riyadh was confronting Nasserite Pan-Arabism, Faisal had asserted that the organizing principle of regional politics was Islam, not Arabism. The Saudi initiative to establish the Islamic Conference Organization in 1969 was but one step toward that goal. Sultan Qaboos faced a determined insurgency in his own country, which was publicly Maoist in its orientation, and had no scruples in asserting Muscat's adherence to the Islamic creed in facing the region's challenges. Most importantly, for Muscat, Riyadh, and Abu Dhabi, the recent rapprochement between Muscat and Riyadh paved the way for the final termination of the Buraimi dispute. In 1974, Riyadh abandoned its claim to the Buraimi Oasis, with both Oman and Abu Dhabi dividing it amongst themselves.[28]

THE END OF DHOFAR'S REBELLION

Gaining regional and international legitimacy for the new regime was indeed extremely important, not only for the sake of political legitimacy outside the country, but also for propping up military and political aid from states that now were willing to extend their support to the Sultanate. General Johan Graham, who assumed command of the Sultan's Armed Forces in early 1970, depicted the deteriorating situation:

> In Dhofar the ado [enemy] had by the Spring of 1970 established themselves over the whole of the Jebel. The morale of the civilian population was low and many were unsympathetic to the SAF. By night the ado were coming down on the Plain for mine laying and ambushes, to probe the defenders of RAF Salalah or to engage Dr's hedgehogs with RCL and mortar fire.[29]

Simply put, the Sultanate was on its way to losing the war. Describing the ideological and strategic imperatives of the PFLOAG, Muhammed Ahmad Ghasani, a responsible member of the executive committee of the general command of the movement, stated,

> In accordance with the experience of the Chinese revolution under the leadership of the great Chairman Mao, our people's Front has formulated a line of self-reliance, depending on the broad masses of poor people to carry out a protracted people's war, and using the countryside to encircle the cities and seize the cities ultimately, thus developing the revolution to the whole of the Arabian Gulf to defeat and drive out the British colonialist.[30]

With the establishment of a PFLOAG office in Aden and the forging of ties with various groups at various times, such as China, Iraq, Cuba, Libya, and radical Palestinian organizations, such as the Popular Front for the Liberation of Palestine and the Popular Democratic Front for the Liberation of Palestine, the PFLOAG became steadily more threatening. As more sources of support emerged, PFLOAG was able to extend its territorial control throughout the western part of Dhofar, resulting in the capture of a major town, Rakhyt, in August 1969. The rebels sought to buttress their domination over the "liberated" areas "by forced collectivization of land, political indoctrination in Marxist-Leninist dogma, and strengthened ties with the PDRY hinterland, as evidenced by the beginning of a road from Hawf, in PDRY, to Rakhyut."[31] John Akerhurst, commander of the Dhofar Brigade during the last part of the campaign, reported that at its height, in 1970–1971, PFLOAG's strength was 2,000 full-time guerillas, 4,000 part-time militiamen, and an uncertain number of potential sympathizers in the midst of the Dhofari population.[32]

In Muscat, Sultan Qaboos began to initiate a totally different strategy to counter the growing strength of the PFLOAG. He immediately recognized that socioeconomic factors were just as important as military means.[33] The scope and the speed of social and economic reforms throughout the Sultanate in general and Dhofar in particular proved to be a key factor in ending the insurgency. As Akehurst commented at the end of the insurgency, much of the "the Sultan's victory was due to rapid and continuous civil aid efforts made wherever government forces took control of a village, which gave the local population an incentive for seeing that the guerrillas did not return."[34] Central to the conclusion of the insurgency was the way in which the government pleaded its case to the population in Dhofar. Using transistor radios, distributed freely to every part of the region, the authorities disseminated messages constantly conveying the promise of new hope and dignity under the new regime. Qaboos' messages delivered as early as October 1970 gave an account of the history of the struggle. The Sultan cautioned his people of the danger to their way of life:

> The weapons they use and the uniforms they wear come from the countries of communism and, far worse, the Chinese communists, with Chairman Mao's little Red Book and all its doctrines are forcing the people of the Jebel to reject the Holy Koran and their traditional way of life ... a new life is already open to the people of Dhofar—this new life will bring them the benefits of security, medicine, schooling, and work, exactly as in the rest of the Sultanate.[35]

In addition, he notably promised a benevolent pardon for the insurgents who were willing to put down their arms.[36]

Although the statements made by Sultan Qaboos in 1970 refer to China's role in supporting the PFLOAG, by 1971 Chinese aid was essentially over. A number of developments convinced Beijing to alter its Middle East policy: the Soviet invasion into Czechoslovakia, the Brezhnev Doctrine, and more ominously the escalation of Sino-Soviet arms clashes. As a result, Beijing started to accept U.S. policy in the Persian Gulf and Arabian Peninsula region while cultivating friendly relations with the independent states of the region. Particularly alarming for Beijing was Moscow's successful bid in signing two treaties of friendship and cooperation with both India and Iraq in August and April 1971. This pressured China to establish diplomatic relations with both Kuwait in March 1971 and Iran in August 1971. China attempted to limit Soviet influence in the region (through Iraq) by establishing relations with both Iran and Kuwait.[37] China's approval of U.S. role in the Persian Gulf and its concern over Soviet penetration are best demonstrated in a memorandum submitted to President Nixon in March 1973 by Henry Kissinger, Assistant to the U.S. President for National Security Affairs, describing his meetings with Mao and Zhou in February 1973:

> In literally every region of the world the Chinese see the Soviet hand at play ... Mao and Zhou urged us to counter the Russians everywhere, to world closely with our allies in Europe and Japan, and to take more positive action to prevent the Soviets filling vacuums or spreading their influence in an area like the Middle East, Persian Gulf, Near East, south Asia and Indian Ocean.[38]

Muscat's direct concern, however, was the end of Beijing's military and political support for all national liberation movements in the region. Beijing recognized that continued support for the PFLOAG would only hamper its efforts in establishing good relations with countries of the region, and thus play into Moscow's growing influence in both Iraq and South Yemen. According to Hashim Behbehani, who interviewed several Popular Front for the Liberation of Oman (PFLO) officials after the war in 1972, Beijing called on PFLOAG to confine its aims to Oman. Since PFLOAG refused, Chinese aid was terminated. Even though the PFLOAG finally did comply with Chinese wishes in 1974 and changed its name to Popular Front for the Liberation of Oman, Beijing remained indifferent. By 1972, PFLOAG had replaced Chinese aid with aid from the Soviet Union.[39] Expressing Chinese fear that a power vacuum created after the British withdrawal might be filled by the Soviet Union, Chi Pengfi stated in a speech delivered in Tehran on 14 June 1973 that

> at present, the situation in the Persian Gulf is arousing general concern. The intensified expansion, infiltration, and rivalry by certain Big powers are gravely menacing the peace and security of this part of the world. Iran is an important country in the Persian Gulf and you have every reason to feel uneasy at this situation.[40]

The note about intensified infiltration by certain "big powers" naturally referred to the Soviets, who, according to Yodfat, saw that their efforts to penetrate the region by diplomatic means (establishing relations with the newly independent, or soon-to-be independent, Emirates) had not yet materialized. As the date for British withdrawal from the Gulf area approached, they boosted their aid for revolutionary elements directed against existing regimes. The Soviets believed that the "events in the PDRY would be repeated in the Gulf area, with the PFLOAG playing the same role as the PDRY's National Front for Liberation. They concluded that since the situation in Oman was fairly similar, it should therefore yield similar results."[41] In other words, the Soviets erroneously calculated that the insurgents might win the war.

Since Sultan Qaboos' accession, the new government had received nothing but scathing commentary from both Soviet officials and the Soviet propaganda machine. They accused the Sultan of being a British puppet whose reforms were simple ploys to deceive the masses. As Katz asserts, "none of Moscow's commentary about Oman has ever been favorable, nor has Moscow called for diplomatic ties with Muscat as it has with the other governments of the region with which it does not have relations."[42] Soviet aid to the PFLOAG, however, was never direct, since this could have adversely affected the Soviet relations with Iran. Soviet arms arrived from Iraq and through South Yemen, as part of its aid to that country.[43]

Soviet aid, notwithstanding, by early spring 1973 it became apparent that the Sultan's Armed Forces (SAF) were beginning to gain the upper hand. The SAF were able to marshal 3,500 combatants and some 45 aircraft against an insurgency totaling approximately 2,000. This success was without a doubt owed to Sultan Qaboos' ability to mobilize outside support largely from Britain and Iran.[44] The British motives in the Persian Gulf and by extension in the Sultanate were clearly articulated in the following secret record.

> British interests in the Gulf, up to and beyond British military withdrawn are that the oil which constitutes about 40 per cent of British ... oil imports annually, should continue to flow reasonably and that British companies continue to benefit from very large investments ... that no hostile power, especially the Soviet union, should ... seriously ... damage these ... that development in the Gulf should not damage British relations with Iran ... [that] the cohesion of CENTO ... [and protecting] British overflying rights in Iran [be maintained]; [and] that the use of staging and broadcasting facilities at Masirah [be retained].[45]

By April 1971, SAF included 49 seconded British officers, 71 on contract and approximately 60 pilots. As the war drew to an end in 1975, the British presence had mushroomed to 700, including 220 officers in private contract, 60 Special Air Service (SAS)[46] members, and 75 servicemen from the Royal Engineers. In addition to the role British personnel played, British equipment and weapons were a dominant factor in the war effort.[47]

In some respects, the Shah's objectives and those of Her Majesty's Government coincided in Oman, giving rise to close cooperation. Tehran's involvement in Dhofar reflected the Shah's alarm over a potential Communist "penetration on his southern flank, in addition to the northeast." Consequently, he declared that PFLOAG represented the "forces of subversion, destruction, chaos and murder" and enthusiastically championed Sultan Qaboos' efforts.[48] According to Marschall,[49] the Shah's involvement signaled to Marxist regimes as well as to revolutionaries that radical movements would not be allowed to threaten Tehran's interests in the Persian Gulf. Elaborating on the matter, a British diplomat stated:

> In the Dhofar rebellion, the British-Iranian relationship is of interest. Britain did not provide any troops but officers who worked together with the Iranian military. Iran being involved as an equal partner with Britain was important for the Shah, as it confirmed his view of Iran's position as a global power.[50]

One can hardly overemphasize the role Iran played in wining the war in Dhofar. This was not only due to its military aid, as shall be discussed, but also undoubtedly to its political muscle. Iran's military aid started as early 1973, with Iranian paratroopers already stationed in Oman. They were instrumental in clearing the Thamarit road in December (once available, the archives of the period might indicate even an earlier date; given that Sultan Qaboos and the Shah had already held several meetings by then). Their role, however, was not acknowledged until February 1974.[51] Estimated numbers of Iranian forces operating in Oman vary from one scholar to another. Marschall[52] suggests that there were approximately 30,000 to 35,000 troops (which seems to contradict the numbers given by experts of the region that are available to this research).[53] Peterson puts Iranian troops stationed in Oman between 3,500 and 5,000 troops.[54] Katz[55] puts the numbers between 4,000 and 4,500. Peterson claims that a large Iranian presence may be explained not only by the Shah's self-perception as the guardian of the Persian Gulf, but also by the potential for combat experience for the Iranian troops:

> The crack ranger battalions of the 1973 Operation Thimble had been replaced by units of decidedly lesser quality which were rotated out at frequent intervals in attempts to give many elements as much battle experience as possible. However, this policy resulted in alarming losses among Iranian combat forces, reportedly consisting of over a quarter of the 400 total deaths suffered by the Sultanate and its allies throughout the entire rebellion.[56]

Variations of numbers notwithstanding, the Iranian troops and air support were positively instrumental in ending the insurgency in Dhofar.[57] While Iranian Phantom F-5s patrolled the PDRY border, "Iranian destroyers shelled that part of the Dhufar coast then under rebel control. The Iranians were at the center of Rakhyut's recapture in January and played a prominent role in the 'big push' of December."[58] It was rather ironic that most Arab countries either were hostile, were neutral, or extended little help to the Sultanate in the initial stages of the war in Dhofar (Sultan Said had to face a similar situation, with one exception—not a single Arab country was willing to help). Libya, for example, wavered between support for the Sultanate and a diatribe of accusations and threats. This was culminated by Moammar Al-Qadhafi's invitation for the PFLO to have a representative in Tripoli. By 1975, Qadhafi had started passing Russian SAM-7 missiles to PFLO and at various times remarked that if foreign troops were not withdrawn, the Sultanate would be invaded, presumably by Libya itself. Jordan was a notable exception in the Arab world; it provided troops and equipment to the Sultanate. Amman, however, had to withdraw its troops after being pressured (one would assume by its fellow Arab countries) to pull out its troops within six months. The idea of Arab troops fighting alongside Iranian troops against fellow Arabs was not acceptable.[59]

It had been more than ten years since the beginning of the Dhofar War, and rebel positions seemed to be as steady. In January 1975, General Perkins, the commander of the Sultan of Oman's Armed Forces, wrote:

> By the end of January 1975 the long Dhofar War was well into its tenth year. Government forces, compromising the Sultan's Armed Forces (SAF) and an Iranian Brigade, had recently secured important areas but at a stiff price. The enemy, the People's Liberation Army, controlled politically by the Popular Front for the Liberation of Oman (PLA and PFLO), appeared as resilient and skillful as ever, certainly still well supplied. None of us present could see the end; yet victory was only ten months away.[60]

By December 1975, Sultan Qaboos declared his government's final victory in the Dhofar rebellion.[61] Superior military strategy won the Sultanate the war in Dhofar, but that victory to a significant degree was enhanced by the favorable regional environment. Within the same month that the Sultan declared victory, it was "reported that PDRY Foreign Minister Muti had visited Jedda for talks, after the Saudis had begun moves to mediate a PDRY-Oman agreement."[62]

The question is why now? Why did the Sultanate's wealthier neighbors, Saudi Arabia, Bahrain, Kuwait, Qatar, and the United Arab Emirates, not provide substantial aid earlier despite the fact that the war in Dhofar posed a real danger to them as well? Once the war was over, Riyadh, Abu Dhabi, and Kuwait all became eagerly involved in attempts to mediate between the Sultanate and the PDRY. After South Yemen, Iraq had been the second most important supporter of the rebels since the beginning of the insurgency. Although the mediation was partly aimed at ending the leftist threat to their own governments, it is equally convincing that "their action regarding the southern part of the Peninsula was equally motivated by resentment over Iranian soldiers on Arab soil."[63]

Certainly, Sultan Qaboos recognized that the presence of Iranian troops in Oman could serve the Sultanate in multifaceted ways. The leaders of Arabian Peninsula tended to look at Iran suspiciously (a perception that was justified by Tehran's occupation of the Gulf islands of Abu Musa and the two Tunbs in November 1971). By insisting on Muscat's need to keep Iranian forces in Dhofar, Muscat was pressuring the Arab Gulf states to compel South Yemen and Iraq to end their support for the insurgency.

The United States' direct involvement in the Dhofar War was negligible. In 1973, the Sultanate became eligible for U.S. military aid through the Foreign Military Sales Program. Between 1973 and 1976, the Sultanate purchases did not exceed two million dollars. This was more of a symbolic gesture since the equipment arrived in 1976, a year after the war had been won.[64] As Peterson rightly argues,

> much of the international concern over the war in Dhufar focused on the ideological schism of the struggle and the high stakes involved, i.e. the Gulf with all its petroleum wealth. Thus, it is not surprising that the 'domino theory' was frequently mentioned and the comparison with Vietnam made.[65]

The end of the war could be attributed to a number of factors. Among them was the external military aid: British, Iranian, and Jordanian. So, as Zahlan asserts,

> Oman's oil revenues after 1973 ... provided the Sultan with numerous advantages: he was able to spend lavishly on upgrading his defense forces; and he was able to provide the province of Dhofar with many social and economic reforms, thus tackling the original reasons for the Revolution.[66]

Amnesty was granted to all Dhofaris who were willing to put down their arms. Moreover, many were appointed by the Sultan to senior positions in the government.[67] The author seems to be implying that if the same resources were available to Sultan's late father, the results would have been the same. This evaluation is utterly erroneous. The role of Sultan Qaboos' personal leadership in the outcome of war cannot be overemphasized. The Sultan was a

> professional soldier, and thus defense and security were of paramount concern. Qaboos readily admitted that his own military experiences, meaning Sand Hurst, service in the British Army on the Rhine, and the Dhofar war, were major influence on his life.[68]

His political acumen from the start of the war proved itself in linking sociopolitical factors with military objectives.[69] As we saw in the last chapter, Sultan Said was either unwilling or unable to demonstrate the same political imagination.

THE SULTANATE'S STRATEGIC AND SECURITY CONCEPTIONS

The end of this long war unquestionably brought with it a newly found status to the Sultanate. Only a few years earlier, the country was called "Muscat and Oman and Dhofar," although the latter was seldom appended to "Muscat and Oman." Qaboos' resolve and determination to end this artificial divide and create a unified country was evident from his earliest announcements made in August 1970, when he declared that henceforth the country was to be known as The Sultanate of Oman.[70] Regionally and internationally, the world took notice of the Sultanate's victory. The country's strategic value, the involvement of various countries in the conflict, the scale of the war itself, and Muscat's successful modernization were all noteworthy. Without a doubt, the country's experience of the war was a decisive factor in the rebirth of Oman as a country whose voice is relevant and indeed important. This became apparent in subsequent years "when the discussions about Gulf security developed in the later 1970s which ended with the formation of the Gulf Cooperation Council (GCC), Oman's opinions were influential and necessary to the debate in a way that would have been inconceivable a few years earlier and pre-1970 would not even have been sought."[71]

This was already clear from one of the earliest efforts to establish a Gulf security formula on 16 July 1975. As the Ministers of Arab Gulf states, Iraq, and Iran were attending the Islamic Conference meeting at Jidda, Riyadh elicited its accord on a set of standards regarding Gulf security. Specifically, Riyadh sought few key principles:

> (1) exclusion of the superpowers from the region; (2) denial of foreign military bases; (3) military cooperation among Gulf countries to ensure freedom of navigation; (4) peaceful resolution of regional disputes; and (5) a collective guarantee of the territorial integrity of countries of the region.[72]

Essentially, these principles or standards recognized a common denominator of external threats as an alliance of Gulf countries with superpowers, perceived security issues principally in terms of relations among Gulf countries, and called for the bare minimum in military cooperation (the latter is not even conceived necessarily on a full collective basis).[73] For various reasons, these principles were simply unacceptable for various states in the region. When Muscat, for instance, made the appeal that all "littoral states extend financial support to the joint Iranian-Omani naval patrols in the Strait of Hormuz, Saudi Arabia and the UAE [United Arab Emirates] objected, proposing instead that security arrangements be worked out within the 'Arab Nation.'"[74] For both Muscat and Tehran, the idea that foreign troops (British and Iranian forces still engaged in Dhofar) must be pulled out of the area was unrealistic and uncalled for, given that in Dhofar Soviet aid was still channeled through South Yemen. Baghdad, on the other hand, argued that collective arrangements were unnecessary; rather, cooperation in the form of bilateral arrangements between individual states should be a norm. It allowed Baghdad to pressure individual counties such as Kuwait or the United Arab Emirates. In addition, the regional states frowned on the professed exclusion of the superpowers as being

> directed at their Soviet connection but having no effect on the 'organic' connection of Iran and Saudi Arabia and the United States. They wanted the denial of foreign bases to apply to American base rights in Bahrain but not to the Soviet presence in their own Umm al-Qasr naval base.[75]

In Muscat, the exclusion of foreign forces from Dhofar, without a concrete commitment that troops and resources will be provided for the war effort, was understandably perceived as unrealistic and even dangerous. Second, Muscat was already engaged, as early as September 1974, in negotiating with the United States on terms under which landing rights were sought for Masirah Island. Arrangements were reached only after the Sultan's visit to

> Washington in January 1975, where he met President Ford, Secretary of State Henry Kissinger, Secretary of Defense James Schlesinger, and CIA Director William Colby … The move was interpreted as a sorely needed counteraction against the growing Soviet presence in the region.[76]

Riyadh, however, was still hopeful that its proposed scheme would eventually gain the approval of the countries of the Arabian Peninsula at least. To that end, Saudi Minister of Interior Prince Nayef bin Abd Al-Aziz toured the Gulf countries in October 1976 to promote a pact on internal security along the same Saudi scheme mentioned earlier. Kuwait, fearing Iraq, and Oman, with its special relationship with Iran, called instead for a regional security scheme that included both Iraq and Iran. A conference took place in Muscat on 25 November, with the participation of Kuwait, Bahrain, the UAE, Saudi Arabia, Qatar, Iraq, and Iran.[77]

This conference, like previous ones, was destined to fail. Once again, different security concerns of each state precluded the possibility of a common formula and understanding of what constitutes Gulf security, let alone a formal alliance or agreements between the Persian Gulf states. Muscat's relations with Tehran were again a key factor in the conference. At this juncture, it is important to remember that Riyadh played a key role mediating between the PDRY and the Sultanate of Oman in ending the PDRY's support for the PFLO. Once diplomatic relations were established between the PDRY and Riyadh on 10 March 1976 (a watershed event for both states, which had had no diplomatic missions since 1967) Riyadh attempted, although unsuccessfully, to bring about reconciliation between Oman and South Yemen.[78] The efforts did succeed, however, in mediating a cease-fire premised on South Yemen's withholding of all aid to the PFLO, in exchange for the withdrawal of all foreign forces from the Sultanate. The agreement

> underscored the common interest between Saudi Arabia and PDRY in getting Iran out of Oman, but was also a source of continuing friction between them, since the Saudis expected PDRY to cease aiding the rebels but could not themselves deliver the withdrawal of Iran's force.[79]

Yet again, Muscat demanded a regional security agreement before asking the Iranians to leave. When the demand was not met, Muscat

> concluded an agreement with Iran in January 1977 calling for the reduction but not the complete removal of Iran's military presence. The mutual Saudi-PDRY recognition of the preceding March did not therefore lead to an exchange of ambassadors between the two countries, and Saudi assistance to PDRY remained at a modest level."[80]

There were simply too many differences between the parties concerned on what constitutes security and how best to secure the Persian Gulf for the Muscat summit to succeed. There was no consensus on the status of foreign fleets in the Persian Gulf, on how best to cooperate militarily to guarantee the safety of navigation, or on whether military facilities should be granted to Western powers. Iran, Iraq, and the Arab Gulf monarchies identified different sources of tensions in the region and, as a consequence, conceived of different security arrangements.[81] The Sultanate's Minister of State for Foreign Affairs captured the prevailing mood by noting that "it is apparent that the present atmosphere is not suitable to reaching a formula for mutual co-operation. There are many reservations and many options to clear up first."[82] Qaboos recognized that "separate arrangements would have to be reached with Iran and Iraq but that another effort should also be made to join the Arab monarchies together. In an appeal to his fellow rulers, he asked for the establishment of a $100 million Common Defense Fund that would be responsible for safeguarding the security of the Strait.[83]

Sultan Qaboos' resolve to procure serious and reliable security arrangements between the countries of the Persian Gulf, as a precondition for withdrawal of Iranian forces and for ending the American presence in Masirah Island, in the face of Iraqi and Arab Gulf states pressure, was the beginning of a sense of independent foreign policy initiatives. In fact, as early as 1971,

> India's support of Oman at the UN was reciprocated by the Sultan Qaboos in 1971 during the debate over Bangladesh. Unlike the majority of Arab states, Oman abstained notwithstanding it [sic] nascent membership status. It was the only Muslim state not to fully support Pakistan.[84]

In 1977, despite the pressure from Arab countries, Muscat supported Egyptian President Anwar Sadat's visit to Jerusalem in November 1977 (after all, Oman was one of the three Arab countries that supported the Sadat initiative), the subsequent U.S.–brokered Camp David Accords of 1978, and the bilateral peace treaty between Egypt and Israel in March 1979. When Baghdad, as a response to President Sadat's visit to Israel, invited Sultan Qaboos to attend the October 1978 Rejectionist Front Summit, the Sultan declined. When another invitation was issued for the Foreign Ministers to meet in Baghdad on 27 March 1979, Muscat once again decided not to attend. Baghdad's harsh response came from Saddam Hussein, when he declared through the Iraqi paper *Al-Thawra*: "We regard every Arab ruler who does not implement the summit decisions as a traitor. It is therefore our duty to instigate his people against him and to provide them with the necessary means to topple him."[85] According to Kechichian,

> Qaboos declined the invitation not only because he thought that the Summit was unnecessary, but because he did not believe in joining 'rejectionist' fronts. Oman would not join a pack dominated by weak ideas and even weaker concepts. This was more than a technical matter.[86]

Even after the Israeli invasion of Lebanon in 1982, Muscat continued to regard the Camp David Accords as the foundation for a possible resolution of the Arab-Israeli conflict. The Sultan declared that

> the Camp David accords had been and still were the only means that achieved a constructive step in the direction of reaching a peaceful solution to the Middle East issue. We believe it is necessary to regard Camp David accord as alive, and that every effort designed to attain further progress should be based on it.[87]

It is logical therefore that in 1983, official Muscat, through its Foreign Minister Yusuf al-Alawi, "took the unusual step of calling upon Arab nations to recognize Israel, since Israel will remain in existence."[88]

Outside the Middle East, the Soviets vilified Oman for approving the Camp David Accords and for not breaking diplomatic relations with Cairo, as was the case with most of the Arab states. The Soviets had other reasons to denounce the Sultanate's foreign policy either in official comments or through its propaganda machine, namely the establishment of diplomatic relations between Oman and the People's Republic of China in 1978, which the Soviets perceived as "as part of the two countries efforts to form a broader anti-Soviet alliance."[89] Only a few years after the Dhofar War, and despite China's early involvement, the representatives of two countries met in London to sign a joint communiqué in May 1978. It stated:

> The Government of the People of China and Government of the Sultanate of Oman have decided to establish diplomatic relation at ambassadorial levels as from May 25, 1978, and to exchange ambassadors ... The Government of the Sultanate of Oman recognizes the Government of the People's Republic of China as the sole legal government representing the Chinese people. The two governments have agreed to develop friendly relations and cooperation between the two countries on the basis of the principles of mutual respecting for state sovereignty and territorial integrity, mutual non-aggression, non-interference in each other's internal affairs, equality and mutual benefit, and peaceful co-existence.[90]

Indeed, the communiqué expressed one of Beijing's key priorities in the region: recognizing Beijing as the only legitimate representative of all of China. It should be noted, however, that the Sultanate still allowed a Taiwanese trade mission to remain in the Omani capital of Muscat.[91] A number of key factors prompted both Muscat and Beijing's to establish diplomatic relations. China's motives were mainly driven by a concern over Soviet penetration of South Yemen and Iraq as a prelude to an overall domination of the Persian Gulf region. In addition, China recognized that its relations with Oman might open the door for other states in the region to establish relations with Beijing, while terminating their ties with the Taiwanese government. This was particularly true of Saudi Arabia, which was one of the key states with which Taiwan enjoyed diplomatic relations (the others were South Korea and South Africa).[92]

As far as Muscat was concerned, the establishment of diplomatic relations with Beijing intended to put a complete end to any possible future support that China might lend to the PFLO. In addition, the Sultanate's shared concern with Beijing regarding Soviet penetration in and around the region was also a key factor in Muscat's decision to establish diplomatic relations with Beijing. The Sultanate reasoned that diplomatic relations with China would serve as counterweight to the Soviets. Sultan Qaboos said:

> The Soviet Union is pushing forward a scheduled and fixed policy of expansionism in this region. This policy is no way different from the savage acts of the old colonialists during their time. This has been obvious for some time, undoubtedly, the Soviet Union has two intentions: ultimately gaining control of the Middle East, in particular, the oil region; and second, carry out expansion towards the Indian Ocean in order to control African countries and then the entire Far East.[93]

THE SULTANATE OF OMAN, THE IRANIAN REVOLUTION, AND THE SOVIET INVASION OF AFGHANISTAN

The year 1979 proved to be one of the most eventful years in the history of the region: the Iranian Revolution and the Soviet invasion of Afghanistan were watershed events that continue to reverberate to our present day. These events reinforced the Sultanate's regional and global significance stemming from its geographic position in the southeast corner of the Arabian Peninsula overlooking the Strait of Hormuz and the entrance of the Gulf, and controlling the apex of the Indian Ocean. Although Muscat shares with Tehran the sovereignty over the Strait of Hormuz, it should be stressed that the designated traffic lanes through which tankers navigate "are all on the Omani side of the dividing line: so in fact Oman is responsible for the protection of all the tanker traffic through the Strait of Hormuz."[94] Within a year, Muscat found itself between two of the Middle East's most radical regimes: PDRY to the immediate south and the revolutionary Islamic Republic of Iran across the Gulf to the north.

> Among the six, his [Sultan Qaboos'] country alone straddled the Hormuz Strait. Omani land, the narrow and isolated tip of the Musandam Peninsula, stuck out into the center of the strait. Sultan Qaboos and the Shah had undertaken the patrol of the strait together. What was Qaboos to do with the revolutionary leaders in Tehran?[95]

Less significant was a situation taking place in Afghanistan: "since the December 1979 invasion of Afghanistan … Soviet troops in that country, now numbering close to 100,000, [had] been positioned a mere 300 miles—less than an hour's flying time—from Oman's borders."[96] However, the most difficult development for the achievement of Soviet goals in the region was the resurgence of American resolve, exemplified by the Carter Doctrine,[97] the U.S. naval buildup in the Indian Ocean and Gulf of Oman, and the determination to proceed quickly with the establishment of the Rapid-Deployment Force (RDF). Muscat's immediate response varied from attempts to maintain correct, if not warm, relations with Iran to a resolute call for the Persian Gulf states and the international community to share in the responsibility in safeguarding the Strait. Muscat dispatched a delegation headed by the Minister of State for Foreign Affairs, Alawi bin Abdullah, to meet with Ayatollah Ruhollah Khomeini. Alawi was informed in Tehran that agreements signed by the previous regime would be honored and that Iran would work closely with Oman to ensure regional security. At the conclusion of the meeting, the Minister declared, "Iran is our neighbor, we have close historical, religious and geographic links with her and we are eagerly looking forward to expanding pure relations with her in all fields in order to make the region a safer place to live in."[98] In addition, Muscat dispatched another mission, headed by Muscat's former ambassador to Iran, to all Gulf countries, including Iran, calling for the preservation of freedom of navigation through the Strait of Hormuz and the financial and technical support of major industrialized countries. The mission, however, was aborted,

> not only because of the Iranian preferences to go it alone, but also because of a visit the Iraqis made to Bahrain and Kuwait in order to sabotage the mission. The Iraqi newspaper Al-Thawra, the mouthpiece of the Ba'th party, charged that the 'Omani plan' was 'a new imperialist alliance.' The plan was suspect form the very beginning, because the sultan had a well-known preference for closely cooperating with the West in security matters. Long before the Soviets invaded Afghanistan, for example, he advised the Americans: 'What we need is a clear drawing of the line against Soviet involvement in the area.' 'The U.S position,' he added, 'should be clear without ambiguity. You should not allow the Russians to undermine your friends and, in the process, America itself.'[99]

The Sultan demanded a clear commitment from the United States not only to protect the security of the Persian Gulf but also to consider a possible role of NATO in the region. In one of his interviews, he wondered

> why countries friendly to the West, that have the strategic location, possess vital resources for the industrial world and hold common interests with the West, are not invited to join NATO as associate members or observers, thus becoming an integral part of the Western defense system.[100]

Illustrating his unfailing realism, Qaboos commented in another interview, given on 15 December 1979, that "if the big powers find that their interests in the region are threatened, they will not seek permission from me or anybody else to intervene."[101] Six months later, Sultan Qaboos made a bold decision that was denounced by almost every Arab capital: Muscat signed the United States–Oman military access agreement in June 1980, allowing the U.S. military use of Omani facilities. This was in exchange for

> assistance in upgrading four of Oman's airfields and the provisions of military and economic credits, the agreement stipulates that US forces, upon the Sultanate's invitation, be allowed access to Omani military facilities in the event of a regional confrontation requiring Western intervention ... Pursuant to this agreement, the Sultanate has been the only GCC member state—and apart from Morocco, Egypt, the Sudan and Somalia, the only Arab country—to conduct joint exercises with US military forces ... In addition, the US has spent more than a quarter of a billion dollars in connection with holding three joint training exercises with Omani forces in 1981, 1982, and 1983, and in improving facilities at Masirah, Khasab, Thamarit and Sib.[102]

The Sultanate's Minister of State of Foreign Affairs, Alawi bin Abdullah, stated that the exercises were being conducted with a state that is a

> friend of all the area states. On this basis, the maneuvers could not be interpreted as being directed against any Gulf State. The United States was a country which has

transcended the stage of friendship to the point where it could be said that it was an allied state, despite the fact that there was nothing written in this respect.[103]

The response, however, from all of the Arab Gulf countries was one of critique and accusations. Bahrain's Foreign Minister stressed that "the defense of the Gulf must be undertaken by the states of the area, and any request by any foreign state for bases or facilities will be rejected."[104] He further commented that

> there is no organization in the Gulf area that supports Oman's steps to grant facilities or military bases in the area. The act of bringing U.S. forces into the area would complicate matters and would render the dangers of conflict and competition between the United States and the USSR in the area more possible and more serious.[105]

Kuwait's reaction was expressed even more strongly in both the Prime Minister's and the Foreign Minister's rejection of the presence of American forces in the region. Kuwait's Foreign Minister demanded that all major powers should withdraw their fleets from the Gulf and neighboring area, and thus "keep this important strategic region of the world away from international conflicts."[106] The United Arab Emirates emphasized,

> It is true that the Arab Gulf states have condemned the Soviet military intervention in Afghanistan … however, their position on Afghanistan was decided at the Islamic Conference … and their awareness of the Soviet danger does not mean that they should accept foreign forces. Just as they reject and condemn any Soviet expansion, the Gulf States, on the basis of the same independent national will, reject U.S. protection.[107]

Whereas the Saudis were content that there were no foreign "bases" in Saudi Arabia, Iraq responded by condemning the Soviet invasion, which was followed by a call for an Arab charter, which states that

> the presence in the Arab homeland of any foreign troops or military forces shall be rejected and no facilities for the use of Arab territory shall be extended to them in any from or under any pretext or cover. Any Arab regime that fails to comply with this principle shall be proscribed and boycotted both economically and politically as well as politically opposed by all available means.[108]

For its part, Muscat denied that the agreement granted the United States a base, insisting that it was a facility that could only be used with Muscat's approval.[109] On 18 November 1980, on the occasion of the Sultanate's 10th National Day, the Sultan commented on Muscat's motives behind the agreement:

> Oman has given repeated and, we regret to say, largely unheeded warnings about these dangers. We have invited our brothers to join with us and aid us in preserving the stability of the area—not only vital to ourselves but to the whole world—but to no avail. Therefore, threatened as we are—and we still have vivid and bitter memories of the realities and form of that threat—we have had no other choice than to seek the assistance of those who will provide us with the means to defend ourselves.[110]

Speaking with more directness, the Sultan stated in an interview,

> I would like to reveal one of the reasons behind this agreement (with US on facilities). The strategic location of Oman and the possible threats, however remote, made it indispensable that Oman should enlarge its military establishments and airports. Consequently, we asked the GCC brothers to help us in this task, particularly as our oil resources are very limited in comparison to theirs. The required improvements involved about $2 billion, a sum which most brothers declined to spend, while the US showed readiness to finance these projects. That is how we came to agree on the facilities.[111]

In another interview, the Sultan went into even further details explaining Oman's decision:

> We must make clear that the questions of facilities has been overblown and given different interpretations. Some have even gone as far as saying they are bases in the guise of facilities. This is unthinkable from the outset, and we refuse to discuss it in any way. However, because of the conditions created in the world, and our area in particular, if was necessary to have to have some kind of understanding between us and our friends, without specifying a particular state. Also, while the United States is on one side of the international scale, it has become necessary for the area that there be a balance because the opposite side has become heavy and the Eastern Camp's presence has become large ... particularly in South Yemen and Ethiopia as well as Afghanistan in the north, which is only 300 nautical miles from here. As for the U.S. naval presence, Oman has nothing to do with it—it is in the Indian Ocean and not under the sovereignty of a particular state.[112]

Indeed, Oman's insistence on using the term "facility" rather than "base" was not merely for public consumption. As Acharya maintains:

> In the case of these "arrangements [military facilities], host country intentions in granting access could not be confirmed until actual clearance was received at the onset of a particular crisis. Even in the case of Oman, the GCC member most sympathetic to the U.S strategy in the region and the only one in need and receipt of American military and economic aid, U.S. discretion in using the facilities was limited and uncertain.[113]

This is further confirmed in a Senate Foreign Relations Committee staff report in 1984 that "concluded that the U.S.-Omani 'agreement' was predicated on assisting the United States in meeting a potential Soviet threat to the region. Oman did not commit itself to United States use of these facilities to meet threats originating from within the region."[114] As the following memorandum to national security advisor Zbigniew Brzezinski illustrates:

> My old friend Stephen Groueff, now Public Relations Adviser to the Omani Embassy, invited me to lunch today ... The Omani Ambassador left for home consultations last night in connection with what Stephen termed 'current misunderstandings' ... The Omanis have interpreted our desire for facilities as relating primarily to their own

security, which they see most directly menaced by South Yemen. They envision no U.S. military presence of consequence unless and until Oman itself is endangered directly. They do not envision Oman as a staging area for American operation toward Iran or Iraq, Afghanistan or other more distant points.[115]

The simple fact is that the agreement met significant needs of both Washington and Muscat. Given the Soviet invasion of Afghanistan, the Iranian revolution, and the looming threat of war between Iraq and Iran, the Unites States needed access to facilities or bases outside its traditional points of operation in the Indian Ocean and the Persian Gulf region: Saudi Arabia, Bahrain, and Diego Garcia. For various reasons, all three were viewed to be inadequate for meeting U.S. needs in the area in the light of new environment. Bahrain, for example, was home to the U.S. Middle East Force, but it was too small for significant military activity. Moreover, Bahrain being in the Gulf, its ability to assist large ships such as aircraft carriers was negligible. Saudi Arabia's military facilities were more than adequate for various military uses, but could be very costly politically for both Riyadh and Washington because of the Saudi status in the Arab and Muslim world. Diego Garcia, on the other hand, is too far away from the Persian Gulf, especially for daily operations. Muscat, therefore, was an ideal point of access in the region given that it lacked both the logistical and the political problems of Saudi Arabia and Bahrain.[116]

The Sultanate's motives for the agreement varied.[117] As articulated by Sultan Qaboos in his interview, Muscat recognized possible threats to its security, and wished to obtain U.S. assistance in modernizing its military facilities, an assistance that was not forthcoming from its wealthier neighbors. One may assume that these "threats" emanated from Tehran; however, it is more likely that Muscat was more concerned with both South Yemen and the Soviet Union. After all, the Sultanate was the only Arab state in the region that was in complete agreement with Washington in recognizing the Soviet Union as the main threat to the Persian Gulf.[118] In addition, Qaboos was able to extract a

> side-letter to the agreement in which there is a formal undertaking by the US to support Oman in the event of aggression against the Sultanate. Excluding President Truman's letter to Ibn Saud this was the only case of such an agreement between the US and an Arab county until after the Kuwait War of 1991.[119]

An alliance with a major power was motivated chiefly by strategic concerns, but one should not discount the economic dimension of the agreement. A salient reason behind the Qaboos' decision was Muscat's lack of great wealth in comparison to the rest of the Arab Gulf states. The war in Dhofar and the requirements for building a modern state were extremely expensive for Muscat's modest resources.

The Soviet invasion of Afghanistan, however threatening, was soon to be superseded by a closer threat: the Iran-Iraq war, which began with Iraq's invasion of Iran on 22 September 1980. For Muscat, this was a double tragedy and a strategic hazard. First, the war was preceded by the Iranian revolution, which removed the most important regional deterrent to a possible Soviet advance in the Gulf. The new regime, notwithstanding its promises for security cooperation with the Sultanate in the Strait as mentioned earlier, was visited by a delegation of the PFLO in April 1979. Muscat simply ignored this visit and reiterated its position (which it kept throughout the ordeal of the war) that the Iranian Revolution was an internal matter.[120] Second, the spillover of the conflict to the Sultanate was a real possibility that Muscat could not dismiss. Importantly, this was not necessarily a question of supporting subversive acts against the Sultanate, as occurred in Iraq or later in Kuwait, or by supporting indigenous dissidents, as was the case in Bahrain in late 1981.[121] As Ramazani pointed out, the

> Iranian geo-strategic challenge to Oman is unique. Omani shorelines (1,005 nautical miles) lie mainly outside the Persian Gulf, but the isolated 51-mile Omani enclave that lies within Gulf waters looks Iran straight in the eye across the strategic Strait of Hormuz. The Iranian challenge to Oman, therefore, interconnects uniquely with the Iranian challenge to all Gulf States at the Strait of Hormuz ... 'joint Iranian-Omani patrol of the Strait of Hormuz' that has been set up by the two monarchs [the Shah and the Sultan] was scrapped by the revolutionary regime, resulting in Oman undertaking unilateral military efforts—with the help of the United States—to keep a watchful eye on the strategic waterway.[122]

THE SULTANATE OF OMAN AND THE GULF COOPERATION COUNCIL

Ironically, the war between Iran and Iraq "forced" the creation of the long-sought-after Gulf Cooperation Council, composed of Bahrain, Kuwait, Oman, Qatar, Saudi Arabia, and the UAE on 25 May 1981. The Iran-Iraq war was certainly not the main motive behind this organization; rather, it was a combination of events such as the Soviet invasion of Afghanistan, the impact of the revolution on the region, and the concern over a possible American intervention in the area. The Iran-Iraq war was "a precipitative factor at the inception of the GCC, but only later did it become a primary concern of GCC members."[123]

Since the inauguration of the GCC, the Sultanate was the strongest advocate of defense cooperation in the GCC body. Yet Muscat was acutely aware that this institution should not be construed as a military force directed at Tehran. Indeed, Sultan Qaboos indicated in an interview,

> To be perfectly frank, I say that here in Muscat we do not believe it to be in the interest of security in the Gulf that Iran feels we intend to establish an Arab military pact that will always be hostile to it, or that we are about to from a joint force, whose main task is to fight Iran ... There is no alternative to peaceful co-existence between Arabs and Persian in the end, and there is no alternative to a minimum of accord in the region.[124]

Graz rightly points out that

> Oman, despite the old friendship with the Shah, managed to stay neutral, refusing to join in the condemnation of Iran by the Arab foreign ministers meeting in Tunis in September 1987. The inevitable result was, once again, that it was charged with lack of Arab fervor.[125]

If anything, the Sultanate has consistently pursued an evenhanded approach to the first Iran-Iraq war. It refused to make any attempts to structure the GCC as an anti-Iranian front. More importantly, Oman has encouraged Gulf states to engage Iran if only to ensure the safety of the Strait. The confusion seems to arise from the Sultanate's conception of what arrangements the GCC should adopt to ensure the security of its members. As Allen explains:

> Oman has led opposition to a GCC defense pact. Qaboos opposes both an integrated military structure and formal alliance in favor of strong independent defense forces with close cooperation in training and exercises. Two specific concerns are that an alliance might be perceived by Iran as an Arab military pact against the Islamic Republic and the conditions by which the GCC's rapid deployment force will be permitted to intervene in any member state. Sultan Qaboos has also been at odds with his neighbors on the role that the United States should play in defense policy. Oman favors close cooperation, as demonstrated by its access agreement and joint military exercises, whereas other members wish to distance the organization from both of the great powers.[126]

In an interview, Sultan Qaboos articulated his views on the fundamental need of the GCC states to work closely with the West:

> We want to look after our own affairs and have the capacity to do so under normal circumstances. After all, why have we bought so many weapons? If there should be a major armed confrontation we would like to have advice on military planning and borrow expertise from our friends. We do not want their soldiers … But in the ultimate scenario where all odds are against us, I do not see how we can avoid asking our friends from outside and all those who want to see this region stable and peaceful.[127]

Muscat's emphasis on cooperating with the West and granting military facilities to the United States was consistently coupled with a declared policy of neutrality toward Iran and Iraq. This balance was not violated even despite the fact that the Sultanate's navy was involved in a "showdown" with the Iranian navy in 1980, when Muscat claimed that Iran violated Omani waters. Muscat also refused to allow the Iraqi air force to make use of Omani facilities or airspace to attack the Islamic Republic and protected all shipping across the straits, which was Iran's primary outlet for its oil transportation.[128] However, this is not to assume that Muscat was oblivious to the possibility that its neutrality might not spare it from the spillover effect of the Iran-Iraq war. Sultan Qaboos' assessment of Iran in 1983 was ominous:

They are going to cause problems because they are going to use subversive mechanisms in the area, and that is going to create some instability ... But we are very determined to prevent them from threatening, intimidating or overthrowing the present government.[129]

The above remarks notwithstanding, Muscat continued to follow its declared policy of active neutrality throughout the war. The Sultanate's position toward the Iran-Iraq war was clarified by Sultan Qaboos' interview given to the Beirut weekly *Monday Morning* in late 1983:

In any war situation, there is a possibility of hostilities getting out of hand. That's why I believe every possible step—on the national, regional and international level—should be taken to stop the [Iran-Iraq] war. I understand from the Iranian declarations that Iran will not follow through its threats with steps on the ground unless all its oil facilities are crippled or destroyed. In such a situation, the Iranians will have nothing to lose. I believe too that the Iraqis are wise enough to evaluate what they are doing.[130]

This position proved to be useful for all parties concerned, whether inside or outside the region, as an Omani official explained:

Oman always played a dual role. Oman dealt with the war according to its point of view that we should not be drawn into the conflict because Oman will be there, Iran will be there, no matter what government, so the only solution is to keep talking to them. At the same time, Oman did not isolate itself from the region, it was a part of the GCC. This dual policy was encouraged by the West—the US and Britain used Oman. Washington asked Muscat many times to mediate with Iran, especially when there were US casualties in the Gulf. Even Iraq did not object to this Omani role. Saudi Arabia was not happy because it did not want to see anybody take the initiative. They wanted to be the leaders of the GCC, all decisions should be taken from Riyadh. But Oman had the influence to stop the deterioration of the relationship between the Gulf and Oman. Oman defused the tension many times.[131]

Elaborating on the same subject, H.H. Sayyid Haitham, Secretary General of the Omani Foreign Minister at the time, said,

The war produced some negative reactions from our neighbors towards Iran. During the first year, it was not clear for Oman what direction the war would take. We did not want to be allied to either party. We were neutral, we had no interest in continuing this war. This was very much appreciated by Iran, but it made a number of neighbors very unhappy.

We looked far ahead and saw that GCC had no strength against Iran and Iraq. Also, being Iran's neighbor, it was not wise making an enemy. In the beginning of the 1980's, Iran kept its distance from Oman. They were not sure because the rest of the GCC was different. Our approach began in 1985. In 1986, the visits started, first junior officials, then senior officials. From then on they increased steadily. There were always visits by Foreign Ministers and the Embassies played a great role as well. But we only mediated if we could see the way to success.[132]

Muscat's mediation was paying off for all parties concerned. In 1987 and 1988, the Sultanate repeatedly used its office to repatriate Iranians killed or injured during the engagement with American forces in and around the Strait.[133] It is true that Oman supported the 1987 GCC-LAS summit resolution condemning Iran's aggression in the Gulf, but it is equally true that Muscat rejected UN, LAS, and GCC resolutions threatening to collectively sever diplomatic ties with Iran.[134] After the 1987 hajj (pilgrimage) incident between Iran and Saudi Arabia over quotas and demonstrations, Oman again was at the center of the mediation efforts between Iran and Saudi Arabia and between Iran and the GCC. After Riyadh broke off diplomatic relations with Tehran in April 1988, Foreign Ministers of both states met in Muscat in May 1989. Muscat was also active in promoting the implementation of UN Security Council Resolution 598, calling for a cease-fire between the parties. Certainly, Muscat was "relieved" when Iran and Iraq finally accepted a cease-fire on 20 August 1988. Oman's Minister of Information Abdulaziz bin Mohammed Al-Rowas stated that

> Oman was deeply concerned that its long term interests with Iran would be permanently affected by the war. 'History and geography' dictate our foreign policy goals towards Iran, he posited, and 'these are permanent features.'[135]

It was no surprise then that the GCC officially commissioned Muscat to mediate between Iran and Iraq.[136] Muscat's position regarding the peace talks was articulated by the Omani Undersecretary of the GCC, Said al-Maskery:

> All Gulf attempts [to bring peace talks] should concentrate on backing the UN Secretary General's efforts … The Iranian government's general approach had changed since Rafsanjani came to power. We always hear positive statements. But it depends on his ability to carry out in practice what he says … I think that if Iran wishes to develop relations with the GCC states, it must be convinced of the need to improve relations with Saudi Arabia.[137]

Just as the Sultanate was a key mediator between Iran and Saudi Arabia and Iran and the GCC countries, the Arab Gulf states were also instrumental in the improvement of the PDRY-Omani relations, which led to the normalization agreement of October 1982. Under Omani tutelage in November 1981, only few months since the establishment of the GCC, the GCC sent two military missions to determine the extent of the threat posed by South Yemen to the Sultanate.[138] By January 1982, when the next GCC Defense Ministers' meeting took place, South Yemeni threat was the main focus of the discussions. Politically, both Kuwait and the United Arab Emirates played a key role in mediating between the Sultanate and the PDRY. Finally, recognizing the PDRY's serious economic needs, Riyadh approached the PDRY with an economic package but linked its assistance with a change in Aden's political behavior.[139] Once diplomatic relations with Muscat's longtime adversary were established, the establishment of diplomatic relations between Oman and the Soviet Union should not have come as such a surprise:

In September 1985, out of a clear blue sky, Oman suddenly announced that it was establishing diplomatic relations with the Soviet Union. Even the British diplomats, still the best connoisseurs of the Sultanate, were surprised by what had long been considered the most anti-Soviet country in the Middle East. The Americans were more than surprised; they were furious. They told the Omanis what they thought warning them of all the dire consequences of a Soviet diplomatic offensive in the Gulf; the Omanis politely told them to mind their own business.[140]

Oman's Foreign Policy (1990–2004)

MUSCAT AND THE GULF WAR (1990–1991)

The end of the 1980s appeared to signal a period of relative stability in the Middle East, particularly in the Persian Gulf region. This optimism seemed to be justified given the end of the Iran-Iraq war and the dramatic events taking place in the Soviet Union, Central Europe, and Germany that culminated with the end of the Cold War. The 1991 Gulf War, precipitated by Baghdad's invasion of Kuwait in August 1990, brought an abrupt end to this optimism and thrust the Middle East yet again into the center of an international crisis.

Muscat's response to Baghdad's invasion of Kuwait was in accordance with that of the international community. Officially, the Sultanate affirmed its position that Iraq's invasion of Kuwait set a dangerous precedent, threatened the stability of the international order, and represented a direct challenge to the integrity of the United Nations. Muscat at once condemned the invasion and called upon Iraq in the strongest of terms to withdraw from Kuwait.[1] In August 1990, the Sultanate initiated a resolution condemning the invasion at a meeting of the Arab League. In the meantime, the Omani Foreign Minister traveled to New York and Washington to discuss the merits of the United Nations–sponsored coalition force against Baghdad.[2] Muscat's diplomatic initiatives to counter this new crisis were not limited to the Middle East or Washington and London. Recognizing the growing importance of China in the region, Qaboos dispatched a senior adviser, Omar Al-Zawawi, to Beijing to meet with the Chinese President. At the meeting, China's President, Yang Shangkun, affirmed Beijing's opposition to Iraq's invasion and called for an unconditional withdrawal from Kuwait.[3] Muscat was assessing China's role in a future settlement of the crisis, since China's permanent membership in the Security Council. More important was Muscat's recognition that China still retained "a formidable presence in the region, primarily by continuing to sell arms to Iran and Iraq.

True to its long-term foreign policy principles, Muscat focused on the effect of such sales rather than simply on immediate gains."[4]

Along with its diplomatic activities to counter Iraq's aggression and deter it from further advances, the Sultanate was a participant in both Desert Shield and Desert Storm. Indeed, between December 1990 and February 1991, Muscat deployed troops to Saudi Arabia.[5] Furthermore, and perhaps more importantly for the coalition forces, Muscat granted the United States access to critical air and seaport facilities in Oman and the authorization to use pre-positioned U.S. equipment in various Omani facilities.[6] Indeed, this war demonstrated that Muscat's previous positions concerning the security of the Persian Gulf were justified. As early as in December 1988, only a few months after Tehran had accepted the Security Council's Resolution 598 calling for a permanent cease-fire in the Iran-Iraq War, Sultan Qaboos traveled to Riyadh and argued for a new vision for regional security. Qaboos reasoned that swift foreign policy initiatives were needed to bring both parties into a new security framework before a possible future conflict could erupt.

MUSCAT AND REGIONAL SECURITY

Unfortunately, "neither he nor members of his delegation were successful in persuading their Saudi counterparts of the urgency to act decisively towards Iran and Iraq. It was, as the monarch would recognize[,] a 'lost opportunity.'"[7] The basis for a collective arrangement that would include Iran, Iraq, and the Gulf Cooperation Council (GCC) states in a new security framework was found in UNCR 598, paragraph 8. It was introduced by the Iranian UN representative.[8] An Omani official expressed Muscat's support for the regional security arrangement in these words:

> We could have used Resolution 598 after the Iran-Iraq war. Item 8 calls on the United Nations Secretary General to arrange consultations between the two belligerent parties and the other counties in the region to create stability in the region. Consequently, the GCC Political Department organized a working group which produced a White Paper: The Secretariat led by GCC Undersecretary Saif al-Maskery, Oman, proposed to use this Resolution as an instrument either to have an international agreement between the eight countries in the region for security and stability in the region; or to hold an international conference and issue a regional declaration to keep the Gulf countries stable and secured by all countries together. A declaration has a moral and political obligation. If one party does not fulfill the obligation, it won't affect the others, unlike an agreement. Unfortunately, nothing happened, the suggestions were not accepted by the GCC.[9]

Muscat's declared neutrality in the Iran-Iraq war, and its persistent policy of engaging both sides rather than the unquestionably backing Iraq, proved prophetic. As the following quotation demonstrates, the support that members of the Gulf Cooperation Council lavished on Saddam was staggering:

> During the first two years of the war, Saudi Arabia, the UAE [United Arab Emirates] and Kuwait provided nearly $30 billion in grants and loans to Iraq. The Saudis reportedly financed the Iraqi purchase of French weapons. From 1982 onwards, the direct military ads stopped. Kuwait and Saudi Arabia, instead, agreed to produce Iraq's quota of 1.2 million barrels of oil per day on its behalf and transfer the proceeds to Baghdad. Saudi Arabia also permitted the 650 kilometer long Iraqi pipeline on the Saudi port of Yanbu free of charge having the initial capacity of 5,00,000 b/d.[10]

When the Gulf crisis of 1990 occurred, Saddam was quick to make overtures to Iran in an attempt to secure Tehran's neutrality or possible support in the conflict. To that end, Saddam unexpectedly announced that he was suing for peace with Tehran and was unconditionally accepting all Iranian claims since the ceasefire, including the reinstatement of the Algiers Treaty of 1975. Extremely concerned, both Kuwait and the UAE sent envoys to Tehran to block Iraqi initiatives aimed at winning Iranian support. On 22 August 1990, Kuwait's foreign minister arrived in Tehran and openly expressed his country's regrets over past mistakes toward Tehran. The UAE Foreign Minister followed with messages of reconciliation. Tehran accepted Saddam's offer of a formal settlement, yet it unequivocally condemned Iraq's invasion, called for its unconditional withdrawal from Kuwait, and offered to defend the other Gulf states from further aggression. It should be noted that the decision to condemn the Iraqi invasion and to remain neutral in the conflict was accompanied by heavy debates within the Iranian government. Many hardliners called for supporting Iraq and fighting the forces of the United States and its allies to keep the Gulf out of bounds for foreign powers.[11] Pragmatism, however, dictated that accepting the foreign presence was a necessary evil. An intricate balance between the two positions was expressed by Iran's President Rafsanjani: "We have no objection to them [foreign powers] obstructing aggression; anybody may help in anyway. However, it would have been better if the regional counties would have done so."[12]

The Sultanate's previously stated position that granting the U.S. facilities in the Gulf was important for the security of the GCC states proved accurate (ironically, Kuwait was the most vocal opponent among the GCC states of such an arrangement). Kechichian argues that the "West in general, and the United States in particular, could not have achieved their successes in the liberation of Kuwait were it not for the pre-positioned equipment in Oman."[13] While rather exaggerated, this opinion clearly indicates the importance of the facilities granted to the United States in Oman for Operation Desert Storm.[14] Omani facilities were equally essential for British forces as well in their part of Operation Desert Storm: Operation Granby. Although the Dhofar War had ended more than two decades ago, Britain had continued to participate in Oman's military affairs. There were roughly 500 British officers and non-governmental organizations seconded or contracted to the Omani military. British military forces regularly trained Omani troops: for example, the Royal Navy's Flag Officer Sear Training for Oman's new Muheet-class frigates and British Special Air Service training of the Omani anti-terrorist task force. They also assisted in surveillance of the border with Yemen. The British made regular use of Omani facilities, maintained intelligence posts near Muscat and Qabl in the Musandam Peninsula, and used the Omani base at Goat Island in the Strait of Hormuz.[15]

Following the liberation of Kuwait, Muscat continued to pursue its independent attempts to resolve the challenges facing the region. Its policies proved to be different from those of other GCC member states, and also from Washington's. The devastating experience of the Gulf War could have rallied members of the GCC to cement their security integration and act decisively toward combining their resources. The Gulf War could have become the defining moment that would accelerate Gulf integration. Instead, the end of the war brought to the surface divergent perspectives and disputes among the members of the GCC.[16] These differences were reflected in their relationship with Iraq and Iran and in their position on the security of the Gulf.

At the conclusion of the Gulf War on 3 March 1991, the six members of the GCC, along with Egypt and Syria, met in Damascus in a U.S.-brokered effort to formulate the structure of a permanent security force to protect Kuwait against future aggression. As the nucleus of an Arab security force, Syria and Egypt would remain in the Gulf after the war, contributing troop contingents on a reimbursable basis. The Damascus Declaration, termed "six plus two," soon came apart when differences developed over the merit of a long-term Egyptian and Syrian presence in the Gulf. Iran, which had restored diplomatic relations with Saudi Arabia in 1991, saw Gulf security as the responsibility of the Gulf states alone and opposed a permanent Egyptian and Syrian military role in the region. Nonetheless, Egypt and Syria remained committed under the agreement to send military aid to Kuwait and the other Gulf states if a threat arose. Egypt in turn was opposed to any possibility that Iran might in the future be a part of a security framework to guard Arab Gulf states. Differences between Muscat and Cairo over the degree of the Iranian threat both to the Sultanate and to the region came to the fore during Hosni Mubarak's visit in May 1993. For Egypt, Iran was both a strategic threat to Cairo's influence in the region and a supporter of Islamic fundamentalism. Oman, on the other hand, never made references to Iran as a "strategic threat," and furthermore perceived the fundamentalist issue as an internal affair of Tehran.[17] Essentially, GCC states preferred to rely on the United States and other major Western powers rather than on Egypt and Syria, let alone Iran, possibly believing that the Egyptian and Syrian government had different agendas from those of the Gulf countries.[18] Although on paper Kuwait supported the Damascus Declaration and the inclusion of Egyptian and Syrian troops, its preference for U.S. troops was well known. The only GCC state to support Iranian participation in future security arrangements to some extent was Oman. Muscat's support for an Iranian role in the future of Gulf security, however, had yet to appear in a concrete proposal or "security arrangement" between the states of the Persian Gulf. As for the GCC, its Secretary-General announced that Iran would not be given a direct role in the Gulf security system.[19] At the 1991 Kuwait GCC Summit, Sultan Qaboos was entrusted by the Council to chair the Higher Committee on Security and to formulate postwar regional security arrangements. Muscat seized the chance to encourage reconciliation between Saudi Arabia and both Iran and Iraq. In addition, the Sultanate "assiduously vaunted the notion of a 100,000 man strong GCC army despite opposition from the rest of the council states."[20] Muscat's plan called for a force that would be separate both from the national armies and from the small Peninsula Shield Force stationed in Saudi Arabia. The plan also called for the establishment of a unified command. In essence, "Muscat wanted to avoid a repetition of the crises that emerged during Operation Desert Storm when national contingents, ostensibly attached to a multinational force, remained under their own national commands."[21] Omani officials commented that the true uniqueness of Muscat's proposal was that it afforded GCC residents "for the first time the opportunity to defend themselves, their own sons, their countries and their resources."[22] Oman's proposal was rejected, prompting Sultan Qaboos to express his frustration and disappointment with GCC progress in strengthening security cooperation among the member states.[23] The Sultan stated, "Certainly, I would have liked to have seen more progress in this direction"; however, the proposal was never enacted, with various states citing budgetary constraints and disagreements over how a genuinely collective GCC army should be commanded.[24] In the daily Arabic newspaper, *Al-Sharq Al-Awsat*, Alawi commented on the Omani proposal of raising a 100,000-man-strong Gulf Army:

> (Al-Husayni) Sultan Qaboos raised the idea of forming a Gulf army of 100,000 men. What has become of that idea? (Bin-'Alawi) That idea emerged immediately after the war to liberate Kuwait. There were great fears. It was the product of experience, but it emerged in the context of deterrence. We came to the conclusion at the time that if another problem occurred, God forbid, the difficulty that the Western allies would have would be in relation to infantry, armor, and troops, whereas they have no difficulty with air forces or naval forces.[25]

This bold proposal was hardly surprising in the context of Muscat's conventional position, which has always been in strong favor of self-defense in a region where, despite rhetoric to the contrary and enormous defense budgets, few countries maintain ground forces adequate to deter even relatively small threats. Indeed, Oman has maintained a "small (by world standards) but impressive (by Gulf standards) army, well trained and disciplined. Beyond its own self-defense, Oman has recognized that the small states of the Gulf must, as Benjamin Franklin remarked, 'hang together or assuredly [they] will all hang separately.'"[26] At the same time, Muscat recognized that no members of the

Gulf Cooperation Council could single-handedly mount a strong defense designed to repel any of the major powers in the region, as was clearly demonstrated in the second Gulf War. During the time "when it was utterly anathema to support any public U.S. role in the Gulf, Oman was the only GCC state officially to grant the United States access to military facilities in its territory."[27]

MUSCAT'S POLICY TOWARD IRAN AND IRAQ IN THE 1990s

As in earlier times, Muscat's policy toward both Iran and Iraq during the 1990s continued to simultaneously accommodate and differ from other GCC members' policies. On many occasions Muscat came into a direct conflict with Washington's polices. In essence, Muscat's accordance with members of the GCC and Iran regarding Iraq was reflected in two principles. First, the preservation of the territorial integrity of Iraq was paramount. Second, the GCC demanded the full implementation of all the UN Security Council resolutions passed after the invasion of Iraq.

The general agreement notwithstanding, from the early 1990s Muscat was quietly working toward a conciliatory approach to both Iran and Iraq. Muscat's policy toward Iraq particularly frustrated Saudi Arabia and Kuwait. Their distress was reflected during the GCC Foreign Ministers' Conference in April 1993, when the organization failed to appoint the Omani candidate to a third three-year term as assistant secretary-general for political affairs. Both Riyadh and Kuwait felt that Oman was "too soft" on Arab states that supported Iraq during the 1990–1991 Gulf crisis.[28] Oman's quiet diplomacy to reintegrate Iraq into the Arab embrace was also in direct conflict with Washington's "dual containment" policy toward Iraq. The dual containment policy was formulated by Martin Indyk, a senior fellow for the Near East and South East Asia on the National Security Council, for the Washington Institute for Near East Policy on 18 May 1993. It essentially sought to isolate both Iraq and Iran internationally. Iraq's isolation was to be achieved through stringent sanctions that would eventually lead to the fall of Saddam, while isolating Iran was designed to pressure Tehran to change its foreign and domestic behavior.[29] This policy received a resounding welcome in Israel, where Foreign Minister Shimon Peres told the Knesset, "I admit, in all modesty, that it is better to let the United States, rather than us, stand at the head of this campaign. Were we alone, it would make sense to lead the fight. But if the U.S. wants to lead, its influence and connection are greater than ours."[30] By 1998, however, containment of Iraq was replaced by a single purpose of regime change. That year, the U.S. Congress announced that it had authorized military aid to Iraqi opposition groups attempting to depose Saddam (this legislation later became known as Iraq's Liberation Act).[31]

In the Gulf, Muscat's stance echoed this view and maintained that it was futile for Oman and members of the GCC to continue formulating their Iraqi policy on the basis of a possible regime change in Iraq given that Saddam might survive indefinitely.

> Instead, the Gulf States should try to readmit him [Saddam] to the international community through the Arab door—in terms they can influence rather than waiting and being caught off guard when the Western powers eventually come to terms with Iraq. Oman's position is that it is in its and the GCC's interest to adopt a more conciliatory approach to both the big regional powers. Such a policy, according to Omani officials, is preferable to accepting the dubious logic of dual containment.[32]

To that end, Muscat never broke relations with Iraq, and the Iraqi ambassador continued to reside in Muscat. Defending Muscat's diplomatic relations with Iraq, Omani Information Minister Al-Rawas remarked that "we do not cut any diplomatic ties with any country. We may freeze them or we may withdraw one of our diplomats but never cut such relations completely."[33] Adding that Iraq would eventually come back to the international community, he emphasized, "When we open an embassy, we open it with the people. This is our strategy, and all of the Arabs know it very well."[34] More disconcerting for Kuwait and Saudi Arabia in particular, was Oman's willingness "to work with whoever is in charge in Baghdad," as expressed by Abdullah Ali al-Qatabi, President of Majlis al-Shoura (the Consultative Council).[35] Clearly, in Muscat's view, UN resolutions did not require the overthrow of Saddam. This meant that a regime change in Baghdad was not a prerequisite for integrating Iraq into a regional security arrangement. Muscat's position was in stark contrast to the support received by Iraqi opposition groups bent on the overthrow of Saddam from various regional and international powers. Since 1982, Tehran had helped establish the Supreme Assembly for the Islamic Revolution in Iraq as an umbrella for all the Iraqi Shia parties. Similarly, both the United States and Saudi Arabia supported the Iraqi National Congress as the main group dedicated to regime change in Iraq. Jordan also supported and hosted an Iraqi opposition group, the Iraqi Accord. Moreover, Omani officials continued to make statements expressing sympathy toward the Iraqi people suffering under the United Nations sanctions that followed the invasion. To its credit, Muscat's media never vilified Saddam, just as it never vilified Khomeini before him, in contrast to most Arab media. Thus, it was less difficult for the government in Muscat to receive envoys from Saddam's Iraq shortly after the war to discuss reconciliation. When asked about the visit of Iraq's Foreign Minister to Oman in 1995, Oman's Foreign Minster Alawi remarked:

> [Bin-'Abdallah] We, for our part, are seeking to hold consultations with Iraq to ensure implementation of the resolutions imposed on it. I believe that this policy has succeeded in bearing fruit to a certain extent, the most important result being Iraq's judicial recognition of the independence of Kuwait. This is no easy or small matter. We view things from this angle and not from the angle of the existence of a conflict between so and so nor from the angle of sympathizing with one side to spite the other. There is no such thing at all.[36]

Oman's perceived sympathy led many to believe that once Oman assumed the Arab seat in the UN Security Council in January 1994, it would support the lifting of sanctions against Iraq. Contrary to this, Muscat maintained resolute support for the sanctions against Iraq while it attempted to ease the impact of sanctions on the Iraqi people. When then U.S. ambassador to the United Nations Madeleine Albright visited Muscat in February 1995, Sultan Qaboos seized the chance to discuss and draft a new UN Security Council resolution that would have allowed Iraq more flexibility to sell oil and use the proceeds for the purchase of humanitarian supplies for the Iraqi people.[37] In an interview with Arabic Newspaper, *Al-Sharq Al-Awsat*, Alawi elaborated on the new Resolution 986:

> As you know, the Sultanate of Oman played a major part in Resolution 986. The idea of the resolution was formulated here when Madeleine Albright came here on a visit and met with Sultan Qaboos. The sultan raised the issue for the first time, because no people should be left to starve. So the idea emerged of coming up with a humanitarian plan, and she went back to submit a draft resolution with Britain and Canada; but that was not the draft that Sultan Qaboos discussed with her, nor was it the resolution that was later passed. That idea was not put forward and it remained just a draft, and we therefore entered into long discussions with them over six weeks or more on the articles of the resolution, and we achieved what we achieved after the Russians and the French introduced some amendments. So we were of the opinion that we had a moral responsibility to see the resolution implemented. That is why contacts between us and Iraq are continuing.[38]

Among Gulf monarchies, Qatar and the UAE eventually began to move closer to Muscat's position. The UAE restored its diplomatic ties with Iraq and began humanitarian aid shipments to the besieged country. In a conference titled "The Future Prospects of Kuwaiti-Iraqi Relations" that took place in Kuwait on 13–15 May 2000, Qatar's Foreign Minister openly called for the rehabilitation of Iraq. However, he was careful not to call it an initiative, but simply an idea.[39]

The Sultanate's opposition to the U.S. dual containment policy also manifested itself clearly in Muscat's relations with Tehran. Although it is beyond the scope of this chapter to trace the sources of the dual containment policy toward Iran specifically, it is vital to bear in mind the context in which it originated, as articulated by Gary Sick, the National Security Advisor to President Carter:

> The U.S. 'dual containment' policy toward Iran had a mixed parentage. As indicated above, the original impetus and much of the subsequent momentum of this policy originated with Israel. From the beginning, it was entwined with U.S. policy on the Arab-Israel peace processes, the administration's most important foreign policy initiative. It also resonated in U.S. domestic politics, including the Clinton administration's efforts to maintain the strong support of the U.S. Jewish community; but it also played extremely well with the Congress and with the American public more generally, where the image of Iran was indelibly associated with terrorism and with

the hostage crises of the 1980's. There was also a palpable yearning within the Washington establishment for an all-purpose enemy that would provide a focus for our strategic planning and justify agency budgets in a period of retrenchment. Finally, it may be suspected, that harsh criticism of Iran satisfied a desire for revenge against a regime that had humiliated the United States and contributed greatly to the electoral defeat of President Carter. As a member of Warren Christopher's team that negotiated the settlement of the hostage crisis in 1980–81, I have some sympathy for that view.[40]

Muscat continued to have balanced relations with Iran and continued to advocate the re-integration of Tehran into both the Gulf and the international community. When asked about his reaction to the dual containment policy toward Iran, Sultan Qaboos responded, "Iran is the largest country in the Gulf, with 65 million people. You cannot isolate it."[41] The need to engage Iran was articulated by the Sultan in other interviews as well. Without directly criticizing the U.S. policy, he emphasized the active participation of all regional states to safeguard the vital interests of both regional states and the world community in the Persian Gulf region:

> As I have indicated earlier, my principal concerns is that every state that has a vital interest in Gulf security should play its full part, energetically and constructively to maintain that security … It can readily be understood that, given the fact that this region produces a commodity that is vital to the rest of the world-oil—the whole international community has an interest and responsibility in assisting in every way possible the maintenance of peace and security in this region.[42]

It should be noted that President Bill Clinton's adoption of dual containment in 1993 represents a significant shift from the previous administration's policy toward Iran. In his inaugural address in January 1989, President George H.W. Bush mentioned the Americans "held against their will in foreign lands," in a clear reference to the American hostages in Lebanon. "Assistance can be shown here," he stated, and, "Good will be long remembered. Good will begets good will. Good faith can be a spiral that endlessly moves on." In an informal Oval Office press conference later in the day, he added, "People in the past facilitated the release of our citizens, and I'd love to see that happen again, and I won't forget it" if it does. Such comments were recognized to be directed to Iran, where they were warmly received.[43] Significant improvement of relations between Washington and Tehran were further reinforced during and after the Gulf crisis. This is clearly demonstrated in a statement delivered by James Baker, United States secretary of state during the Gulf Crisis, to the House Foreign Affairs Committee on 6 February 1991. The secretary identified five challenges to the newly envisioned world order that must be pursued: greater security for the Persian Gulf, regional arms proliferation and control, economic reconstruction and recovery, search for peace and reconciliation in the Middle East, and reduction of U.S. energy dependence. More specifically, in regards to the Persian Gulf states, Baker asserted that Gulf security must be based upon "new and different security arrangements" that addressed the "role of local states, regional organizations, and international community."[44] In this arrangement, Iran was viewed as a major power in the Gulf, which must be engaged. These statements were echoed by President Bush, who stated that a country as big as Iran cannot be possibly treated as an enemy by all countries of the region. The president indicated that Washington wanted better relations with Iran and no animosity. As an indication of Washington's good will, following the Gulf War, the World Bank extended to Iran its first loan since 1987, an act that was undoubtedly made possible by the U.S. decision to remain neutral on the matter. Furthermore, in June of 1991, the U.S. Treasury allowed American companies to purchase 250,000 barrels of Iranian crude oil, which officially resumed the Iranian oil sales to the United States, which had ceased in 1987. On its part, the Iranian government demonstrated good will and improved relations between the two countries by releasing Jon Pattis, an American engineer who had been sentenced to ten years on spying charges.[45]

Clinton's presidency, however, significantly reversed this trend, as evidenced by Secretary of State Warren Christopher's testimony before a Senate committee upon his return from a trip to the Middle East:

> We think that Iran is one of the principal sources of support for terrorist groups around the world. When I was in the Middle East, I found that to be a common judgment among many of the leaders that I met with, that Iran was greatly feared at the present time because of their support for terrorist groups ... Their determination to acquire weapons of mass destruction, I think, leaves Iran as an international outlaw.[46]

Muscat, on the other hand, had repeatedly rejected the premise that Iran posed a fundamental threat to security and stability in the region. Instead, it asserted that a prosperous and stable Iran would enhance and consolidate the chances of comprehensive peace in the Persian Gulf and the whole of the Middle East.[47] When Iran acquired three Kilo-class submarines from Russia, a step much criticized by the Gulf states as detrimental to the stability of the region, Muscat refused to overreact, its joint submarine warfare exercises with the United States and the United Kingdom notwithstanding.[48] Expressing sympathy toward Iranian rearmaments efforts, H.H. Sayyid Haitham, secretary general of the Omani Foreign Ministry, remarked "Iran after its war with Iraq feels very weak. They think that U.S. forces in the Gulf are directed against them. So they have a reason to arm. It is an internal affair. There are no grounds for us to feel threatened. We are not in confrontation with them."[49] Tehran, for its part, continued to assert that its armament was not designed for territorial conquests or to threaten the Persian Gulf states. Iran's UN ambassador remarked:

> We are surrounded by turmoil. In the West, we have Iraq, which has attacked its neighbors twice ... In the east, we have Afghanistan; in the north, we have republics with their own problems ... It is very easy to make the case that we need to keep our

military capacity and buy some arms for defensive purposes. If the Americans claim that this military expenditure is to threaten the states in the Persian Gulf, that is a baseless accusation. I think they make this claim to sell more arms.[50]

The Iranian government appreciated the Omani position, as expressed by an Iranian official:

Our relationship with Oman was better than with other countries in the region. Nowadays, it is the best. After the Gulf crisis we have been holding joint military maneuvers; the Iranian Defense Minster visits Oman almost every year. Omani mediation has always been welcomed by Iran, the Foreign Ministers have a good relationship.[51]

Indeed, Muscat remained Iran's main mediator and supporter in the GCC[52] by concentrating on attempts to further a dialogue between the GCC and the Islamic Republic. Its efforts bore fruits in March 1991 when full diplomatic relations were restored between Riyadh and Tehran in a meeting that took place in Muscat.[53] This step was accompanied by Oman's continued efforts to negotiate Iran's role in the future Persian Gulf Security arrangement. In his visit to Tehran in March 1992, Foreign Minister Alawi raised the possibility of Iran's consultative role in the formation of future regional security arrangements. Military relations became a visible element of the increased cooperation between Oman and Iran. In 1993, Rear Admiral Shihab bin Tariq, commander of the Royal Navy of Oman, visited Tehran, where he met with the Iranian president Rafsanjani. The meeting ended with an announcement by Shihab "that the two countries had agreed to cooperate in the maintaining security in the Straits of Hormuz."[54] In 1995, Sultan Qaboos reiterated that he did not regard Iran as "a long term threat to the stability of the region."[55] In 1996, after a highly publicized three-day visit, Alawi remarked in a statement to *Al-Sharq Al-Awsat*:

I would rather not elaborate at present on the outcome of the good and open dialogue between us and our Iranian brothers. I can, however, assure you that the atmosphere, in all my meetings with the Iranian President (Hashemi-Rafsanjani), with the Majles Speaker (Nateq-Nuri), and with the scholars, was excellent. However, this fruitful action now requires us to bear the Prophet's saying in mind, and 'use circumspection in one's endeavors.[56]

In Muscat, the Omani minister stressed that "both Muscat and Tehran, in addition to the other states in the region, wish to help achieve stability in the region."[57] *Al-Awsat* cited the assessment of the visit by the experts on the Iran-Gulf relations as "reaffirming a permanent channel for open dialogue between Iran and all the Arab Gulf states."[58] As a sign of a remarkable improvement of relations, for the first time since the revolution, the Omani and Iranian navies began to exchange visits and port calls. In April 1995, Iranian Navy commander Admiral Ali Shamkhani toured the Omani naval base at Wudam. In March 1997, Oman's air force commander al-Aridi visited Iran "within the framework of joint efforts by both sides to familiarize themselves with each other's capabilities, strengthen the bridges of trust, and boost the climates of mutual reassurance."[59] He was also to discuss ways for a practical formula for joint regional security arrangements to establish security in the shared Gulf waters. He stated that

> Iran is an influential neighboring state. We and Iran share the coasts of the Strait of Hormuz, which is vital to countries, the region, and the world. Thus it is our duty to protect it ... This is why we decided some time ago to break this imaginary barrier and to sit down as military officials from both sides to hold discussions so that matters can proceed in a balanced manner.[60]

Muscat was obviously hoping that its attempts at "constructive engagement" could prove to be more a practical method of dealing with Iran than the U.S. focus on dual containment. Muscat's foreign policy makers had supported strong U.S. military presence in the region, yet they warned that putting too much diplomatic and economic pressure on Tehran might jeopardize the stability in the region.[61] As such, "Oman's relations with Iran are a part of a carefully calibrated network of relations with all other Gulf countries (often mutually antagonistic) and its arrangements with external powers."[62] This is clearly the case with the Sultanate's excellent relations with its neighbor the United Arab Emirates, which had strong reservations against the possible reintegration of Iran into a regional security arrangement, given its unresolved dispute with Tehran over the three islands in the Gulf: Abu Musa, Greater Tunb, and Lesser Tunb. In 1971, when Iran expanded its presence in the region through the control of the three islands, both Iran and Abu Dhabi were able at the time to arrange a joint management of the islands. However, in 1992 Tehran expelled from Abu Musa the foreigners who were employed by the UAE in medical clinics and a power generation station.[63] Since then, the UAE and, along with it, the GCC and the Arab League have called on Iran to end its "occupation" of the islands.[64] In the following interviews conducted with Alawi in 1995 and 1996, the foreign secretary responded to various questions concerning Oman, the UAE, and Iran that may shed some light on Muscat's stance on the issue:

> (Al-Husayni) By virtue of your relations with Iran, can you persuade it to do anything about the islands, such as withdraw? (Bin-'Alawi) Listen, our position in the GCC is clear. We will say nothing at all on this issue because it is a bilateral issue. There has been much hardening of positions, making it difficult for anyone to propose ideas, but, despite that, the brothers in the UAE are openly saying that they will seek a settlement of the issue only by peaceful means, and all they are saying at present is: If the problem cannot be solved bilaterally, why not go to the international courts? Iran holds an opposite view. It refuses to go to the International Court of Justice. As a result of the two viewpoints, there is tension. Our position is clear. The Iranians and the UAE know it. We can add nothing to that. (Al-Husayni) What is your

known position? (Bin-'Alawi) We have told the GCC what our position is. We believe that the UAE has a right to the islands. That is the official position, but we will not be a judge. As long as there are negotiations.[65]

As far as the UAE was concerned, however, Iran's occupation of the islands constituted the fundamental obstacle to any collective security arrangements that may have included Iran. In this context, a UAE paper claimed that

Iran with its 'king of kings' [shahinshahiyya] attitude has not abandoned its dream of being the regional power as policeman and of setting down conditions in the area. The revolution did not change these priorities … After the second Gulf War, Iran started to reemerge as the regional power.[66]

The Saudi point of view, although expressed without references to Iran's "occupation of Arab lands," is, nevertheless, similar to the ones expressed by the UAE. This is how a Saudi official described Riyadh's diplomacy toward Iran before 1997:

Today, Iran is a much bigger threat to the Gulf than Iraq. Iraq is now contained. Iran in the long run is much dangerous. Its arms build up signals hostile intentions. If Iran acquires nuclear weapons, it would lead to a major disaster. This is why the US must stay in the region. Iran cannot be part of a security agreement. In the beginning, Saudi Arabia said we needed to include Iran in a regional security agreement, but that was just rhetoric. We string them along. We say: 'Let's talk in six months, let's discuss further.' We do not want to provoke them. At the same time, we bring in the US. Saudi Arabia never had any intentions of including Iran, but we speak softly.[67]

With the election of Mohammed Khatami in 1997, a new level of rapprochement began to emerge. While much credit for this rapprochement resides with Khatami's presidency, Crown Prince Abdullah's role in these developments was equally important. As Okruhlik asserts, "It is not at all clear that rapprochement would have occurred between Fahd and Khatami as it has between Abdullah and Khatami. The impetus comes as much from Saudi Arabia as from Iranian leadership."[68] This was clearly demonstrated in the Eighth Summit of the Organization of the Islamic Conference, hosted by Iran in 1997. At the conference, the Crown Prince issued important statements that demonstrated the remarkable distance that Tehran and Riyadh had traveled to come closer together in a relatively short span of time. The language used by Abdallah evoked "the immortal achievements credited to the Muslim people of Iran and their invaluable contributions through our glorious Islamic history." He referred to the summit as a "historic meeting" and remarked that it was incumbent on the Muslims "to turn over a new leaf in dealing with ourselves and in coexisting with others," adding that it was an obligation to remove the obstacles preventing cooperation in the hope of "making our way toward a better future."[69] Remarkably, Kuwait's ambassador to Washington went as far as saying that

"Kuwait is not concerned about Iran's nuclear program. We think that Iran is on the verge of an internal explosion. It will explode much earlier than it can develop a nuclear bomb. The power base of the regime is eroding."[70]

Despite the close contacts and interests shared between Muscat and Tehran, as demonstrated by various officials of both countries, Muscat's and Tehran's positions on Gulf security fundamentally differed. While Oman's conception of Gulf security is tied to Western commitment and continuous presence in the region, Iran perceives Western presence as the primary cause of insecurity and instability in the Gulf. As Iran's Foreign Minister Kamal Kharrazi stated:

> [We] believe the presence of forces outside our region ... Their presence will turn the region into a military barrack, cause greater instability, lead to proliferation of conventional and non-conventional weapons, pollute the environment and in the long turn impede political, social and economic development of the countries of the region.[71]

An opposing view rooted in an unwavering sense of realism is articulated by Oman's Secretary of Foreign Affairs in the ensuing candid interview. This lengthy interview superbly encapsulates Muscat's fundamental views on security of the Persian Gulf and as such, it is cited verbatim from the record.

> (Bin-'Alawi) Iran is a neighboring country and so is Iraq: That is a fact, but we do not believe that there is a military or security imbalance. There can be no balance between Iraq and Iran, therefore there must be a third party to ensure that balance ... The Iraq-Iran war occurred when there was no such third party. (Al-Husayni) Who do you mean by third party? (Bin-'Alawi) The third party had always been the presence of the Western states. We saw how the Iraq-Iran war occurred as soon as Britain left the Gulf ... (Al-Husayni) Who is it now? (Bin-'Alawi) Our Western friends: either the United States, or Britain, or France. They have interests which they care about. The conflict is basically over these interests. So these states are present and they represent balance. (Al-Husayni) Can you guarantee that the third party will prevent any aggression attempt against any Gulf state? (Bin-'Alawi) War is not the aim, or rather the origin. Deterrence is. War will not occur if there is deterrence and will occur if there is no deterrent. (Al-Husayni) Is there such as deterrent now? (Bin-'Alawi) Yes, there is. And I do not believe that Iran will fight the Gulf states, and I do not believe that Iraq will repeat its mistake, as long as the deterrent is there. (Al-Husayni) Are you satisfied with the present deterrent force in the Gulf? Do you not notice that it imposes certain decisions on some Gulf States? (Bin-'Alawi) The decisions you mean would be imposed regardless of means or methods. That is the reality. If you go to the market place you will notice that the big stores attract more people. That, briefly, is the reality in the Gulf now. (Al-Husayni) But a small store might have very special goods. (Bin-'Alawi) A small store has only its own special clients, but everyone goes to the big store, at least to browse. (Al-Husayni) Here you are not browsing. The big store has come to you and opened its doors in your grounds. (Bin-'Alawi) Everyone has now entered the big store. The meaning here is that close cooperation with friends is one of the GCC's strategies, one of its

firm and meticulous strategies. The Iranians know that and so do the Iraqis. Iraq and Iran have come to understand this situation. We know that neither Iraq nor Iran is run by fools ... Iran has problems with Afghanistan and has problems with Central Asia. It has borders with Russia and problems with Pakistan. It has an assortment of problems, therefore Iran cannot concentrate just on one region even though that region is more important than any other to Iran. Reality makes it necessary for Iranian officials to rise to the level of responsibility. The apprehension we have is not a result of the existence of the Iranian revolution, because some of us had the same apprehension even in the days of the shah, who had good ties with the West when we had—as we still have—good ties with the West ourselves ... For some time after the shah's demise we used to say that we could protect ourselves, only to discover later that that was not true. That is now clear. We are states and all states, large or small, have the same scale of operation, respect, and sovereignty ... But politics from time to time require that one should express some inner anxiety. (Al-Husayni) But it has been noticed that the third power in the region almost deprives you of free and independent decision-making ... (Bin-'Alawi) I do not believe that to be true ... For instance—and the readers can verify this—when the United States wanted to use some bases in the Gulf States (during the Irbil operation in northern Iraq), these states refused to respond. Therefore the claim that the West has denied us the right to express our will and make decisions is not true ... (Al-Husayni) You say that the West has not deprived you of your decision making freedom, yet the West, and particularly the United States, is "stealing the wealth and resources" of the Gulf with arms deals and contracts. You have just mentioned that you tried to defend yourselves but could not do so. Is not that Western assistance costing you a fortune? (Bin-'Alawi) As I said, the world is interlinked and interwoven. They did not come to us and to the other Arabs and tell us to buy those arms. They did not say that. We were the ones who sought to purchase those arms. That is exactly the situation which prevailed in the Arab world in the sixties in relation to the Soviet Union. The Russians did not go to the Arabs and tell them they must buy their arms whether they liked it or not: The Arabs went and purchased the arms.[72]

Indeed, in contrast to members of the Gulf Cooperation Council whose positions vacillated between perceiving Iraq as a counterbalance to Iran (especially during the Iran-Iraq war), or Iran as a counterbalance to Iraq (post–Gulf War), Muscat recognized that there could be no balance between the two states. As expressed by Alawi in the above interview, a balance could be ensured only by a third party.

Essentially, Muscat's policies toward Iran have been characterized by a strong sense of realism and pragmatism, which recognized real threats and attempted to deter them through cooperation both regionally and internationally. Oman pursued a "dual-track policy towards Gulf security: as a strong advocate of closer defense cooperation with the other conservative Gulf states and as a willing ally in providing the United States with facilities needed to maintain its over-the-horizon presence."[73] A crucial element of this design was a constructive engagement of both Iran and Iraq.

MUSCAT AND YEMEN

Muscat's distinct approach to both Iran and Iraq could also be seen in Oman's initiatives in toward both Yemen and Israel. The unification of North and South Yemen in May 1990 set forth a new stage in the relationship between Oman and the Republic of Yemen. High-ranking officials of both states attended an official ceremony to sign the Oman-Yemen border agreement in October 1992, which was ratified in December of the same year.[74] Alawi stressed that the agreement was the fulfillment of the Omani leadership's objective to coordinate polices with its southern neighbor. Muscat had certainly made important concessions to Yemen, a fact readily recognized by Yemen's Foreign Minister: "There would be no compensations to the Omani Government or Omani citizens for areas whose ownership was transferred to Yemen after the signing of the border agreement."[75]

The border agreement with Yemen was another stepping stone in realizing Sultan Qaboos' objective to demarcate Oman's sea and land borders with all of its neighbors starting with Iran in 1972, Saudi Arabia in 1992, and the UAE in 1993. In 1997, the construction of the 243-kilometer highway linking Oman's southern province Dhofar with Yemen began. This left the maritime border with Pakistan as the only boundary left to be demarcated.[76] Ironically, reactions to the border agreement with Yemen were muted. Saudi Arabia, Qatar, and the United Arab Emirates issued no official statements. Kuwait confined its comments to a mere congratulatory cable.[77] Despite the importance of the border agreement with Yemen, a civil war that ensued between North and South Yemen in 1994 threatened to undo all that was accomplished. The crisis between the two Yemens was expanding to the members of the GCC states, with an increasing pressure from Saudi Arabia, Kuwait, and the UAE to support the breakaway Democratic Republic of Yemen. Kuwait's support for the rebel leaders in the South was without a doubt partly derived from Ali Abdullah Saleh's support for Iraq during the occupation of Kuwait. Oman, however, carefully resisted all pressure from GCC allies to support the rebel Democratic Republic of Yemen while extending asylum to its leader Ali Salem Al-Baidh at the end of the fighting. This move ensured the reaffirmation of proper relations between the two neighbors when president Saleh visited Oman in September 1994[78] and as Oman adopted more forthcoming policies toward Yemen.[79] Qaboos was clearly determined to maintain close and friendly relations with Yemen and more importantly to support a United Yemeni front to prevent regional powers from using Yemen's internal conflicts to destabilize the Arabian Peninsula: "By holding both parties responsible for all of their actions, Muscat earned unparalleled credibility in Sanaa, where a new understanding emerged on how critical Oman had become to long term Yemeni interests."[80] Indeed, despite the reservations from members of the GCC over Yemen's role in supporting Saddam during the Gulf crisis 1990–1991, Sultan Qaboos visited Yemen and called upon the GCC to consider admitting Yemen[81] as a member of the organization.[82] Allen and Rigsbee claim that by December 1996, Yemen formally requested membership in the organization.[83] However, an interview with Alawi at the same period records the Foreign Minister stating that "all that has been reported is untrue. Yemen has not submitted any official request to join the GCC."[84] It is important to note that Yemen did submit an application to be a member of the GCC, as recorded by various media outlets in 1997.

THE SULTANATE OF OMAN AND THE ARAB-ISRAELI CONFLICT

The Sultanate's initiatives and contacts with the State of Israel also fell outside the parameters of the GCC. Indeed, in this in this area as well, Oman demonstrated a distinct approach to the issue. Let us first recall that another source of threats to the security of the Persian Gulf and by implication to the Sultanate resides with the Arab-Israeli conflict. The Persian Gulf region is not immune to the effects of such conflicts. Revolutionary forces in Iran used the Shah's support of Israel as evidence to his subversion to U.S. interests. While Gulf monarchies did not support Israel, they still felt the fangs of Pan-Arabism and nationalist movements, and more recently Islamic fundamentalism, accusing them of their subservience to the United States and by extension to Israeli policies. The strategic relationship between the Persian Gulf and the Arab-Israeli conflict was demonstrated through the Arab oil embargo in the 1970s and the landing of Iraqi scuds in Israel during the Gulf War. In fact, from the early days of the Gulf War, Saddam tied the withdrawal of Iraqi forces from the Gulf to the withdrawal of Israel. Israel, on its part, had included Saudi Arabia "in the second of three concentric circles of countries to which it must extend its strategic position."[85] In 1977–1978, for instance, Israeli pilots would frequently fly over Tabuk area, and drop empty fuel tanks on the runway to demonstrate their capabilities.[86] In 1988, when Riyadh acquired silkworm missiles, Israel threatened to launch a preemptive strike against the Kingdom of Saudi Arabia. The threat to carry out such an attack, prompted the Kingdom to declare that the "missiles do not carry nuclear warheads and they will not be used against Israel."[87] This was followed with another declaration in April 1988 (with the advice of the United States) to join the Nuclear Non-Proliferation Treaty.[88] Essentially, Israel represents a credible threat not only to Iraq and Iran, as demonstrated by the past Israeli attacks of Iraq's nuclear site and its repeated threats to attack Iran, but also to Arab monarchies. It seems highly unlikely that a war may ensue between a GCC state and Israel, but as demonstrated above, it is not completely improbable either, since Israel has made previous threats to attack Saudi Arabia. Much more threatening for the Gulf monarchies, however, has been the failure of various peace initiatives between Israel and the Arabs. In essence, the spillover effect to their own increasingly politicized populations disenchanted with the future of Palestinians has manifested itself in various forms of protest against their own governments' perceived incompetence. This linkage became vividly clear during the Clinton administration. It was clearly demonstrated in a nearly unanimous Arab boycott of the Middle East North Africa economic conference held in Doha on 16–18 November 1997, when America's key Arab allies, such as Egypt, Saudi Arabia, Morocco, and others, refused to attend despite U.S. pressure. Albright, who was in attendance for no more than four hours, provoked several Arab complaints when she called on Israelis and Palestinians to be "prepared to make decisions soon that will enable us to move forward and reach agreements." Arab delegates protested this comment, which put an equal blame on both parties of the conflict. Even Qatar's Foreign Minister, who represented the host country, stated:

> I think it is wrong to lay equal blame on the Arabs and Israelis, because the blame should be laid on Netanyahu's government … I believe that the Israeli government's position is, as my lord his highness the emir said, the reason for the stumbling of the peace process.[89]

Muscat, on its part, as discussed in the previous chapter, was a key supporter of a comprehensive and honorable peace between the Arabs and the Israelis. Muscat supported the Egyptian President Anwar Sadat's visit to Jerusalem in November 1977, the U.S.-brokered Camp David Accords of 1978, and the bilateral peace treaty between Egypt and Israel of March 1979 over the opposition from the majority of Arab states. Since the early 1990s, "Oman has been an active participant in all aspects of the multilateral peace-process working groups created by the Madrid Peace Conference of 1991."[90] The dramatic developments on the Arab-Israeli peace front after the Madrid Peace Conference, held in October 1991, have vindicated Oman's consistent policy toward the issue, as the Palestine Liberation Organization and Israel signed the Oslo Accord in September 1993 and a peace treaty was signed between Jordan and Israel on 26 October 1994. This was a time of great hope that a final settlement between the Arabs and Israelis was finally on the horizon.

The period of 1993 and 1994 became the time when unofficial contacts between both Tel Aviv and Muscat first took place at the UN headquarters in New York. By February 1994, the Israeli deputy foreign minister, Yosi Beilin, met with a special Omani envoy to further discuss contacts between the two countries. This was followed by Muscat's willingness to host the April 1994 meeting of the Middle East multilateral working group on water resources. Since Israel was a participant of that group, Oman encouraged Tel Aviv to send its representatives to Muscat. This marked the first-ever official visit to an Arab Gulf state by Israeli delegates.[91] Before long, Oman, like other GCC states, removed its economic sanctions on foreign companies dealing with Israel. In December 1994, Prime Minister Yitzhak Rabin visited Oman. Although the late Israeli prime minister's trip did not last for more than twenty-four hours, "its occurrence showed Oman's intentions to follow its own path concerning relations with Israel."[92] Muscat's ambassador to the Arab League was sent to brief the Arab League on the outcome of the Rabin's visit. The Arab sources stated that

Rabin's visit to Oman was part of the efforts to advance peace process on the "basis of Security Council Resolutions concerning the establishment of a comprehensive, just, and durable peace."[93] By 30 September 1995, Oman became the first Gulf Arab state to have officially established trade relations with Israel.[94]

After Rabin's assassination in November 1995, Oman sent a high-ranking minister to attend Rabin's funeral.[95] This was followed by Muscat's invitation to the new Israeli Prime Minister Shimon Peres to visit Muscat on 1 April 1996. Prime Minister Shimon Peres came to Muscat with a large delegation of economic and political advisors, further indicating the potential for improved relations between the two countries in various fields. In a joint statement, both Muscat and Tel Aviv stated that their meeting "reflects the development of bilateral ties and is part of the support of the Middle East peace process."[96] Peres added: "As for my visit here, again it is a demonstration of how both Arabs and Israelis can build a new Middle East without wars, without hatred, with economic cooperation."[97] The visit resulted in an agreement between both countries to have trade representatives on behalf of both counties. An Omani official noted that the "decision of the two countries will contribute to better contacts between private companies in Oman and Israel and encourage cooperation in the areas of investment and trade."[98] While back in Israel, the Foreign Ministry stated that "this announcement is important for Israel because it is the first time that a Gulf country has official relations with us."[99]

Significantly, although Muscat's relations with Israel inevitably became an object of discussions and debate in the Arab media, they were not condemned by the GCC:

> (Al-Husayni) Some Arabs blame you and say that you were hasty in establishing links with Israel, thus jeopardizing their maneuvers. Is it true that the Palestinians were the ones who asked you to initiate contacts with Israel? (Bin-'Alawi) That is what they called "rushing into something." Had we rushed, we would have spared ourselves all the problems. The truth is that the only one who rushes is someone who wants to be ahead of others, while the one who moves ahead fast is first to arrive. International competition is for those who have the strength and the willpower to go fast ahead of everyone else. Regrettably, we thought that it was bad to rush. It has now become clear to some that that would have been beneficial. At any rate, we work within the context of the general Arab approach and we prefer to remain in the middle ... What we are saying is that war is not always fought with the sword, that it can be fought with wisdom and vision.[100]

At the time, it seemed that Oman's initiative toward Israel, noticeably followed by Qatar, could have been the beginning of a diplomatic breakthrough between the GCC as a block on one hand and Israel on the other. Speaking of the organization's "constant principles" vis-à-vis the peace process, the GCC Secretary General outlined the following:

> For these countries have affirmed their conviction that peace is a strategic option to which there can be no alternative. They will recall in this regard their participation in

the Madrid conference and the multilateral talks and their support for the Oslo Accord and the other accords that followed it. They will also recall the fact that two GCC member countries, namely the Sultanate of Oman and the State of Qatar, have embarked on advanced diplomatic initiatives toward Israel. This GCC position is closely dependent on the Israeli Government's respect for the principles on which the peace process was founded, namely land for peace, and the implementation of UN resolutions headed by Resolutions 242, 338, and 425.[101]

Muscat's hopes of a comprehensive and honorable peace between the Arabs and the Israelis came to a halt when Prime Minister Binyamin Netanyahu came to power in June 1996. As far as Muscat was concerned, the new "Israeli Government has not honored the agreements signed by the State of Israel. The Arabs cannot accept that fait accompli and that peace. Even if the Arabs did, the Palestinians would not."[102] Muscat specifically cited the continuation of the building of Israeli settlements on the West Bank. Although some media outlets were reporting that Muscat welcomed Israeli participation in two commercial exhibits that were held in Muscat during the months of March and April 1997, the Israeli newspaper *Ha'aretz* reported in April 1997 that the authorities in Muscat have asked Israeli firms not to come to the exhibits.[103] *Ha'aretz* continued to claim that Muscat had refused an Israeli diplomat entry into Oman where an Israeli trade office had been operating since 1996 in a step toward normalization. Muscat also withdrew its trade representative from Israel.[104] Qatar also suspended its contacts with Israel. Essentially, for both Muscat and Doha, the normalization was aborted by what they perceived to be Israel's inflexibility at the peace negotiations. Although normalization with Israel came to an end, Muscat was always careful to state its "willingness to restore communications with Israel and to exert any effort needed to move forward the peace process in the Middle East."[105] Along the same lines, Qatar's foreign minister, Hamad Al-Thani, stated after a meeting with his Israeli counterpart, David Levi, "that in the absence of any progress in the peace process, namely on the Palestinian track, we won't change our position."[106] By 1998, as indicated in the following excerpt, the chances of normalization of ties between Oman and Israel were essentially over:

(Diyab) Do you have any contacts of any kind whatever with Israel? (Ben 'Alawi) None at all. Basically there is no room for talk of such a thing. There is an Israeli office in Muscat but it does not function and there is nobody in it. Israel participates in a local research center (with headquarters in Muscat) like many other countries. For its part, Israel too tries to keep contacts with us to a minimum. This kind of thing also takes time. This thread which has been established has its objective. Once the objective ends, there will be no need for the thread. (Diyab) Does this mean that you will close down the Israeli office? (Ben 'Alawi) That is, of course, on the cards. We had given Israel the chance to serve peace. Then came the new Israeli government (the Binyamin Netanyahu government) and matters developed in the way they did. Naturally, every chance eventually runs out.[107]

Indeed, the "Omani Secretary General for Foreign Affairs, Sayyid Haitham bin Tariq al-Said, expressed great relief and optimism when Ehud Barak was elected as Prime Minister in May 1999."[108]

> (Maydani) Contacts between Oman and Israel were suspended some time ago. Are there any contacts between you at present? (Bin-'Alawi) Our contacts are still frozen. (Maydani) Is there any specific thing you are awaiting to resume these contacts? (Bin-'Alawi) This issue is linked to the movement in the peace process. The negotiations on the Palestinian and Syrian tracks are facing obstacles. We are expecting moves by the Israeli party. Syria is not responsible for the suspension of the negotiations because Israel suspended them … It is not right for some to say that what was agreed on with others is gone with them. Relations among people do not proceed in this way, otherwise we would have to go back to square one in every stage of any negotiations.[109]

Essentially, Muscat took the initiative among the GCC states in its initiatives toward Israel. As Kechichian argued:

> Qaboos recognized that no Arab leader could champion the Palestinian cause better than Yasser Arafat. He further reasoned that all ought to consider individual long-term interests, as the Chairman of the Palestine Liberation Organization did in later 1993 … After all, Qaboos welcomed Arafat in Muscat after the Oslo Talks—when the entire Arab world shunned the Palestinian—and was not about to allow anyone to dictate what policies the Sultanate ought to pursue.[110]

Yet it is not clear to whom Kechichian is referring to when he states that Muscat "was not about to allow anyone to dictate what policies the Sultanate ought to pursue." Certainly it was not the West, Arab states, or members of the GCC organization, all of whom were represented in the Madrid Peace Conference of 1991. The only country that was not supportive of Muscat's initiative toward Israel was Iran. However, we should recall that Iran had limited its actions to no more than a mere critique in public pronouncements. Muscat, on the other hand, made an effort to assuage Iranian concerns over Muscat's rapprochement with Israel by sending its foreign minister to Tehran in 1996. The visit was seen as a "key to relieving the strain in Iranian-Omani relations, in the wake of former Israeli Prime Minister Shimon Peres' visit to both Doha and Muscat and Iranian attacks on both visits."[111]

MUSCAT, WASHINGTON, AND THE PERSIAN GULF

The linkage between events in the Persian Gulf and the Arab-Israeli conflict became were even more pronounced in 1998 when President Clinton unleashed Operation Desert Fox, targeting Iraq for its expulsion of the United Nations Special Commission, which had been designated to verify the destruction of Iraq's weapons of mass destruction.

With each day [of] the US-led air strikes, popular protest in the Arab world rose sharply. Besides demonstrations in Cairo, Rabat (100,000-strong), Tripoli, Amman, Beirut and Damascus, there was one in Muscat, the first such event in the history of Oman. This, and the condemnation of the American military action as "unjust aggression" by Jordan's parliament, followed by a similar resolution on December 27 by the 16-member Arab Parliamentarian Union—providing the first non-governmental, pan-Arabic forum on Iraq since the Gulf War—buoyed Baghdad.[112]

Saudi Arabia was quick to stress that it would not allow the use of its territory and military bases to deliver a military strike against Iraq. In a statement published by *Al-Sharq al-Awsat*, Prince Sultan said "the Saudi Government has not received an official request from the United States to provide military facilities to strike Iraq." He also emphasized that the "the Kingdom of Saudi Arabia supports a peaceful solution if this solution can be reached to end the crisis; however, the Kingdom supports all Security Council resolutions and the need for Iraq to implement them." Another report claimed that all the officials with whom U.S. Defense Secretary William Cohen met during a tour of the region's capitals called for intensifying political and diplomatic efforts to force the Iraqi government to retract its decision to suspend cooperation with the United Nations Special Commission (UNSCOM) inspectors, and to refrain from using armed force, particularly if the objective behind it is only muscle flexing. The report noted that "although the UAE condemns the recent Iraqi escalation toward the international inspection teams, it is nevertheless opposed to military action against Iraq."[113] The UAE reasoned that a military strike against Iraq would not help the UN inspectors in their task, "because any strike, regardless of its size, will have a limited impact with regard to forcing Iraq to cooperate, and will cause further suffering for the Iraqi people who are paying the price of the international blockade." In addition, the UAE declared that the timing of the Iraqi escalation

> was not right since it came at a time when some influential international forces were busy trying to persuade the United Nations to carry out a comprehensive review and assessment of the UN inspectors' task. This has clearly been an embarrassment to these forces in front of those who believe that the Iraqi leadership cannot be trusted.[114]

The sources said that, unlike in the past, the latest Iraqi escalation did not have a political cover, since it was a violation of the agreement that Baghdad signed with the UN Secretary General with regard to the inspection committees' work. This placed an additional burden on those who were trying to help Iraq end the blockade. In Muscat, an Omani diplomatic source elaborated on his country's position on the crisis between Iraq and the United Nations. "Baghdad [had] to implement all the resolutions concerning Iraq's invasion of Kuwait, including allowing UNSCOM to do its work without any hurdles being placed in its way." The diplomat added that Baghdad was "gradually losing the friends who were supporting it," in a reference to the Security Council's recent unanimous condemnation, which was supported by Russia, France, and China, which had shown some sympathy toward Iraq in the past. On what Oman's position would be, should a resolution be issued to put an end to the oil-for-food program, an Omani diplomat commented, "First, we hope that matters will not reach that point, particularly in view of the fact that the program is a humanitarian decision aimed primarily at easing the suffering of the brotherly Iraqi people."[115]

If Saddam had planned to use the combined outrage in the Arab world over the bombing of Iraq and the suffering of the Palestinians to force the Arab states to condemn the United States–United Kingdom action and call for the lifting of UN sanctions, he miscalculated. This was clearly demonstrated in the final statement issued by the 16th session of the Foreign Ministers of the Damascus Declaration Member States (composed of GCC member states plus Egypt and Syria) in Doha on 12 November 1998; however, the Damascus Declaration was intended by the GCC governments to demonstrate to their own citizens that the Gulf War was not another example of their subversion by the "imperialists." Voices of resentment and opposition were resonating throughout the Gulf, and as Piscatori points out, the Islamic opposition in the Gulf was using the sanctions as evidence of the GCC states' conspiracy to destroy a Muslim neighbor. In the view of tense domestic atmosphere, the document was carefully worded to condemn at length the Israeli occupation from the outset, and as such ameliorate the effects of the lack of Arab support to Iraq with a resounding support for the Palestinians. It also called upon Iran to end its alleged occupation of UAE islands, and finally it stressed the importance of combining the efforts of the member states to fight terrorism.[116] Curiously enough, in a document that was no less than ten pages long and was intended to reflect the current crisis of Iraq, Baghdad received a single paragraph warning Iraq of the consequences of its actions:

> The ministers discussed the current crisis between Iraq and the United Nations … They asked Iraq to reverse its decision to halt cooperation with the UN Special Commission and resume its full cooperation in accordance with the relevant Security Council resolutions and the Memorandum of Understanding signed by the Iraqi Government and the UN secretary general in February 1998. The ministers said that the Iraqi Government is to blame for any consequences of its refusal to reverse its decision—consequences, which may expose innocents among the fraternal Iraqi people to further disasters and tragedies.[117]

Iraq continued to claim that it had fully cooperated with the UN inspectors over its alleged weapons of mass destruction and that therefore the time had come to end the crippling sanctions imposed on the country. The UN Security Council continued to insist that UN inspectors must be allowed back into Iraq. For a brief period, there was a glimpse of hope for Iraq, with a new resolution passed on 17 December 1999. Under the resolution, sanctions could be suspended if Iraq were to cooperate with the inspectors over a period of nine months. Baghdad, however, rejected the resolution and refused to cooperate with the newly created United Nations Monitoring, Verification, and Inspection Commission (UNMOVIC), headed by Hans Blix. The saga of Iraq's crisis continued to vacillate between Iraq's rejection of further inspections, citing its cooperation, and further UN Security Council resolutions demanding full and unconditional access to what Iraq considered sensitive cites.

THE SULTANATE OF OMAN AND SEPTEMBER 11

The saga, however, was put to an end by circumstances that neither Iraq, nor the United States, nor the international community had anticipated: the terrorist attacks of 11 September 2001 on the United States. Once again, the Persian Gulf became the center of an international crisis near the turn of a new decade (the Iranian revolution in 1979, and Iraq's invasion of Kuwait in 1990). The United States' response to terrorist attacks was outlined in the president's State of the Union address on 29 January 2002, which conveyed the essence of the United States' new defense strategy in two succinct sentences: "We must prevent the terrorists and regimes who seek chemical, biological, or nuclear weapons from threatening the United States and the world ... I will not wait on events, while dangers gather." The speech famously singled out Iran, Iraq, and North Korea as constituting an "axis of evil." In another speech, delivered on 1 June 2002, in his West Point Commencement speech, President George W. Bush elaborated on the strategic shift since Cold War: "For much of the last century, America's defense relied on the Cold War doctrines of deterrence and containment. In some cases, these strategies still apply ... If we wait for threats to fully materialize, we will have waited too long ... We must take the battle to the enemy ... and confront the worst threats before they emerge."[118]

In Muscat, the authorities voiced their concern about yet another possible war against Iraq. Although the Sultanate had issued formal statements condemning the terrorist attack of 11 September and made its facilities available for U.S. military campaign against the Taliban in Afghanistan, another war on Iraq, in the words of Alawi during a GCC Ministerial Council meeting, "will cause deep anti-American feeling and will provoke revenge and violence in Arab and Islamic countries." In reference to President Bush's address to the United Nations on 12 September 2002, when he denounced the Iraqi leadership as posing a "grave and gathering danger," called for the United Nations to act, and stated that "The Security Council resolutions will be enforced ... or action will be unavoidable," Alawi said "The world cannot accept a weakened role for the United Nations ... [Those who are] thinking they can impose law for their own benefit, they are pushing the world into instability and chaos."[119]

The Sultanate, on the other hand, welcomed the positive steps taken by Iraq to cooperate with the UNMOVIC committee and the International Atomic

Energy Agency, saying that this positive and developing cooperation between Iraq and the committee will lead to settling the pending issues. It also reiterated its hope to avert any military action against Iraq that would jeopardize security and stability in the Gulf region in particular and the Middle East in general, announcing that it backed peaceful initiatives in dealing with this issue.[120] To that end, Muscat welcomed Iraq's foreign minister to Oman on 2 October 2002, delivering a letter from Saddam.[121] Although the contents of the letter are unknown, it is safe to assume that Saddam may have been attempting to use Oman's close relations with the United States to deliver assurances regarding the return of UN inspectors. This also demonstrates Muscat's established position as a mediator among states of the region, and between the states of the region and international powers.

Baghdad's initiatives to avert war came to naught. On 19 March 2003, war began with a U.S. raid targeting a meeting of Saddam with his advisors. On 21 March 2003, British and American land forces entered Iraq, taking control of areas bordering Kuwait. By 9 April 2003, Baghdad fell to U.S. troops. Shortly after, on 1 May 2003, President Bush declared an end to the Iraq War: a swift victory for the United States and Great Britain, the type of victory for which the GCC had hoped. While there was not a single GCC state that openly supported the overthrow of the government of Iraq, there was no question that the states of the GCC assisted the United States' and coalition partners' military operations in Iraq.[122] In many ways, this was expected. Military operations between the United States and members of the GCC had increased throughout the late 1990s in the context of enforcing the sanctions against Iraq. U.S. air patrols with Operation Southern Watch prevented Baghdad from moving its military forces south of the thirty-third parallel. Southern Watch operated on a regular basis out of both Saudi Arabia and Kuwait, with support flights dependent on the cooperation of the other GCC members. In addition, naval patrols designed to stop illegal Iraqi oil exports were enforced with cooperation from all GCC members. In the wake of 11 September 2001, Washington was able to rapidly gather its military forces for a campaign against the Taliban regime and Al Qaeda terrorists in Afghanistan. This rapid mobilization was in large part due to the already well-established U.S. presence in and cooperation with the Gulf monarchies.[123] Even Saudi Arabia, the most publicly reluctant GCC member, quietly allowed U.S. and British special forces to operate from its northern border areas into Iraq (while denying the use of Saudi bases for air strikes).[124]

In Muscat, the rhetoric stayed within the Arab consensus in the "months leading up the war, but official criticism of the United States all but disappeared when the war started. As it did with previous Western military actions in the Persian Gulf region, Oman permitted U.S. and U.K. forces to use air bases with the Sultanate."[125] We should also recall that Muscat's public statements and actions, as in the extensively cited paragraphs throughout this chapter, made it clear that U.S. presence in the region is a force of stability—the rhetoric against the Iraq war notwithstanding.

In essence, both Muscat and the GCC at large were resigned to U.S. actions in Iraq. Previously, both Saudi Arabia and Kuwait had refused to work with Baghdad as long as Saddam was in power. Initially, Muscat, the United Arab Emirates, and Qatar had displayed sympathy and willingness to work with the regime in Baghdad. Once Washington was resolved to attack Baghdad, their interests resided with Washington, especially after the destruction of the Iraqi old guard. Members of the GCC reasoned that a stable, democratic, unified, and wealthy Iraq could be a force of stability in the region, and perhaps more importantly, a long-term counterweight to Iran. This is especially true given that the alternative, the failure to create a stable and unified Iraq, could lead to a degree of instability in the Arab Gulf states themselves. A successful and emboldened insurgency in Iraq with an increasingly militant Islamized ideology is undoubtedly bound to carry its activities throughout the Gulf states, particularly to Saudi Arabia. The 13 May 2003 attack in Riyadh that killed at least 29 and injured 184, including 10 Americans, is a clear example.

Specifically, the change of regime in Iraq would not end the rise of extremism in the region, the proliferation of destabilizing military capabilities, drug trafficking, territorial disputes, environmental disasters, and internal political challenges to stability. Moreover, neutralizing the Iraqi threat, coupled with heightened local opposition within the Gulf to the U.S. military presence would exert mounting pressure on the United States to reduce its regional deployments and as such shift much of the burden of dealing with these problems to the member states of the Gulf Cooperation Council, as well as Iraq. Moreover, "as long as Washington's relationship with Iran, the largest and most powerful Gulf state, remains hostile, there will be a need for an American military presence in the area. A friendly regime in Baghdad might mitigate that need, but will not eliminate it."[126] In short, the "U.S. victory in Iraq—its historical significance notwithstanding—has not resolved many of the difficult security challenges that marked the prewar security environment in the Gulf."[127]

Iran remains a major strategic challenge both to the United States and to the smaller Gulf states, regardless of the Iraq war. Bahrain, with its Shia majority, and the United Arab Emirates, with its territorial dispute with Iran over three Gulf islands (Abu Musa, Greater Tunb, and Lesser Tunb), both see Tehran as a greater threat than Baghdad.[128] However, one should not ignore the remarkable improvements of relations between GCC member states and Iran since Khatami's presidency. As an example, Saudi-Iranian trade reached $1.4 billion in 2001; Iran made agreements with Kuwait in the spring of 2003 to supply this Gulf state with gas and water. In December 2002, the Kuwaiti defense minister had even emphasized the importance of military cooperation with Iran and praised Iran's role in the region.[129] Differences with the UAE notwithstanding, in 2002, Iran received the highest share of Dubai's external trade. In fact, trade between Iran and Dubai exceeded those of the eleven other Middle East and African states that have commercial ties with Dubai. The late UAE president, Shaikh Zaid, noted in December 2002 the "satisfactory development of relations with Iran" in his annual National Day address. Moreover, President Khatami was invited to visit the UAE in May 2003.[130]

These improvements of relations notwithstanding, relations between member states of the GCC and Iran in general, and Iran and Oman in particular, could not be adequately assessed without taking into consideration the attendant consequences of Washington's increased hostility toward Tehran. Rather than welcoming the moves toward détente and potential rapprochement between the GCC countries and Iran, Washington remained mired in its own myopic vision of Iran's position and role in the region. Ironically, Washington only stood to benefit from the GCC countries' efforts to engage Tehran in expanding their joint cooperation on matters of mutual interest and concern.[131] This is especially true of Oman, which has to share the Strait of Hormuz with Iran. However, President Bush's reference to Iran as another member of the "axis of evil," along with Iraq and North Korea, indicated that terrorism was a major concern:

> Iran aggressively pursues these weapons [of mass destruction, particularly nuclear weapons] and exports terror, while an unelected few repress the Iranian people's hope for freedom ... They could provide these arms to terrorists, giving them the means to match their hatred ... The United States of America will not permit the world's most dangerous regimes to threaten us with the world's most destructive weapons.[132]

Not specifically cited above, but repeatedly cited by various U.S. officials, are Iran's opposition to the peace process between the Arabs and the Israelis and the repeated warning for Iran not to "meddle" either in Iraq or in Afghanistan. The importance of Iran's choice of policies cannot be overestimated, since it may have had a direct impact on U.S. efforts to bring stability to Iraq and Afghanistan, maintain the security of the Persian Gulf, and restart the Middle East peace process.

Muscat was naturally aware of all U.S. concerns regarding Iran, which were essentially the same as those of the Clinton administration, with the exception of the Bush's administration willingness to use force against Tehran and U.S. presence in both Afghanistan and Iraq. Despite this and Muscat's close relations with Washington, cooperation between Muscat and Tehran, which was described by both sides as "strategic," continued to progress. In what could be considered a diplomatic victory for Iran, in terms of both world public opinion and diplomatic support from regional states, Muscat welcomed President Khatami to Oman in a first visit by an Iranian president to the Sultanate since the Shah. During the meeting, both sides declared their common stand on a number of issues. The two-day visit of President Khatami beginning on 6 October 2004 was marked by extensive coverage in the Omani media and resulted in various bilateral agreements between the two states. In a joint statement, both sides "expressed common views on a broad range of regional and international issues, notably Iraq, the Middle East conflict, and International terrorism." Both leaders stressed the importance of safeguarding Iraq's territorial integrity and the need to give the UN the central role in this regard. They welcomed Security Council Resolution 1546, which declared the end of occupation and the hand-over of sovereignty to the interim government. They also expressed their strong condemnation of Israeli repression of the Palestinian people and their "full support for Syria in claiming the return of the Golan Heights and the right of Lebanon to restore the rest of its territories in Shebba as per Security Council resolutions" Both sides also "stressed the right of nations to develop their nuclear capacities for peaceful purposes in accordance with the non-proliferation treaty of the International Atomic Energy Agency. They strongly condemned Israel's refusal to submit its nuclear installations to inspections, noting that Israel's stand contradicts all international accords." And lastly, both emphasized "importance of differentiating between terrorism and legitimate resistance."[133]

Muscat was the only capital among the GCC states that issued joint statements supporting Iran's positions on key issues, especially Iran's nuclear program. This was no easy task given the international pressure on Iran and the sensitivity of supporting Iran when the United States has declared Iran to be part of the "axis of evil." However, Muscat's previous foreign policy initiatives indicate Muscat's independent and at times surprising moves. The government's previously declared position that constructive engagement with Tehran rather than confrontation was based then and currently on key substantial positive signs coming from Iran. In almost every single issue declared by Washington as a point of contention with Iran—support for terrorism, attempts to sabotage the peace process, nuclear ambitions, Iran's influence in both Iraq and Afghanistan—Muscat observed evidence of Iran's responsible behavior that could even yield beneficial results if Tehran were sufficiently engaged.

There are many remarks and public statements coming not only from the so-called reformers but from what Nikolas Gvosdev called "pragmatic conservatives," indicating Iran's willingness to work with the United States on various issues. Ahmad Tavakkoli, a leading pragmatic conservative elected to the new Majlis, candidly remarked, "We do not regard relations with America ideologically as being either absolutely necessary like prayer and fasting or absolutely forbidden like wine."[134] Another conservative, Rumania, acknowledged, "By intervening in Afghanistan and Iraq, the Americans have become our neighbors. We have to be realistic. One day, ties will have to be reestablished." Echoing Rumania's remarks, another key figure of the pragmatic right, Mohammad Java Karajan, who served as an adviser to Khomeini, also observed, "It is in our interest and in the interest of America to defuse the tensions between us and to move toward good relations."[135] Clearly, if the survival of the regime required foreign investment and an improved relationship with the United Sates, Tehran's pragmatic conservative were willing to make the necessary adjustments.[136] Indeed, one can detect clear signs from Tehran, in its approach to the Middle East peace process, that demonstrated the primacy of the "national interest" over ideological influences. Rafsanjani's remarks, which constituted a rebuke to hardliners, is noteworthy: "To put the country in jeopardy on the ground that we are acting on an Islamic basis is not at all Islamic."[137] This is a reflection of an Iranian internal debate over the efficacy of the form, as opposed to the substance of supporting the Palestinians. Questions were raised, such as,

> Why support for the Palestinian cause entails support for groups using violence. Why does it undermine support for the Palestinians own elected representatives? How does the adoption of radical solutions help the people in the region? Can Iran not help diplomatically? Does a militant, rejectionist approach advance Iran's national interest? What price is Iran willing to pay for such policies?[138]

Most importantly in this regard, was the fact that Tehran neither opposed the peace plans sponsored by Saudi Arabia which were unveiled at the Beirut Arab Summit of 2002, nor the road map announced that year by the Quarter (the United States, the European Union, the United Nations, and the Russian Federation). President Khatami declared in 2003 that Tehran would not oppose a peace agreement that was acceptable to the Palestinians, noting, "We do not intend to impose our views on others or stand in their way." Indeed, if the international community restarted a viable peace process buttressed by a regional consensus, it would be improbable for Tehran to persist with its lonely struggle on behalf of radical Palestinian forces.

Washington had also accused Iran of supporting Al Qaeda terrorists. Public assertions that members of Al Qaeda were taking refuge in Iran across the border from western Afghanistan came from none other than Zalmay Khalilzad, the administration's special envoy to Afghanistan: "Hard-line, unaccountable elements of the Iranian regime facilitated the movement of Al Qaeda terrorists escaping from Afghanistan."[139] The head of Iran's Intelligence Ministry, Ali Yunesi, acknowledged for the first time in 2003 that Iran was holding both "small and big elements of Al Qaeda."[140] Holding Al Qaeda members, however, is a far cry from actively supporting the group.

> Those allegations strained credulity, however, given Iran's vigorous opposition to the Taliban government in Afghanistan and its Al Qaeda supporters. Al Qaeda is a Sunni Muslim group that espouses the views of the most extreme proponents of the Salafi school (often called Wahhabi) of Islamic thought, which regards Shism, the religion practiced by most in Iran and by Hizballah in Lebanon, as heretical. One can imagine some low-level tactical contact between the two groups, particularly in view of their shared opposition to the Western presence in the Gulf region. Claims of an alliance, however, lack evidence and logic.[141]

Ironically, the U.S. and Iranian views concerning the future of Iraq have much more in common than is usually assumed. Both countries support the development of a pluralistic, decentralized government. One expert notes that a "democratic, inclusive Iraq is likely to be a fractious, even polarized state too preoccupied with its internal squabbles to resume its hegemonic Gulf policies."[142] Despite its strident public objections to the U.S. intervention, Tehran recognized the positive potentialities of cooperating with the United States in achieving shared objectives; Iran had no wish to witness a weak Iraq become a failed state, as Afghanistan did. Deputy Foreign Minister Hussein Adeli recently noted, "We don't mind joining forces with all countries including [the] Americans to do something over there [Iraq]." In April 2004, Rafsanjani himself declared, "We helped the Americans in Afghanistan and are ready to do the same with them in Iraq."[143]

Nonetheless, it does seem highly unlikely that Iran's relations with the United States will improve in the face of Iran's nuclear ambitions, Iran's cooperation in both Afghanistan and Iraq notwithstanding. Although Iran insists that its nuclear ambitions are strictly for peaceful uses, Washington alleges that Iran's nuclear programs point to the ultimate goal of acquiring nuclear weapons. Muscat, as articulated earlier, supports Iran's right to use peaceful nuclear energy. However, it cannot be positively ascertained whether Muscat's position toward Iran's nuclear ambitions arose from confidence over Iranian claims or from Muscat's realization that Iran's path to the nuclear club is only a question of time. Due to the complete absence of public official statements or opinions—beyond what has already been quoted—over Iran's nuclear ambitions, it can only be speculated why the Sultanate chose to support Iran publicly in this tense period. The most probable conclusion suggests that Muscat believes that Iran's transformation into a nuclear state is not necessarily inevitable.

The saga of Iran's nuclear programs and its policies continues to attract intense debate. There are more ominous signs of a possible attack on Tehran. Nevertheless, Muscat's position toward Tehran will be marked, as it has been in the past, by cautious pragmatism.

Conclusion

This research is the first systematic study of the foundations and practices of Oman's foreign policy since 1995. While most of the literature on the subject matter focuses on a narrow time period defined by the rise of the current Sultan Qaboos till the present, this work seeks to extend and reappraise the historical literature that influences and properly contextualizes our understanding of modern Oman's place in the world. It is necessary then to explore a persistent historical consciousness that gives an indication of the motives behind the foreign policy decisions emanating from Muscat. This rooted historical consciousness remains grounded in the tumultuous events that took place during the reign of previous Sultan. Thus, by reexamining the set historical narratives from the 1930s to the 1970s, we can better understand the significance of foreign policy positions to which Muscat still holds. An accurate understanding of Oman's consistent emphasis on the need for security, regional stability, and the balance of power remains inchoate without a return to the very foundations and experiences that characterize the process of state-building that gave rise to modern Oman.

This process of reexamination first calls into question the entire edifice of assumptions that, until now, tarnished the reign of Sultan Said bin Taimur. The essential claim remains that the literature concerning the period in question treated Sultan Said as either a tyrant, an incompetent administrator, or a tool of the colonial United Kingdom. This view obscures the significant actions taken by the Sultan and, concurrently, the set of perceptions that emerged during and after his reign. Thus, it is argued that this period was instrumental in formulating Oman's understanding of itself within the region and the international arena as a whole.

The thrust of this research lies in reexamining the conventional wisdom regarding both the persona of Sultan Said and the customary political/historical narrative of Said's reign. It underscores the importance of Oman's modern political development: the attempt of the Imamate to gain international recognition as an independent state separate from Muscat's authority; the insurgency of the 1950s, followed by the intervention of regional and international powers; the Dhofari rebellion; and finally an assessment of Sultan Said's failure to lead the Sultanate. These were the major challenges facing Muscat during Said's reign, and indeed, these are the major themes recounted in the prevalent literature on Oman. The literature, however, has overlooked and often undermined the significant role that Said played in the Sultanate's political development from the early 1930s to 1970. What is often overlooked is that the state of affairs of that Sultan Said inherited when he came to power was a government that was crippled by debt, incompetent leadership, and a significant, and often intrusive, British influence in Muscat's domestic and external relations. Instead, the beginning of Sultan Said's reign marked a forceful attempt to reassert Muscat's authority throughout the interior with a set of political and financial reforms. First and foremost was the replacement of the then British finance minister, Bertram Thomas, by Sultan Said himself. This act itself had a dramatic symbolic significance in that it sent a message of renewed independent authority vis-à-vis Whitehall. By the 1950s, however, internal and external circumstances would force Sultan Said to backtrack on his independent policies and appeal to the British for substantial aid. Much of the conventional literature argues that this necessity for calling upon the British for assistance was the direct consequence of a continued mismanagement of the country on the part the Sultan himself. However, this claim is not consistent with, on the one hand, a continued legacy of British involvement in Muscat's affairs for more than two centuries and, on the other hand, the particular geopolitical context of the 1950s that greatly diminished the freedom of movement that Sultan Said could have had in responding to the Imamate challenge. This was the geopolitical context in which two nominal enemies, pan-Arab nationalist Egypt and arch-conservative Saudi Arabia, found common cause in allying themselves with Muscat's internal enemies. In consequence, the only recourse left to Sultan Said—given that the United States was a de facto supporter of Saudi Arabia—was again to compromise the independent policies first set forth at the beginning of his reign. What must be emphasized, nevertheless, is that Sultan Said did not become a passive agent for Whitehall's machinations throughout the region. Though the geopolitical constraints forced the Sultan into a position of working with the British, the archival evidence demonstrates a deeply complex and nuanced relationship.

From the British perspective, the situation in the 1950s was even more multifaceted, given its strong but waning influence throughout the region. The inherent motivations that induced cooperation with Sultan Said were, in part, contingent upon a greater awareness of the future geopolitical and economic alignment of the Gulf states. Their desire to protect the Persian Gulf from the influence of Gamal Abdul Nasser and the persistent need to appease Saudi Arabia, all the while living up to the responsibilities toward the other Gulf states, were major considerations of the British during that crucial period. Though some of the literature assumes that Omani oil remained the driving force for

British motives, the archives sufficiently demonstrate that Omani oil was a secondary consideration at best. In contrast, the references to oil made by the British leadership focused on Kuwait and the need to structure British policies toward protecting its influence there.

Aside from the continuous relationship between the British and Oman, this study begins to reexamine the interaction between Oman and China. Though some previous authors do intimate some facets of China's role within Oman during the 1950s and 1960s, this is the first time that archival sources have been systematically consulted and analyzed. China's role is particularly illuminated through the earliest periods of the Imamate challenge and the Dhofari rebellion, a rebellion that eventually brought the downfall of Sultan Said. Indeed, it is at this stage that the archives clearly demonstrate Sultan Said's failure in envisioning a political strategy beyond the mere application of brute force. Nonetheless, it is at that particular juncture where the conventional literature refracts the totality of Said's reign into a singular moment of failure and impotence.

There is a tendency to compartmentalize and underestimate the connections among the various crises facing Muscat during Said's reign. For instance, the Imamate challenge of the 1950s is treated as a contained threat that withered away by the late 1950s with no real consequences for subsequent events. In contrast, this work demonstrates that the conflict over Buraimi, for example (involving Riyadh, Muscat, London, Abu-Dhabi, and Washington), had remarkable implications for the subsequent Imamate challenge, the Anglo-American relationship, the Dhofari rebellion of 1965, and even the future government of Sultan Qaboos. Reaching this conclusion is possible only through the use of primary sources that include top-secret documents, many of which are recorded and analyzed for the first time in this research. An array of various classified memos, cables, notes, and documents sharpens our understanding of the motives behind the actions of Muscat, Riyadh, and London. Some of the archives display a remarkable candidness of British policies toward Riyadh and disclose the difference between London's official foreign policy pronouncements, and the objectives of Whitehall. The actual words of Sultan Said, King Faisal of Saudi Arabia, Sheikh Zaid of the United Arab Emirates, and various British prime ministers punctuate this project and convey more convincingly and intimately the spirit of the times. As such, some previous conclusions that were accurate in their assessments are now buttressed with newly discovered evidence, while many other conclusions are rejected through the evidence of the archives and the forcefulness of a new analysis.

The archives are also used to demonstrate Muscat's foreign policy from 1970 to 1989. The archives detail Muscat's early challenges beyond the accustomed treatment of the period. The historic step of the Sultanate's membership in both the Arab League and the United Nations, while battling a determined insurgency, is carefully detailed and analyzed. In contrast to the common account of the period, the Sultanate's admission to both institutions is not treated as a foregone conclusion after Qaboos' accession in 1970. Primary sources demonstrate the potential for rejecting the Sultanate's membership in either institution. This research provides the first attempt to convey the complicated admission of the Sultanate to the Arab League and the United Nations and explains the motives of key actors in either supporting or denying the Sultanate's admission.

Muscat's most important challenge in the early 1970s was the Dhofari rebellion, a rebellion that involved local, regional, and international actors. The research deals with the most important events from early 1970s until 1989: the Soviet invasion of Afghanistan, the Iranian revolution of 1979, the 1981 facilities agreement with the United States, and the Iran-Iraq war. The aim is not only to narrate the events but also to investigate the key interests and policies that informed Muscat's foreign policies in the Persian Gulf. The analysis was concerned with a number of questions: What is the role of Oman in the Gulf Cooperation Council? Do Muscat's interests converge or clash with those of other Gulf states? What is the Sultanate's concept of Gulf security? Would new alternative security arrangements be open to Muscat? The literature fails to systematically explain the motives and the behavior of regional states toward Oman and, in turn, Muscat's actions in the region and beyond. Detailed analysis of Oman's relations with regional states, as well as with international actors, is important for the narration of a country's foreign policy. However, to have a comprehensive understanding of Muscat's foreign policy, it is necessary that the narration not be restricted to Muscat's historical relations with one country or another in a chronological fashion. Local, regional, and international levels interconnect in a complicated web of actions and reactions that must be analyzed and rendered intelligible to the reader. Muscat's relations with Tehran, for example, disclose how important it is to have a broad approach that connects local, regional, and international developments in order to analyze Muscat's polices in the Persian Gulf. Moreover, this example between Muscat and Teheran illuminates the Sultanate's foreign policy objectives within the Persian Gulf, while simultaneously serving as a prime example of Muscat's heightened sense of realism.

An attempt to explain and analyze post-1970 Omani foreign policy remains incomplete without a reappraisal of the conventional narrative that describes Sultan Said's reign. The positions taken vis-à-vis central regional issues such as the Arab-Israeli conflict, the Iranian revolution, the Iran-Iraq war, both Gulf wars, and Oman's role in the Gulf Cooperation Council are often described as being uniquely independent. In determining the merit of such a characterization, previous studies have appealed to either a legacy of history that has its roots in Ibadi Islam or the capable leadership of Sultan Qaboos as distinct from his predecessor. Though this study does not dispute the merits of such conclusions, it does argue that they present an incomplete explanation for Muscat's past and contemporary foreign policy. The historical roots that underline Oman's position in the world cannot be taken to start at the 1970s with the rise of the current Sultan. The internal and external crises that plagued Oman from the 1930s to the 1970s had major formative consequences for the post-1970 government. These various crises often pitted a friendless—with the exception of the British at certain times—Sultanate against a kaleidoscope of external actors that sought to undermine its sovereignty and authority. Saudi Arabia, Egypt, Iraq, South Yemen, China, and the Soviet Union all participated at one time or another in various capacities and with different means in the singular aim of destabilizing Muscat. This historical consciousness on the part of the future Omani government could not have been expiated with simply a change of government. Security thus consistently remains the singular theme that runs through its major initiatives in the era of Sultan Qaboos. The current emphasis on self-reliance, regional balancing, and the support of a major role for the United States in the region while remaining at the fringes of great power politics points to a deeply rooted fear of internal and external instability. What is most apparent in appraising Muscat's regional role is not only a disparity with its Arab neighbors and brethren concerning substantial political issues, but also the fact that Oman often anticipates geopolitical trends. Oman's steady desire to see a resolution of the Arab-Israeli conflict, for example—while standing with Egypt at the conclusion of the Camp David Accords, when all other Arab states had forsaken them—demonstrates a persistent willingness to view the region in an entirely different lens. While it became more fashionable for other states to support the peace process with the cajoling of the United States, Oman anticipated such a geopolitical condition and thus became viewed as a progressive ally. Furthermore, because of Oman's particular position of independence, all the while remaining above the fray or regional disputes, it has assumed a particular ability to serve as a mediator: between the Gulf Cooperation Council (GCC) and Iran, Saudi Arabia and Iraq, and the United States and Iran, among others.

It should also be mentioned that Oman occupies a geostrategic place that deeply influences its relationship with major world powers. The Sultanate of Oman has a 1,200-mile coastline along the Arabian Gulf, the Gulf of Oman, the Arabian Sea, and the Indian Ocean. It is adjacent to the sea-lanes leading to Europe and Asia, Iraq and Iran, and its fellow members in the GCC. It is difficult to overemphasize Oman's role as the gatekeeper to the Persian Gulf, and its role as a guarantor of one of the world's most strategic lifelines, Strait of Hormuz. The Iran-Iraq war, the Gulf War, and the U.S. policy of dual containment all highlight Oman's strategic importance to the world and its role in maintaining the safety of the Strait.

The post-September 11 global environment has reemphasized Oman's geostrategic location in the region. The lead up to the second Gulf War in 2003 clearly shows, on the one hand, Oman's reticence at the possibility of regime change in Iraq alongside the possible consequences of destabilizing the region, and, on the other hand, a continued cooperation with the United States and the United Kingdom by allowing them facilities and overflight rights. Nonetheless, the cooperation with external powers does remain nuanced and eclectic. In the case of Iran's nuclear program, Muscat was the only actor within the Gulf region to support the Iranian acquisition of peaceful nuclear technology.

It is safe to assume that Oman's foreign policy in 2005 and beyond will display similar characteristics as those in previous decade. That is to say, close alliance with the United States and Western powers, all the while seeking a balance among the major regional powers of the region. Particularly vis-à-vis Iran, Muscat has sought and continues to seek a general deescalation of potential conflict. Within the Arabian Peninsula, Oman will remain a strong advocate within the organization of the GCC for a significant military expansion of forces under the command of that organization. While other Gulf states remain susceptible to pan-Arab or pan-Islamic movements that seek to bypass or overthrown the state, such as the recent radical Wahhabi-inspired attacks in Saudi Arabia, Oman does not seem as vulnerable. The articulated difference that the local Ibadi population posses with respect to other Gulf states in terms of its religious and historical consciousness serves as a barrier to the appeals of transnational political identities of Arabism and Islam.

This work represents the first systematic attempt to record and explain Muscat's foreign policy during the crucial period between 1990 and 2004. Most importantly, however, this research brings to the fore the archival evidence collected in both Britain and the United States. There remains, however, much to be discovered through archival research in other states. This historical undertaking has repercussions on the literature of both regional studies and the relationships between small states and great powers. A critical reexamination of the history of Oman's foreign policy formation through archival research demonstrated that there could exist unexplored narratives that challenge the conventional wisdom. Likewise, a similar approach to other Middle East states can uncover a different historical account that recontextualizes the foreign policy of states in a different and more nuanced approach. For example, it was argued that the traditional perception of Saudi Arabia as a persistent foe of any form of communist movement in the Middle East was inaccurate in the case of their support for the radical communist Dhofari rebellion. This demonstrates that small states can exhibit a wider range of foreign policy choices than previously recognized. Moreover, the perception that the asymmetry that characterizes relations between small states and great powers translates itself into restricted foreign policy alternatives for small states is inconsistent in the examples put forward here of Sultan Said, Sheik Zaid, and King Faisal. This work demonstrates, in contrast, that small states with limited resources can conduct successful and distinct foreign policies.

It is hoped that future research will be able to build upon this work by accessing different archival material from Saudi Arabia, the United Arab Emirates, Kuwait, Egypt, and Russia, among others. This continued scholarship would likely challenge our conventional understanding of the foreign polices of Middle East states.

Appendix I

Imams of Oman

Eighth Century

al-Julanda ibn Mas'ud

According to Arabic chronicles, al-Julanda was the first Ibadhi Imam elected in Oman, his election taking place about the middle of the eighth century.

Eighth to Twelfth Century

Many Imams

The Arabic chronicles list the names of many Imams who held office during this period, and the careers of some are described in considerable detail. There appear to have been a few interregna, but none of long duration.

Twelfth to Fifteenth Century

The First Great Interregnum

No record has survived of Imams being elected during the period from about the middle of the twelfth century to the early years of the fifteenth century. The Arabic chronicles of Oman state that it is possible that there might have been Imams all trace of whom has been lost, as the existing accounts for the whole period are very brief. During this interregnum, the petty princes styled Maliks acquired power in different parts of the country, the most prominent among them being the Nabhanis.

Fifteenth to Sixteenth Century

Many Imams

A new Imam was elected in the early fifteenth century and was succeeded by a number of other Imams over a period of about a century and a half. During this time Europeans first entered the Persian Gulf in force, and the Portuguese established themselves on the coast of the Gulf of Oman.

Sixteenth to Seventeenth Century

The Second Great Interregnum

For a period of some sixty years, roughly from 1560 to 1624, there again appeared to have been no Imams. The Nabhanis reached the climax of their power during this period.

1624(?)–1743

The Imams of the Ya'aribah

Beginning with Nasir ibn Murshid, who held office from 1624(?) to 1640(?), the Imams for a period of over a century came from the tribe of the Ya'aribah. Early in this period the Portuguese finally lost their grip on the coast. From about 1718 to 1728 Oman was torn by a civil war during the course of which factions of the Ghafiris and the Hinawis emerged, and for a time the power of the Ya'aribah became virtually non-existent, though the rule of the dynasty did not come to an end until 1743.

1744(?)–1783(?)

Ahmad ibn Sa'id: The First Imam of Al Bu Sa'id

A man of humble origins, Ahmad rose rapidly to prominence and was elected Imam after he had captured Muscat and expelled Persian invaders from the coast of the Batinah in 1744. His rule was so successful that upon his death his son Sa'id, though not nearly as strong a man, was elected Imam in his place.

1783(?)–1830(?)

Sa'id ibn Ahmad: The Second Imam of Al Bu Sa'id

Sa'id remained titular Imam until his death, though he lacked the capacity to maintain his father's firm grasp on the affairs of the state. Sa'id's son Hamad had effective control of the government from 1785(?) until his death in 1792, during which time he made Muscat his residence. Sa'id's in the last year of his rule remained isolated in al-Rustaq, while his younger brother Sultan gradually acquired power and established himself as the real ruler in Muscat. Sa'id's ibn Ahmad may be reckoned the last member in the direct line of Al Bus Sa'id to hold the office of Imam.

1803(?)–1868

The Third Great Interregnum

No attempt was made by Sa'id ibn Ahmad's successors in Muscat to secure religious authority, and for sixty-five years no Imam was found to fill the gap in Ibadhi society left by this secularization of the rule of Al Bu Sa'id.

1846

Unsuccessful Attempts to Revive the Imamate

Despite the great prestige enjoyed by Sa'id ibn Sultan as ruler of Muscat and Zanzibar, the Ibadhis of Oman were not content to have only a temporal ruler, as indicated by their attempt to elect a new Imam at al-Rustaq in 1846. The office was offered to Hamud ibn 'Azzan of Al Bu Sa'id, uncle of the 'Azzan who was elected Imam some twenty years later, and to two other religious figures, but all three declined the honor.

1868–1871

'Azzan ibn Qais of Al Bu Sa'id

A coalition of Ibadhi leaders captured Muscat in 1868 and the reigning Sultan, Salim ibn Thuwaini, fled to India. 'Azzan ibn Qais was elected Imam of the Ibadhis at Muscat in October 1868, his connection with the dynasty of Al Bu Sa'id being regarded as a recommendation for his holding the office rather than a bar thereto. Control of the state, however, devolved upon a triumvirate of leaders; foremost among them was Sa'id ibn Khalfan al-Khalili, grandfather of the present Imam (this is in reference to Imam Mohammed Al-Khalili). During the revival the Ibadhi, the state held control of the Dhahran, including al-Bahraini, almost all of the interior, and the coast of the Gulf of Oman, but the Imamate collapsed early in 1871 when Turki ibn Sa'id, uncle of ex-Sultan Salim, gained a military victory of Dhank and his supporters took Matrah, where Imam 'Azzan was killed.

1871–1913

The Fourth Great Interregnum

With the reestablishment of secular rule in Muscat the chiefs of the interior resumed their petty rivalries, and no leader with sufficient religious prestige and political stability came forward to re-marshal the forces of the Imamate. Ibrahim ibn Qais, brother of the late Imam, maintained himself independently at al-Rustaq for more than twenty-five years following the fall of the Imamate. Salih ibn 'Ali, the Ibadhi leader in the Sharqiyah, harried the Sultans in Muscat, and his forces even captured the city in 1895, retiring after payment by Sultan Faisal of a substantial sum of money to Salih.

1898

Unsuccessful Attempt to Revive the Imamate

In 1898 it appeared that the Imamate would be revived under Sa'ud ibn 'Azzan, second son of the late Imam, who acceded to power in al-Rustaq upon the death of his uncle Ibrahim ibn Qais in that year. A conference of Ibadhi leaders was called in al-Rustaq, but no decisive steps were taken despite widespread enthusiastic anticipation among the people of Oman.

1913–1920

Salim ibn Rashid al-Kharusi

A desire for security and dissatisfaction with the policy of the Sultan of Muscat encouraged the people of the interior to revive the Imamate in May 1913. Salim ibn Rashid al-Kharusi was the first Imam elected in the twentieth century. After being prevented by British intervention from capturing Muscat in January 1915, the forces of the Imamate withdrew and turned to consolidation of the Imam's position in the mountains and the transmontane regions. Throughout Salim's tenure the British were active in support of Muscat and trying to mediate between the Sultanate and the Imamate. Salim was assassinated by a Bedouin of Oman in 1920.

1920 to the Present

Muhammad ibn Abd Allah al-Khalili

Immediately following the assassination of Imam Salim, the Ibadhi community elected Muhammad ibn 'Abd Allah al-Khalili head of state, and he has held office ever since. An attempt to expand to al-Buraimi in 1925 carried the forces to the Imamate as far as 'Ibri, and after that the Imam has restricted activities to internal matters. Now about sixty-five years old, Imam Muhammad rules principally through the prestige of his religious office and relies for political support upon Sulaiman ibn Himyar al-Nabhani of the Green Mountain and Salih ibn Isa al-Harithi of the Sharqiyah, as well as numerous lesser chiefs.

(Reproduced from Rentz, G., and Foreign Office Research Department (1997). *Oman and the South-Eastern Shore of Arabia*. Reading, United Kingdom: Ithaca Press.)

Sultans of Muscat

From 1803 to the Present

All of these rulers belong to the dynasty of Al Bu Sa'id. For the first two rulers of this dynasty see the table of the Imams of Oman.

1803(?)–1804

Sultan ibn Ahmad

Sultan, who was in actual control of Muscat during the latter part of his brother Imam Sa'id's reign, succeeded upon his brother's death in 1803(?) only to temporal authority; he was not elected Imam or even considered for election. Sultan met his end in 1804 in a minor affray at sea.

1804(?)–1856

Sa'id ibn Sultan

Sultan's two young sons, Salim and Sa'id, appear to have become nominal rulers upon the death of their father in 1804, but Badr ibn Said, their cousin, and an ally of the Unitarians set about to gain actual control of the state. Following almost two years of confusion, Sa'id murdered Badr and was acknowledged as sole ruler by his older brother Salim and other kinsmen. Sa'id's long reign, the expansion of his authority to Zanzibar and East Africa, and his eagerly cultivated relations with European nations and the United States contributed to his fame. Although Sa'id did not use the title Sultan for himself, he was in effect Sultan of both Muscat and Zanzibar. Sa'id owed part of his success to the British, who intervened on several occasions to maintain the integrity of his domains in Muscat. In October 1856 Sa'id died while on his way by sea from Muscat to Zanzibar.

1856–1866

Thuwaini ibn Sa'id

Upon the death of Sa'id ibn Sultan his son Thuwaini succeeded him in Muscat and another son Majid in Zanzibar. The two halves of the realm were officially separated from each other by the Canning Award of 1861, with Thuwaini as Sultan of Muscat to be supported in part by an annual subsidy from the richer state of Zanzibar. Thuwaini was murdered in February 1866 by his son Salim, who succeeded him forthwith.

1866–1868

Salim ibn Thuwaini

Salim, a patricide and a weak character, had to ward off a serious challenge to his right to rule on the part of his uncle, Turki ibn Sa'id. In October 1868 Salim was expelled from Muscat by the forces of the Ibadhis, who elected 'Azzan ibn Qais, a distant relative of his, to the position of Imam.

1868–1871

Interregnum in the Sultanate

'Azzan as a religious leader did not take the title of Sultan. The British continued for a time to recognize Salim as the legitimate Sultan, but about the beginning of 1870 they threw their support behind his rival and uncle, Turki ibn Sa'id. At no time did they accord recognition to 'Azzan, who was killed in January 1871 when the Imamate was overthrown by Turki's forces.

1871–1888

Turki ibn Sa'id

On a number of occasions during Turki's long and uneasy rule his authority was menaced by his brother 'Abd al-Aziz, by his nephew Salim, and by the Ibadhis of the interior. Without British support and active intervention on such occasions, Turki could not have maintained his position. Turki died a natural death in 1888.

1888–1913

Faisal ibn Turki

Faisal was faced by the reviving power of the Ibadhis of the interior throughout his reign. The city of Muscat was captured by then in 1895, but the occupying forces withdrew following the payment of money by Faisal to their leader, Salih ibn Ali. The growing opposition to the Sultan in the interior culminates in the election of al-Kharusi as Imam of Oman in May 1913. Faisal died in October of the same year.

1913–1931

Taimur ibn Faisal

The British intervened with troops for the defense of Muscat and saved Taimur from complete submergence by the forces of the new Imamate in January 1915. During Taimur's reign al-Khalili succeeded al-Kharusi as Imam of Oman in 1920. Taimur abdicated in November 1931 for reasons, according to official statements, of poor health. The accession of his son took place three months later.

1932 to Present

Sa'id ibn Taimur

At the age of twenty-one Sa'id succeeded his father and he has ruled continuously since then. He is officially recognized by both the British and the American Governments as Sultan of Muscat and Oman. Sa'id is well acquainted with lands beyond Oman, having been educated in India and having made a tour around the world in 1937–1938, during which he visited the Untied States and Great Britain. At present he is relying extensively on British experts in the administration of his government, one of whom is in charge of foreign affairs while another commands the Muscat Levies, the Sultan's main military force. Sa'id is known to have been active in trying to expand the area of his authority at the expense of the Imamate (and other independent states in Oman.)

(Reproduced from Rentz, G., and Foreign Office Research Department (1997). *Oman and the South-Eastern Shore of Arabia.* Reading, United Kingdom: Ithaca Press.)

Notes

INTRODUCTION

1. Korany, B., and A. E. H. Dessouki (1991). *The Foreign Policy of Arab States.* Boulder, CO: Westview Press.

2. Hinnesbusch, R., and A. Ehteshami, eds. (2002). *The Foreign Policies of Middle East States.* Boulder, CO: Lynne Rienner.

3. Phillips, W. (1967). *Oman: A History.* Beirut, Lebanon: Librairie du Liban.

4. Akehurst, J. (1982). *We Won a War: The Campaign in Oman 1965–1975.* London: Michael Russell Publishing. D. Smiley (1960). "Muscat and Oman." *Journal of the Royal United Service Institution* 108: 29–47. Smiley, D., and P. Kemp (1975). *Arabian Assignment.* London: Leo Cooper. R. Fiennes (1995). *Where Soldiers Fear to Tread.* London: Mandarin.

5. Peterson, J. E. (1978). *Oman in the Twentieth Century: Political Foundations of an Emerging State.* London: Croom Helm.

6. Wilkinson, J. C. (1987). *The Imamate Tradition of Oman.* Cambridge, United Kingdom: Cambridge University Press.

7. Allen, C. H. (1987). *Oman: The Modernization of the Sultanate.* Boulder, CO: Croom Helm.

8. Riphenburg, C. J. (1998). *Oman: Political Development in a Changing World.* Westport, CT: Praeger.

9. Cordesman, A. H., and Center for Strategic and International Studies (1997). *Bahrain, Oman, Qatar, and the UAE: Challenges of Security.* Boulder, CO: Westview.

10. Kechichian, J. A. (1995). *Oman and the World: The Emergence of an Independent Foreign Policy.* Santa Monica, CA: Rand.

11. Bhacker, M. R. (1994). *Trade and Empire in Muscat and Zanzibar: Roots of British Domination.* London: Routledge and Kegan Paul.

12. Alabdulkarim, A. (1997). *Political Economy and Political Development in the Arabian Peninsula: The Case of the Sultanate of Oman.* PhD diss., University of Southern California.

13. Rigsbee II, W. L. (1990). "American Foreign Policy toward the Sultanate of Oman: 1977–1987." In *Graduate Education and Research.* PhD diss., University of Cincinnati. L. G. Timpe (1991). *British Foreign Policy toward the Sultanate of Muscat and Oman: 1954–1959.* PhD diss., University of Exeter. J. A. Gawlik (1982). *Persian Gulf Security: The United States and Oman, the Gulf Cooperation Council, and Western Allied Participation.* Master's thesis, Naval Postgraduate School. A. Fehmi (1966). *The Question of Oman in the United Nations.* Master's thesis, The American University (Michigan).

14. Kechichian.

CHAPTER 1

1. Wilkinson, J. C. (1972). "The Origins of the Omani State." In *The Arabian Peninsula: Society and Politics.* D. Hopwood, ed. Totowa, NJ: Rowman and Littlefield, p. 67.

2. Peterson, J. E. (1987). "Oman's Odyssey: From Imamate to Sultanate." In *Oman: Economic, Social and Strategic Developments.* B. R. Pridham, ed. London: Croom Helm, p. 4.

3. Wilkinson, J. C. (1987). *The Imamate Tradition of Oman.* Cambridge, United Kingdom: Cambridge University Press, p. 1.

4. Ibid.

5. Risso, P. (1986). *Oman and Muscat: An Early Modern History.* London: Croom Helm, p. 1.

6. Peterson, J. E. (1976). "Britain and the Oman War: An Arabian Entanglement." *Asian Affairs* 63: 285–298.

7. Burrows, B. (1990). *Footnotes in the Sand: The Gulf in Transition, 1953–1958.* Norwich, United Kingdom: Michael Russell Publishing, p. 88.

8. Rentz, G. (1972). "Wahhabism and Saudi Arabia." In *The Arabian Peninsula: Society and Politics.* D. Hopwood, ed. Totowa, NJ: Rowman and Littlefield, p. 9.

9. Ibid., p. xxvi.

10. Ibid.

11. Ibid., p. 4.

12. Wilkinson (1972), p. 69.

13. Ibid., pp. 71–74.

14. Peterson, J. E. (Spring 1977). "Guerrilla Warfare and Ideological Confrontation in the Arabian Peninsula: The Rebellion in Dhufar." *World Affairs* 139: 279–295.

15. Wilkinson (1972), p. 74.

16. Ibid., pp. 74–75.

17. Lewicki, T. (1971). "The Ibadites in Arabia and Africa." *Journal of World History* 13: 65.

18. Ibid.

19. Hoffman, V. (2004). "The Articulation of Ibadi Identity in Modern Oman and Zanzibar." *The Muslim World*, p. 209.

20. Wilkinson (1987), p. 150.

21. Wilkinson (1972), p. 75.

22. Wilkinson (1987), p. 154.

23. Ibid., pp. 154–156.

24. Hoffman, p. 201.

25. Lewicki, p. 52.

26. Ibid., p. 61.

27. Ibid., p. 68–71.

28. Landen, R. G. (1967). *Oman since 1856: Disruptive Modernization in a Traditional Arab Society.* Princeton, NJ: Princeton University Press, p. 45.

29. Riphenburg, C. J. (1998). *Oman: Political Development in a Changing World.* Westport, CT: Praeger, p. 24.

30. Bathurst, R. D. (1972). "Maritime Trade and Imamate Government: Two Principal Themes in the History of Oman to 1728." In *The Arabian Peninsula: Society and Politics.* D. Hopwood, ed. Totowa, NJ: Rowman and Littlefield, p. 90.

31. Riphenburg, p. 28.

32. Townsend, J. (1977). *Oman: The Making of a Modern State.* London: Croom Helm, p. 30.

33. Wilkinson (1972), p. 76.

34. Wilkinson (1987), p. 9.

35. Peterson, J. E. (1978). *Oman in the Twentieth Century: Political Foundations of an Emerging State.* London: Croom Helm, p. 20.

36. Wilkinson (1972), pp. 77–79.

37. Peterson (1987), p. 3.

38. Peterson (1984).

39. Ibid.

40. Wilkinson (1972), pp. 78–79.

41. Bathurst, p. 92.

42. Riphenburg, pp. 30–31.

43. Bathurst, p. 99.

44. Riphenburg, pp. 30–31.

45. Wilkinson (1987), p. 48

46. Wilkinson (1987), p. 48.

47. Kelly, J. B. (1980). *Arabia, the Gulf and the West.* New York: Basic Books, p. 108.

48. Wilkinson (1987), p. 50.

49. Rentz, p. 13.

50. Kelly (1980), p. 108.

51. Riphenburg, pp. 34–35.

52. Ibid., p. 36.

53. Risso, pp. 179–180.

54. Riphenburg, p. 36.

55. Wilkinson (1987), p. 54.

56. Bhacker, M. R. (1994). *Trade and Empire in Muscat and Zanzibar: Roots of British Domination.* London: Routledge and Kegan Paul, p. 197.

57. Allen, C. H. (1982). "The State of Masqat in the Gulf and East Africa, 1785–1892." *International Journal of Middle East Studies* 14: p. 44.

58. Wilkinson (1987), p. 54.

59. Riphenburg, p. 37.

60. Townsend, p. 42.

61. Rentz, pp. 17–18.

62. Ibid.

63. Ibid.

64. Riphenburg, p. 39.

65. Rentz, pp. 34–35.

66. Kechichian, J. A. (2000). "The Throne in the Sultanate of Oman." In *Middle East Monarchies: The Challenge of Modernity.* J. Kostiner, ed. Boulder, CO: Lynne Rienner Publishers, p. 187.

67. Kelly (1980), p. 113.

CHAPTER 2

1. Halliday, F. (1974). *Arabia Without Sultans.* Harmondsworth, United Kingdom: Penguin Books, p. 277.

2. Ibid., p. 274.

3. Halliday (1974). J. Morris (1957). *Sultan in Oman.* London: Arrow. D. Smiley and P. Kemp (1975). *Arabian Assignment.* London: Leo Cooper. P. Thwaites and S. Sloane (1995). *Muscat Command.* Barnsley, United Kingdom: Pen and Sword Books Ltd. P. Searle (1979). *Dawn over Oman.* London and Boston: Allen & Unwin. F. A. Clements (1980). *Oman: The Reborn Land.* London: Longman. A. Hill and D. Hill et al. (1977). *The Sultanate of Oman: A Heritage.* London: Longman. B. K. Narayan (1979). *Oman and Gulf Security.* New Delhi, India: Lancers Publishers. L. Graz (1982). *The Omanis, Sentinels of the Gulf.* London: Longman. D. F. Eickelman (1984). "Kings and People: Oman's State Consultative Council." *Middle East Journal* 38: 51–71. U. Wikan (1982). *Behind the Veil in Arabia: Women in Oman.* Baltimore, MD: Johns Hopkins University Press. N. Kaylani (1979). "Politics and Religion in Uman: A Historical Overview." *Middle East Studies* 10: 567–579. E. Foda (1958). "Controversy over Oman." *Egyptian Economic and Political Review* 4: 12–14. M. Joyce (1995). *The Sultanate of Oman: A Twentieth Century History.* Westport, CT: Praeger.

4. Phillips, W. (1966). *Unknown Oman.* London: Longmans. J. E. Peterson (1978). *Oman in the Twentieth Century: Political Foundations of an Emerging State.* London: Croom Helm. I. Skeet (1974). *Muscat and Oman: The End of an Era.* London: Faber.

5. Peterson, J. E. (2004). "Oman: Change and Development." *Middle East Policy* 11: 125–137.

6. It should be noted that Muscat's application to the WHO was resisted: a "coalition of Muslim and communist states—Iraq, Mali, Sudan, Yugoslavia, the Soviet Union, Saudi Arabia, and the United Arab Republic—spoke against it." M. Joyce (1995), p. 89.

7. Peterson, J. E. (1976). "The Revival of the Ibadi Imamate in Oman and the Threat to Muscat 1913–1920." *Arabian Studies* 3, p. 105.

8. Miller, J. (1997). "Creating Modern Oman: An Interview with Sultan Qaboos." *Foreign Affairs* 76: 13–18.

9. Halliday, p. 275.

10. Wikan, p. 6.

11. Graz (1982), p. 16.

12. Kaylani, p. 573.

13. Narayan, p. 75.

14. FCO8/1072: "The Rebellious Mountains of Dhofar: A Report from the Liberated Areas." Special correspondent of *Pravda*: A. Vasiliev. *Pravda*, 29 September 1969.

15. FCO8/1072: The Dhofar War: British Embassy, Moscow: 29 September 1969.

16. This is a book that is supportive of the conventional wisdom and contains many pictures.

17. Pridham, B. R. (1986). "Oman: Change or Continuity." In *Arabia and the Gulf: From Traditional Society to Modern States.* I. R. Netton, ed. London: Croom Helm, p. 134.

18. FCO8/569: Confidential: Record of Conversation with the Sultan of Muscat: 22 December 1966.

19. Phillips (1966), p. 166.

20. Townsend, J. (1977). *Oman: The Making of a Modern State.* London: Croom Helm, p. 57.

21. Innes, N. M. (1987). *Minister in Oman: A Personal Narrative.* Cambridge, United Kingdom: Oleander. Wendell Phillips (1921–1975) was an American oilman and an archeologist. He first entered Oman in the late 1950s after his expulsion from Yemen by the imamate forces. In Oman, he gained the confidence of Sultan Said bin Taimur, spending considerable time with him in Salalah. He is also the author of two books on Oman: *Oman: A History* and *Unknown Oman.* John Townsend worked for both Sultan Said and his son, Sultan Qaboos. He first visited Oman in late April 1969. Neil McLeod Innes was invited to Oman in 1953 to become Sultan Said's adviser. Apparently Sultan Said had more advice than he could possibly cope with, for he immediately informed Mr. Innes that his job was to "tell Her Majesty's Government what I want, not the other way around. Your title would be Minster of Foreign Affairs." Innes, p. 1.

22. PREM11/4923: Secret: Visit of the Sultan of Muscat and Oman: 20 August 1958. There is also another memo from the British Foreign Office that refers to how the sultan, in previous negotiations concerning the Royal Air force Facilities, "conducted the negotiations entirely on his own and most capably" (PREM11/4923). It should be noted that these memos are by no means the exception.

23. Skeet (1974), p. 164.

24. Allen, C. H., and W. L. Rigsbee (2000). *Oman under Qaboos: From Coup to Constitution, 1970–1996.* London: Frank Cass, p.3.

25. Ibid., p. 4.

26. Vine, P. (1995). *The Heritage of Oman.* London: Immel, p. 487.

27. Bailey, R. W. (1988). *Records of Oman 1867–1947.* Farnham Common, United Kingdom: Archive Editions, p. 425.

28. El-Solh, R. I. (2000). *The Sultanate of Oman, 1918–1939: Administrative Affairs.* Reading, United Kingdom: Ithaca Press, p. 150.

29. "After a sight-seeing tour, which included a visit to Hollywood, Saiyid Said went on by train to Washington, where he was to be the guest of the United States Government for 10 days. Wearing Omani national dress, the Sultan and his party were welcomed at Washington station on 3 March 1938 by the Secretary of State Mr. Cordell Hull … The Sultan lunched with President Roosevelt on 4th March and that evening was the guest of honor at a state dinner given by the Secretary of State … From London, he

went to Paris, where he was received by the President of the French Republic." Bailey (1988), p. 426.

30. El-Solh, p. 220.

31. In India, the sultan was received by the Viceroy at Simla. The remarks of the Viceroy in his annual report give us a hint to the personality of young Sultan Said: "His Highness, who carries an exceedingly shrewd head on his young shoulders, takes a keen personal interest in the administration of his State and evinces considerable strength of character in dealing with problems that confront him." Bailey (1988), p. 425.

32. Porter, J. D., ed. (1982). *Oman and the Persian Gulf, 1835–1949*. Salisbury, NC: Documentary Publications, p. 44.

33. Ibid.

34. FCO8/569: Confidential: Records of Conversation with the Sultan of Muscat: 22nd December 1966.

35. Phillips (1966), p. 166.

36. Bailey (1988), p. 560.

37. It should be noted that Sultan Said, though cooperative, made it clear that these facilities were for the period of the war only. In fact, he drew up regulations for British service and civilian personal stationed in the sultanate so as to avoid possible misunderstandings and conflict with the resident population. These achieved their objectives. Once the war was over, he insisted on the prompt implementation of the agreed withdrawal arrangements. Bailey (1988), p. 560.

38. "In September, at the outbreak of hostilities, the political resident called on the sultan to inform him that Britain and France were at war with Germany. The sultan was repelled by the Axis powers. He had no sympathy with either their methods or their goals, and he was not interested in using the opportunity to distance himself from Britain. Sultan Said immediately expressed his readiness to render such assistance as was within his power." M. Joyce (1995), p. 40.

39. Bailey (1988), p. 561.

40. Bierschenk, T. (1989). "Oil Interests and the Formation of Centralized Government in Oman, 1920–1970." *Orient* 30, p. 213.

41. "When Muhammad's health began to fail in the mid-1940s, Sultan Said ibn Taymur initiated correspondence with the major tribal shaykhs and invited them to Muscat—his goal being the abolition of the imamate after Imam Muhammad's death. The Imam, however, clung to life for nearly a decade longer." Peterson, J. E. (1984). "Britain and the Oman War: An Arabian Entanglement." *American Arab Affairs* 63: 286.

42. Muhammad Abdullah al-Khalili, the imam elected just prior to the signing of the Agreement of al-Sib, was a "wealthy notable who sold his personal estates to sustain the imamate as its resources dwindled, was the twentieth of a long line of imams selected from his immediate tribal group." Eickelman, D. F. (1985). "From Theocracy to Monarchy: Authority and Legitimacy in Inner Oman, 1935–1957." *International Journal of the Middle East Studies* 17, p. 4.

The Sultan prudently realized that "The Imamate ... was noteworthy for the religious and political qualifications of its leader, the order prevailing in its domain ... As long as the Imam Muhammad lived, there could be no personal or tribal challenge to the imamate." Peterson, J. E. (1987). "Oman's Odyssey: From Imamate to Sultanate." In *Oman: Economic, Social and Strategic Developments*. B. R. Pridham, ed. London: Croom Helm, p. 6.

43. Bailey (1988), p. 428.

44. Ibid.

45. Ibid., p. 561.

46. Eickelman (1985), p. 13.

47. Kelly, J. B. (1959). *Sultanate and Imamate in Oman*. Oxford, United Kingdom: Oxford University Press, p. 1.

48. To see the Saudi position, see A. S. Sahwell (1956). "The Buraimi Dispute." *The Islamic Review* 44: 13–17.

49. As Kelly points out, "whoever holds the oasis can dominate the Trucial Shaikhdoms to the north and the Sultanate of Oman to the east and, conversely, no invading force from the west, bent on the subjection of those principalities, could afford to bypass Buraimi and leave the lines of communications exposed." *Kelly*, J. B. (1956). "The Buraimi Oasis Dispute." *International Affairs* 32, p. 323.

50. Al-Khalili wrote in protest to the Saudi governor of Buraimi: "Your statement that in view of repeated requests from your subjects in Oman to appoint a representative on your behalf among them, you have appointed Turki bin Abdullah bin 'Uteishan, has astonished us, because we do not know that you have subjects in Oman." Bierschenk (1989).

51. In a confidential document this correspondence is affirmed, "When Saudi Arabia agent arrived in Buraimi oasis in August 1952, Mohammed Bin Abdullah wrote to the Sultan expressing his concern and showed the latter that he was ready to join with the Sultan in forcibly ejecting the Saudis" (FCO371/126878: Confidential: Note to Be Handed to the Prime Minister: date not available).

52. Eickelman (1985), p. 13.

53. Holden, D. (1966). *Farewell to Arabia*. London: Rediffusion Television, p. 107.

54. FCO 8/62: Confidential: Qateri Interest in the Buraimi Question: 6 February 1967.

A copy of a summary of the Buraimi problem "In October 1955 the Trucial Oman Levies reoccupied the Buraimi Oasis, capturing document which established Saudi bribery and subversive activities beyond all doubt."

55. Burrows, B. (1990). *Footnotes in the Sand: The Gulf in Transition, 1953–1958*. Norwich, United Kingdom: Michael Russell Publishing, p. 107.

56. Phillips (1967), p. 186.

57. Kelly (1959), p. 12.

58. Eickelman (1985), p. 173.

59. Kelly, J. B. (1964). *Eastern Arabian Frontiers*. London: Faber, p. 185.

60. Peterson (1984), p. 287.

61. Phillips (1967), p. 189.

62. Allan, R. (1957). "Between the Saudis and the Sharks." *Reporter* 1 (17), p. 22.

63. This is certainly Landen's argument: R. G. Landen (1967). *Oman since 1856: Disruptive Modernization in a Traditional Arab Society*. Princeton, NJ: Princeton University Press, p. 419.

64. Kechichian, J. A. (1995). *Oman and the World: The Emergence of an Independent Foreign Policy*. Santa Monica, CA: Rand, p. 42

65. Eickelman (1985), p. 14.

66. Landen, p. 420.

67. Joyce, M. (1993). "Britain and the Sultanate of Muscat and Oman and Dependencies, 1958–59." *Diplomacy and Statecraft* 4, p. 93.

68. Timpe, L. G. (1991). *British Foreign Policy toward the Sultanate of Muscat and Oman: 1954–1959.* PhD diss., University of Exeter, pp. 184–190.

69. Ibid., p. 195.

70. Halliday, p. 281.

71. Morris, p. 148.

72. The reader should not, however, be under any illusion that Sultan Said lacked intimate knowledge of events throughout the country, including the interior. "In spite of the physical distance which separated the Sultan from the majority of his subjects while he lived at Salalah, he had extraordinary accurate knowledge of what was going on throughout his territory by means of written messages and visitors coming to see him form all over the interior." Harrison, P. W. (1940). *Doctor in Arabia.* New York: Day, p. 92.

73. Eickelman (1985), p. 15.

74. FCO371/126878: Confidential: Note to Be Handed to the Prime Minister. The date is not available in this document, but it is safe to assume that it was after 1957.

75. Timpe, p. 202.

76. More to the point was the role that external actors played in fermenting this revolt. As Air Vice-Marshall M. L. Heath pointed out, "the more peaceful atmosphere that followed the conclusion of the Agreement of Sib would not have been shattered, nor would the recent troubles have been prolonged had not outside powers, in particular Saudi Arabia, sought to stoke the flames, for the Imam's financial and military support was supplied directly by Saudi Arabia, who recruited, trained, supplied and paid for the 'liberation army of free Oman.'" *The Times London* 1959, p. 9.

77. Kelly (1964), p. 264.

78. Innes, p. 206.

79. Peterson (1978), p. 183.

80. FO371/126878: Secret: From Muscat to Foreign Office: 26 July 1957.

81. FO371/126875: From Muscat to Foreign Office: 16 July 1957.

82. Perersen, T. (1992). "Anglo-American Rivalry in the Middle East: The Struggle for the Buraimi Oasis, 1952–1957." *The International History Review* 14, p. 72.

83. Ibid., p. 74.

84. Melamid, A. (1956). "The Buraimi Oasis Dispute." *Middle Eastern Affairs* 7, p. 63.

85. Perersen, p. 76.

86. Relations between Saud and Nasser were indeed warming up to the point where Saud was following Egypt's tactics in appealing to the Iraqi and Jordanian masses to rise against their leaders. More ominously for the United States was the fact that "when Nasser announced in September 1955 the conclusion of an arms deal with the Soviet Union, which brought the latter into the Arab region for the first time, Saud supported the move and went on to sign the military alliance with the Egypt the next month." Safran, N. (1985). *Saudi Arabia: The Ceaseless Quest for Security.* Cambridge, MA: Harvard University Press, p. 79.

87. Perersen, p. 89.

88. For a good discussion of the United States, Saudi Arabia, Egypt, and London's entanglement in the Buraimi dispute, see Hart T. Parker's *Saudi Arabia and the United States: Birth of a Security Partnership.* Indianapolis, IN: Indiana University Press (1998).

89. Eden, A. (1960). *The Memoirs of Sir Anthony Eden: Full Circle.* London: Cassell, p. 373.

90. Harrison, p. 87.

91. Memorandum of Conversation [John Foster Dulles, Sec of State, US; Saud ibn Abdul Aziz, Crown Prince, Saudi Arabia; other US and Saudi officials]: Secret. Eisenhower Library, Papers as President of the U.S., 1953–61 (Ann Whitman File): 18 May 1953.

92. Memorandum: Department of State: Secret: Issue Date: 8 December 1953.

93. Peterson (1984), p. 280.

94. Macmillan, H. (1973). *At the End of the Day, 1961–1963*. Harper and Row, p. 271.

95. Secretary Dulles reports on conversation with Crown Prince Abdullah of Iraq. Department Of State, Secret: Issue Date: 5 February 1957.

96. Peterson (1984), p. 289.

97. Phillips (1967), p. 204.

98. Smiley and Kemp, p. 13.

99. Phillips (1967), p. 210.

The following document numerates exactly the number of casualties as of March 1959.

The following statement was included in the Army Estimates published on 19 February (Smd. 699):

Numbers. The total of British troops involved at any one time was about three hundred; the sultan's forces are not large but it is not our responsibility to reveal numbers.

Casualties. Total British casualties over the past year or so were of the order of five killed and five wounded (PREM11/4960: Confidential: From Foreign Office to Certain of Her Majesty's Representatives: Operation in Muscat and Oman: 4 March 1959).

100. Smiley and Kemp, p. 13.

101. M. Joyce (1993), p. 91.

102. Ibid., p. 98.

103. Ibid.

104. PREM 11/4960: Confidential: From Foreign Office to Certain of Her Majesty's Representatives: Operation in Muscat and Oman: 4 March 1959.

105. PREM11/4960-100752: Top Secret: Ministry of Defense: 12 August 1958.

In another top secret document, London expresses the same anxieties: "Even if we did mount a large operation of this kind, it is extremely doubtful whether our blockade would be sufficiently effective to compel the dissidents to surrender" (PREM11/4960-100752–10: Top Secret: September 1958).

106. FO371/126878: Secret: Outward Telegram from Commonwealth Relations Office: 19 July 1957.

107. Smiley and Kemp, p. 50.

108. Ambassador Wadsworth reports on information given to him by King Saud regarding arms sent to Oman (Department of State: Top Secret: Issue Date: 29 July 1957).

109. FCO 371 126877: Secret: From Washington to Foreign Office: 25 July 1957.

110. In a response to *Embassy Analysis of U.S.-U.K. Relations in the Persian Gulf* (Department Of State: Issue Date: 18 December 1957), the State Department made the following official statement on the outbreak of the 1957 fighting:

The Sultan of Muscat, while not formally under British protection, has had close relations with the United Kingdom and has in the past requested British assistance in meetings tribal problems. The area of inner Oman is essentially a tribal area where matters of sovereignty in Western sense have not been of major importance. Revolts against the Sultan's rule in the area have occurred in the past. While the United States does not have direct and extensive information on the current difficulties, the department has been generally informed by the British. The matter appears to be a small-scale action involving a limited are and small forces. While certain of the participants of the current revolt have been recently in Saudi Arabia, inner Oman is not an area where Saudi Arabia has claimed sovereignty. The United States has no specific information on reports of outside arms in the area but it is not uncommon for tribes in this are to obtain them from the Outside. The area where the revolt has occurred appears to be clearly within a concession area of the Iraq Petroleum Company, of which approximately one-fourth is American. There are no claims by any other companies. The United States hopes that the present difficulties can be resolved quickly (FO371/126877: From Washington to Foreign Office: 26 July 1957, p. 10).

111. Allfree, P. S. (1967). *Warlords of Oman*. London: Hale, pp. 162–167
112. Smiley and Kemp, p. 61.
113. Allfree, p. 114.
114. According to the Gulf Committee, oil is the primary reason for British involvement. This is inaccurate primarily because no significant oil discoveries were made by 1955. Joyce also claims that British involvement in Oman was to a large extent a question of oil when she quotes Noel-Baker statement in the House of Commons: "Of course, it was for oil that the military operations in Oman were undertaken." M. Joyce (1993), p. 99.
115. Smiley, D. (1960). "Muscat and Oman." *Journal of the Royal United Service Institution* 108: 29–47.
116. Owtram, F. C. (2004). *A Modern History of Oman: Formation of the State since 1920*. London: I. B. Tauris, p. 103.
117. PREM11/4923: Secret: Visit of The Sultan Of Muscat and Oman: 20 August 1958.
118. PREM11/4923-100752: Confidential: Sultan of Muscat and Oman: 17 July 1958.
119. PREM11/4960-100752: Top Secret: From Foreign Office to Washington: 18 November 1958.
120. PREM11/4960-100752: Muscat: 9 April 1958.
121. FO371/126885: Foreign Secretary: Copy of Minutes by the Prime Minster: From Bahrain: 28 August 1957.
122. M. Joyce (1993), p. 92.
123. PREM11/4960-100752: Secret: Record of Conversation Between the Minister of State and his Highness the Sultan of Muscat and Oman in the Foreign Office: 13 August 1959.
124. PREM11/4960-100752: Secret: Prime Minister—Muscat and Oman: 13 July 1960.
125. FO371/12685: British Embassy, Baghdad: 23 August 1957.
126. FO371/126878: From Tehran to Foreign Office: 27 July 1957.
127. FO371/126878: Confidential: From Foreign Office: Telegram No. 1575 to Amman: 27 July 1957.
128. PREM11/4923: Visit of the Sultan of Muscat and Oman: 20 August 1957.
129. Landen, p. 419.
130. Phillips (1967), p. 194.

131. Timpe, p. 207

132. Khalil, M. (1962). *The Arab States and the Arab League: A Documentary Record*. Beirut, Lebanon: Khayats, p. 177.

133. Ibid.

134. Timpe, p. 208.

135. Not every country on that list was enthusiastic about this matter, but some arm twisting by Egypt and Saudi Arabia went a long way, as the following telegram indicates:

I am doing my best to persuade the Iraqis to take a lead in preventing the ventilation of this issue in the General Assembly, but I fear that they will in the last resort follow the wishes of the Saudis. Indeed, the Prime Minster probably thinks we are not sufficiently appreciative of his efforts to keep Saud on our side ... the Egyptians so maneuvered matters that they were able to say to the Saudis: 'you see, you want this badly but the Iraqis are reluctant to support you' and the Iraqis had then to cave in (From Baghdad to Foreign Office: 28 August 1957).

136. FO371/126883: United Nations Security Council: Letter Dated 13 August 1957 from the Permanent Representatives of Egypt, Iraq, Jordan, Lebanon, Libya, Morocco, Saudi Arabia, Sudan, Syria, and Yemen Addressed to the President of the Security Council.

137. Al-Marayati, A. (1966). "The Question of Oman." *Foreign Affairs Reports* 15: 99–109, p. 103.

138. Fehmi (1966). *The Question of Oman in the United Nations*. Master's thesis, The American University (Michigan), p. 13.

139. Cable: Department Of State: Secret: Issue Date: 19 August 1957. British frustration at Washington's position and the importance of Saudi Arabia to the United States can be clearly seen in the following declassified telegram involving the respective representatives of both countries discussing the upcoming inscription or lack thereof in the UN:

I told Mr. Murphy that from the point of view of Anglo-United States relations I wanted to leave no doubt in his mind of the dangers involved in our not acting and being seen to act together ... I said that the State Department might consider that the problem was one of procedure. But I must warn him that from the point of view of Anglo-American relations, it was a good deal more than that ... Mr. Murphy replied that he would not wish to dispute that. But he hoped that Her Majesty's Government would realize that the United States Government was not going to obtain may thanks in the Arab countries for abstaining. The Saudi Arabian Minister had been to see him and had been quite emotional in demanding United States support (FO 371/126883: Secret: Washington Telegram No. 1578 to Foreign Office: 15 August 1957).

140. In China, the *People's Daily* commented that by its abstention, Washington "was actually backing the British aggressors against the Arab people's fight for independence ... Realising its awkward position in the middle East ... the United States was relying on clandestine dealings with Britain in exchange for British support of United States subversive activities against Syria." H. S. H. Behbehani (1981). *China's Foreign Policy in the Arab World, 1955–75: Three Case Studies*. London: Kegan Paul International, p. 167.

141. FO371/126884: From New York To Foreign Office (United Kingdom Delegation to the United Nations): 20 August 1957.

142. Kechichian, p. 44.

143. Fehmi, p. 28

144. Ibid., p. 31.

145. Ibid., p. 35.

146. Ibid., p. 37.

147. Ibid., p. 63.

148. Ibid.

149. Ibid., p. 70.

Here is a sample of the debates raging in the UN through the words of the United Kingdom mission to the UN:

> The Sultanate of Oman and Muscat is a sovereign and independent state. It follows therefore, Sir, that under the charter of the United Nations, neither this Committee, nor the Committee of 24, no any other body of this Organization, can have the right or the competence to discuss the internal affairs of a sovereign and independent State like Muscat and Oman ... under an arrangement freely entered into between two sovereign and independent states the British enjoy facilities for tow Air Force staging posts ... They are not military bases, and they are used to refuel and service aircraft, when this is necessary, on routine flights to the Far East ... There are no British forces in Muscat and Oman. There are—however—as we have made clear in previous debates—some fifty officers and men serving on ... secondment with the Sultan's Armed Forces. These are not mercenaries or soldiers of fortune; they are personnel on ... secondment on exactly the same bases as those seconded by other independent countries (FCO8/580: United Kingdom Mission to the United Nations: 8 December 1967).

150. Fehmi, p. 4.

151. The *New York Times* published an unofficial version on 13 August 1957. Also, I came across another unofficial translated copy from the Arab Information Center of the British Public Record Office (FO371/126884):

THE TREATY OF SIB 1920

In the Name of God, the Compassionate, the Merciful

This is the peace agreed upon between the Government of the Sultan, Taimur ibn Faisal, and Shaikh Isa ibn Salih ibn Ali on behalf of the people of Oman whose names are signed hereto, through the mediation of Mr. Wingate, I. C. S., Political Agent and Consul for Great Britain in Muscat, who is empowered by his Government in this respect and to be an intermediary between them. Of the conditions set forth below, four pertain to the Government of the Sultan and four pertain to the people of Oman. Those pertaining to the people of Oman are:

Not more than five percent shall be taken from anyone, no matter what his race, coming from Oman to Muscat or Matrah or Sur or the rest of the towns of the coast.

All the people of Oman shall enjoy security and freedom in all the towns of the coast.

All restrictions upon everyone entering and leaving Muscat and Matrah and all the towns of the coast shall be removed.

The Government of the Sultan shall not grant asylum to any criminal fleeing from the justice of the people of Oman. It shall return him to them if they request it to do so. It shall not interfere in their internal affairs.

The four conditions pertaining to the Government of the Sultan are:

All the tribes and Shaikhs shall be at peace with the Sultan. They shall not attack the towns of the coast and shall not interfere in his Government.

All those going to Oman on lawful business and for commercial affairs shall be free. There shall be no restrictions on commerce, and they shall enjoy security.

They shall expel and grant no asylum to any wrongdoer or criminal fleeing to them.

The claims of merchants and others against the people of Oman shall be heard and decided on the basis of justice according to the law of Islam.

Written on 11 Muharram 1339, corresponding to 25 September 1920.

This version is similar to the one in a booklet made by the Gulf Committee (not exactly friendly to Sultan Said) in 1974: *The Oman War 1957–1959: A Critical History*. London: Russell Press Ltd., p. 12. The text of the document can also be found in Landen, p. 403, and in David Holden's (1966) *Farewell to Arabia*. London: Rediffusion Television, pp. 249–250.

152. FO371/126878: From Muscat to Foreign Office: 28 July 1957.

This is in contrast to the Egyptian claim found in *Egyptian Economic and Political Review* by Dr. Ezeldin Foda in March 1958: "The British Foreign Office has attempted to suppress the publication of the text and terms of the Treaty of Sib. This in itself suggests that the Treaty is worthy of study."

153. Wingate, Sir R. E. L. (1959). *Not in the Limelight*. London: Hutchison, p. 89.

154. Ibid.

155. Foda, p. 13.

156. Fehmi, p. 101.

157. This view has been expressed in an enclosed booklet that has been prepared by Her Majesty's Government primarily for distribution through the British Information Services overseas. (Muscat and Oman: 19 November 1962: 14). This conclusion is also supported by *The Arabian Gulf States: Their Legal and Political Status and their International Problems*, first published by the University of Manchester in 1968.

158. Khalil, p. 242

159. There were definitely some intrigues surrounding the election process. This is affirmed by none other than one of the most loyal supporters of the imamate institution, the son of Al-Salmi, a famous Omani historian who wrote *Nahdat al-Ayan bi-Hurriyyat Oman* (in Arabic only, Cairo, 1961). As far as Sultan Said was concerned, Ghalib and his supporters were rebels. When the UN mission arrived in Oman, he handed them "photostats of passport applications, one of which was submitted by Talib, the brother of the Imam, dated 1954. That was, in his view, proof that Talib, and also others who had submitted similar passport applications previously, considered themselves 'subjects of the government of Muscat and Oman.'" Fehmi, p. 45.

160. FO371/126879: Telegram to Washington No. 2947: Oman: 22 July 1957.

161. Timpe, p. 228.

162. A confidential text titled "Legality of British Military Assistance for Sultan of Muscat" clearly indicates that although London has no binding treaty to aid the sultanate, it has provided such assistance many times before. (FO371/126879: Confidential: Legality of British Military Assistance for Sultan of Muscat: 26 July 1957).

163. The Foreign Office did not attempt to give British aid on the bases of treaties, as the following record indicates: "Lord Stansgate has already been told that we agreed

to intervene in Muscat, not on the basis of an treaty with the Sultan but in reply to a specific request by him for aid on the basis of a long-standing friendship and in connection with him and his predecessors" (FO 371 126878: The Legality of British Military Assistance to Oman: 25 July 1957).

164. Timpe, p. 230.

165. Phillips (1967), p. 206.

166. Bailey (1988), p. 135.

167. Bailey, R. W. (1995). *Records of Oman 1867–1947*. Farnham Common, Archive Editions, pp. 138–141.

168. FCO8/1667: Secret: Masirah and Salalah: 9 September 1971.

169. PREM11/4923: Secret: Visit of The Sultan Of Muscat and Oman: 20 August 1958.

170. This is even true of books that deal exclusively with foreign policy (Kechchian and Rand Corporation, 1995) as much as it is of books that deal with the general political history of Muscat (Allen and Rigsbee) or historical and political developments (Peterson, 1976) and various articles, such as Kaylani's work, which uses Masirah as an indication of Said's subservience to London (Kaylani, 1979).

171. PREM11/4960-100752: Secret: Record of Meeting Between the Lord Privy Seal and the Sultan of Muscat and Oman in the Foreign Office at 12 Noon on 24 August 1960.

172. PREM11/4960-100752: Records of Meeting between the Lord Privy Seal and the Sultan of Muscat and Oman in the Foreign Office at 12 Noon on 24 August 24 1960.

173. FCO8/1667: Review of Long Term Policy in the Gulf: 3 September 1971.

174. Timpe, p. 270.

175. Allen and Rigsbee, pp. 8–17.

176. Timpe, p. 228.

177. PREM11/4960-100752: Secret: Prime Minister-Muscat and Oman: 13 July 1960.

178. Ibid.

179. Timpe, p. 269.

180. Ibid.

181. PREM11/4960-100752: Secret: Prime Minister: 27 July 1960.

182. PREM11/4932-100752: Prime Minister: 27 July 1964.

183. M. Joyce (1995), p. 77.

184. Bailey (1988), p. 614.

185. Ibid., p. 615.

186. M. Joyce (1995), p. 69.

187. An example of this is an article that appeared in the Pakistani press blaming the British for not doing enough for Pakistan:

Some Arabs, particularly those from the Persian Gulf States, are usually born smugglers. Be it diamonds or gold, opium or hashish (charas), limousines or unimportable silks, one can count on a particular type of Arab to deliver them. Operating from Gawadur, with the help of the local Mekrani population, they have coolly deprived the Government of Pakistan of scores of rupees in import duties (M. Joyce [1995], p. 72).

188. Ibid., p. 73.

189. Ibid., p. 70.

190. Ibid., pp. 74–75.

191. Ibid., p. 67.

192. Ibid., p. 79.

193. PREM11/4923-100752: Secret: Records of Conversation between the Secretary of State and His Highness the Sultan of Muscat and Oman at the House of Commons on Thursday, 12 June 1958, at 4 P.M.

194. Peterson (1976), pp. 87–88.

195. PREM11/4923: Secret: Visit of The Sultan of Muscat and Oman: 20 August 1958.

196. Ibid.

197. PREM11/4923: Secret: Visit of the Sultan of Muscat and Oman: 20 August 1958.

198. M. Joyce (1995), p. 73.

199. The British were very much aware of this, and they would even repeat it themselves to Saudi policy makers, as in the following conversation between British Ambassador and Prince Fahad at the time: "The Ambassador said the he recognized that for King Feisal the Buraimi affair was not simply a question of a piece of land: his pride was engaged and his feelings were very strong" (FCO8/964: Confidential: Record of Conversation between the British Ambassador in Saudi Arabia and Prince Fahd, Second Deputy Prime Minster, at Taif on 8 July 1969).

200. FO1016/760: Confidential: Records of Conversation between the Political Resident and the Ruler or Abu Dhabi in Abu Dhabi: 30 January, 1968. British foreign secretary commented to the *Daily Star* in 1968 that British withdrawal was necessary, for "if we attempted to keep an effective military presence in that area after 1971, much more than local costs are involved. It would place a severe burden on the logistic backing required from our forces which would then be concentrated here in Europe" (*Daily Star* [Beirut], 27 January 1968).

201. For a detailed discussion on British withdrawal from the Middle East, see Abadi, J. (1982). *Britain's Withdrawal From the Middle East, 1947–1971*. Princeton, NJ: Kingston Press.

202. Mordechai, A. (1974). *Oil, Power and Politics: Conflicts in Arabia, the Red Sea and the Gulf*. London: Frank Class, p. 16.

203. FCO8/45: Confidential: Saudi Arabia and the Gulf: British Embassy: 17 January 1968.

204. FCO8/60: Confidential: Jedda to Foreign Office: 1 October 1967.

205. FCO8/60: Confidential: Abu Dhabi/Saudi Relations: 27 March 1968.

206. FCO8/59: Confidential: Buraimi: 16 February 1967.

207. FCO8/59: Confidential: H.B.M. Political Agency, Abu Dhabi: Shaikh Zaid's Visit to Saudi Arabia: 19 April 1967.

208. A4-35 FCO8/59: Confidential: H.B.M. Political Agency, Abu Dhabi: Shaikh Zaid's Visit to Saudi Arabia: 19 April 1967.

209. FO8/59: Meeting Between King Faisal and Shaikh Zaid: 11 April 1967

210. FCO8/59: Confidential: British Political Agency, Abu Dhabi: 11 April 1967.

211. FCO8/59: Confidential: Priority: Bahrain to Foreign Office: 18 April 1967.

Even the late King Hussein of Jordan was becoming involved in this Buraimi dispute, as indicated in the following extract from a letter from Hussein to Zaid of Abu Dhabi:

Translation
H.H. Shaikh Zaid bin Sultan.

I send to Your Highness, my dear brother, my sincere greetings and best wishes for health, happiness and prosperity.

I have received Your Highness' letter dated 18 Muharram 1387. I was very pleased by Your Highness' praise of the mission we sent for Your Highness' services and that of your sister country. I was also very pleased to hear from H.E Sayyid Ahmad al Tarawneh of Your Highness' care and solicitude for the mission … I was grieved to hear from Your Highness that frontier problems remain between you and sister Saudi Arabia. I cordially thank Your Highness for acquainting me with what passed between you and His Majesty my brother King Faisal. Even if you had not given me the details I should have been considered a party to the problem, since our struggle against the forces of evil and heresy, which threaten us all, obliges us all to support each other and put an end to anything which tends to cause any misunderstanding or disagreement.

Usual ending
(signed) Hussein Bin Talal
Amman 2 Safar 1387 A.H.
11 May 1967 A.D.

212. FCO8/59: Confidential: British Political Agency, Abu Dhabi: Meeting between King Faisal and Shaikh Zaid: 11 April 1967.

213. It should be noted that Sultan Said's opinion on the future of the Union of Arab Emirates proved to be prophetic:

though there were too great inherent differences between Bahrain and Qatar on the one hand and the Trucial States on the other for a Union embracing them all to stick together. He thought a Union consisting only of the Trucial States could be brought into being relatively easily if Qatar stopped interfering (FCO8/585: Confidential: Notes on Conversation between the Sultan and the Political Resident: 12–14 May 1968).

214. FCO8/964: Confidential: British Embassy, Jedda: Saudi/Abu Dhabi Relations: 25 June 1969.

215. FCO8/583: Secret: King Faisal's Relations with the Sultan: British Embassy: 19 April 1967.

216. FCO8/583: Secret: British Residency, Bahrain: Saudi Omani Relations: 9 July 1968.

217. Faisal denied that training was taking place:

Indicating that the scope of this assistance has been expanding. I understand that Faisal has denied that military training is being given in Saudi Arabia to the rebel recruits; but the evidence suggests that not only Omani but also Dhofari rebels are receiving military training at Taif. The reports have also mentioned other kinds of help to subversive movements in the Sultanate (FCO8/583: Secret: British Residency Bahrain: King Faisal's relations with the Sultan: 4 April 1967).

218. Summary of Annual U.S. Policy Assessment toward Saudi Arabia: Department Of State: Confidential: Issue Date: 30 March 1966.

219. FCO8/638: Confidential: British Consulate General, Muscat: 31 August 1968.

220. Halliday, p. 284.

221. Kelly, J. B. (1980). *Arabia, the Gulf and the West.* New York: Basic Books, p. 118.

222. For a short review of the Wahhabi onslaught on Oman, see Kelly's (1956). "The Buraimi Oasis Dispute." *International Affairs* 32: 318–326.

223. Behbehani, p. 164.

224. China's political support to the imamate can be clearly seen from the announcements made by China's embassy in Cairo:

The Chinese people sympathize with the Omani people in their struggle against imperialism, Chinese Ambassador Chen Chia-Kang told the Director of Oman office, Mohamed Al-Harsy [al-Harithi] when the latter called on the Ambassador today. The Omani representative told the Ambassador about British aggression in Oman and asked whether he had received the memorandum of the Arab League soliciting support for the Omani people from the Bandung Conference countries. The Ambassador said he had received the memorandum and would forward it to his government as soon as possible (Behbhani [1981], p. 166).

225. Bin Huwaidin, M. (2002). *China's Relations with Arabia and the Gulf, 1949–1999.* London: Routledge, p. 103.

226. Behbehani, p. 164.

227. Ibid.

228. FCO8/1072: Confidential: Omani Rebels: British Embassy, Beirut, Lebanon: 5 March 1969.

229. Behbehani, p. 171.

230. Allen and Rigsbee, p. 27.

231. Ibid.

232. Peterson (1978), p. 58.

233. Ibid., p. 68.

234. Allen and Rigsbee, p. 27.

235. Behbehani, p. 164.

236. Ibid.

237. Bin Huwaidin, p. 103.

238. Halliday, p. 284.

239. Calabrese, J. (1990). "From Flyswatters to Silkworms: The Evolution of China's Role in West Asia." *Asian Survey* 30: 862–876.

240. FCO8/1072: Confidential: Soviet Bloc involvement in Dhofar: British Residency, Bahrain: 21 January 1969.

241. FCO8/638: Confidential: Muscat and Oman-British Residency, Bahrain: 3 September 1968.

242. Smiley and Kemp, p. 40.

243. Burdett, A. (1997). "Preface." In *Records of Oman 1961–1965.* Farnham Common, United Kingdom: Archive Edition Ltd.

244. Clements, p. 64. Kelly also expresses the same opinion when he states that "for the rest of his life he was to be haunted, however irrationally, by the specter of another descent into penury" (Kelly [1980], p. 119).

245. Skeet (1974), p. 164.

246. Peterson (1978), p. 58.

247. FCO8/1667: Secret: British military involvement in Oman: 10 September 1971. The date of this report indicates that despite Qaboos' accession and his prudent and intensive campaign against the rebels, they were still a force to contend with.

248. FCO8/1074: Confidential: A Coastal Trip from Sur to Sohar: British Consulate General: Muscat: 14 October 1969.

249. FCO8/1422: Confidential: Shaikh Ahmad al Harthi: British Consulate General Muscat: 4 April 1970.

250. FCO8/1072: Secret: [Title not available]: 25 November 1969.

251. FCO8/1072: Confidential: Dhofar: British Consulate General, Muscat: 30 October 1969.

252. FCO8/1428: Confidential: Muscat Oman: British Embassy Tehran: 11 March 1970.

253. FCO8/1428: Confidential: Sultanate/Iran Relations-British Residency Bahrain: 24 March 1970.

254. Allen and Rigsbee, p. 28.

255. FCO8/1422: Secret: Security Situation in Oman: British Consulate General, Muscat: 17 June 1970.

SAF's investigations now make clear that members of the political 'cells' in Mutrah, Summail and Nizwa, which they have long had under surveillance, were involved in incidents of 12 June … Inevitably, recent events are now common knowledge here and this has led to a crop of rumours stimulated by the distribution of subversive literature not only in Nizwa, but also in Summail, Muscat and Matrah.

256. FCO8/1669: Foreign and Commonwealth Office: Sultanate of Oman: Annual Review for 1970: 4 January 1971.

CHAPTER 3

1. FCO8/1669: Confidential: Sultanate of Oman: Annual Review for 1970. Her Majesty's Consul-General, Muscat, to Her Majesty's political resident in the Persian Gulf: 4 January 1971.

2. FCO 8/1676: Confidential: Impression of Oman: 5 August 1971. The First and the Last: Her Majesty's Ambassador at Muscat to the Secretary of State for Foreign and Commonwealth Affairs.

3. Mockaitis, T. R. (1995). British Counterinsurgency in the Post-Imperial Era. Manchester, United Kingdom: University Press/St. Martin's Press, p. 76.

4. FCO8/1672: Secret: The Sultanate and ORM: British Consulate General, Muscat: 28 December 1970.

5. FCO8 1674.
Another petition was sent the following month essentially repeating the same objection:

Two Petitions from Ghalib Bin Ali, Imam of Oman, concerning Oman.
     The situation in Oman had not changed being under the succumb [sic] of foreign rule. We strongly object Oman to be a member of United Nations. We beseech you

to carry out the UNO regulations. We request you to distribute our memorandum to Security Council and UNO Assembly (FCO8/164: 22 July 1971).

6. FCO1674: Confidential.
7. FCO8/1676: Confidential: British Embassy Cairo: 28 July 1971.
8. Confidential: Saudi/Omani Relations: 28 June 1971.
9. FCO8/1673: Confidential: 9 July 1971.
10. Skeet, I. (1992). *Oman: Politics and Development*. Basingstoke, United Kingdom: Macmillan, p. 58.
11. FCO8/1671: Confidential: British Embassy, Muscat: 20 September 1971.
12. FCO8/1679: Confidential: 1971.
13. FCO8/1679: Confidential: [No date available, but probably 1971].
14. FCO8/1676: Confidential: Received 20 September 1971.
15. Both ensuing records highlight the Sultanate's dilemma with the Arab league. First,

Arab League: Oman had applied for membership of the Arab League but did not take the institution very seriously. In this they were at one with the Egyptians. No progress had been made at the League meeting at Ambassadorial level, but he hoped that Oman would get in when the ministerial session was held later this year. If Oman was not accepted then 'to hell with them'. There were several Arab states which would recognize Oman, including the Egyptians, and the Arab League would thus be outflanked. Application for the Arab league had in any case only been a stepping-stone for membership of the United Nations. Certain Arab countries, including Iraq, had urged Oman to do something to help them over the position of Ghalib, but there was a limit to what could be done. There was no possibility of recognizing the Imamate, but Ghalib and Talib could return as private individuals. The Kuwaitis were at present acting as self appointed mediators, but he did not know if anything would come of this (FCO 8/1676: Confidential: Record of A Meeting with Tariq: 3 May 1971).

Second,

Interview with Omani Sultan Qaboos and his Prime Minister Tarok Ben Taymour, have been published in Beirut this week by the weekly A. Sayyad and its sister Daily Al Anwar. The two Omani leaders spoke about present conditions in their country, relations with Britain, the other Gulf Emirates and the Dhofar revolution. Here is a report from our contributor in Beirut:

'Sultan Qaboos who took over power from his father last year, said that his country was facing opposition on almost every front. He specifically referred to the opposition to Oman request for membership in the Arab League. This opposition is championed mainly by the Government of South Yemen. Qaboos said that the South Yemeni delegate at the Arab league claimed that a revolution was going on in Dhofar, therefore, Oman could not be permitted to join the League as an independent state. The Omani Sultan went on; 'The Aden delegate forgot that a day earlier his country's Information Minister announced that revolution was going on in Headhammaur. Why, then, should South Yemen be permitted to be an Arab League member?'

The Prime Minister Tarek Ben Taymour said it was not true that Chinese Communist experts were with the Dhofari rebels. He added that some of the rebels might have been to China where they got some training, but there were no Chinese in Oman (FCO 8/1710: Arabic Tropical Programs: Friday, 2.7.71).

16. FCO8/1676: Confidential: Received 29 September 1971.

17. Iraq's position toward the entire issue can be described as an incoherent vacillation between rejecting the sultanate's bid for membership and supporting it. In the end, however, Iraq chose to support the sultanate (FCO8/16178: Restricted: British Embassy Baghdad: 28 July 1971).

18. See the following record:

Confidential
United Kingdom Mission To The United Nations
845 Third Avenue, New York, N.Y. 10022

The Acting Permanent Representative of Sudan dully buttonholed me in the UN today and, having explained that he was speaking as this month's Chairman of the Arab League, went on ... he already spoken to the Soviets Mission and to the French. Malik had assured him that the Soviet attitude would be determined by the decision of the Arabs and, without actually saying so, had implied that this meant that he would if necessary, be prepared to veto a resolution recommending Oman's admission (FCO8/1674: 18 June 1971).

19. FCO8/1674: 8 June 1971.

20. Katz, M. N. (1986). *Russia & Arabia: Soviet Foreign Policy toward the Arabian Peninsula*. Baltimore, MD: Johns Hopkins University Press, p. 114.

21. As Peterson asserts, "The interest appeared as early as Qaboos's accession in 1970 when the Shah sent a congratulatory cable to the new Sultan. The establishment of diplomatic relations in August 1971 was followed by several meetings between the two rulers." Peterson, J. E. (1977). "Guerrilla Warfare and Ideological Confrontation in the Arabian Peninsula: The Rebellion in Dhufar." *World Affairs* 139 (Spring): 279–295, p. 285.

22. FCO8/1674: 17 June 1971.

23. FCO8/1676: Confidential: British Embassy Cairo: 13 October 1971.

24. Kechichian, J. A. (1995). *Oman and the World: The Emergence of an Independent Foreign Policy*. Santa Monica, CA: Rand, p. 72.

25. FCO8/1679: Confidential: Received 16 December 1971.

26. The record in the archives does not indicate from whom or where the assessment originated, but most probably it is from a British representative either in Saudi itself or in Bahrain.

27. FCO8/1679: Confidential: 15 December 1971.

28. Allen, C. H., and W. L. Rigsbee (2000). *Oman under Qaboos: From Coup to Constitution, 1970–1996*. London: Frank Cass, p. 192.

29. Mockaitis, p. 74.

30. Bin Huwaidin, M. (2002). *China's Relations with Arabia and the Gulf, 1949–1999*. London: Routledge, p. 202.

31. Peterson (1977), p. 281.

32. Katz, p. 112.

33. The military cost of battling the insurgency proved to be daunting, as the following quote indicates:

During the Qaboos period of the Dhofar war (1970-75), the military budget increased rapidly, with military expenditure starting from a low in 1970 of $123 million (15.2 per cent of GNP), and rising in 1971 to $144 million (15.9 per cent of GNP), in 1972 to $242 million (25 per cent of GNP), and in 1973 to $366 million (37.5 per cent of GNP). Following a slight decline in 1974 to $283 million (28.3 per cent of GNP), military expenditure was again up in 1975 to $645 million (40.9 per cent of GNP). Allen and Rigsbee, pp. 65–66.

34. Katz, p. 112.

35. Mockaitis, p. 77.

36. Ibid.

37. Bin Huwaidin, pp. 104–105.

38. Ibid., p. 106.

39. Katz, p. 113.

40. Bin Huwaidin, pp. 104–105.

41. Yodfat, A. (1983). *The Soviet Union and the Arabian Peninsula: Soviet Policy towards the Persian Gulf and Arabia.* London: St. Martin's Press, p. 14.

42. Katz, p. 114.

43. Yodfat, p. 14.

44. Peterson (1977), p. 284.

45. FO106/756: Secret: British Interests In The Persian Gulf: 2 September 1969.

46. A report on 8 January 1972 in the *Manchester Guardian*, a weekly newspaper, put the number of the SAS operating in Oman only at twenty-two, in contrast to Peterson's numbers indicated above.

47. Peterson (1977), p. 285.

48. Ibid., p. 286.

49. Marschall, C. (2003). *Iran's Persian Gulf Policy: From Khomeini to Khatami.* London: Routledge Curzon, p. 9.

50. Ibid.

51. Peterson (1977), p. 286. It may not be a coincidence that the Sultanate's acknowledgment of Iranian participation came in February 1974, the same year that the PFLO had held a press conference on 7 January in Beirut. The press conference was meant to indicate the cooperation of the "imperialist forces" against the "people's revolution in Dhofar." The Shah Army Attack Oman Revolution." *Workers World* 16: 12 (1974).

52. Marschall, p. 9.

53. The only source that this researcher came across that corroborates Marschall's estimation of Iranian troops in Oman is the article cited in the above footnote. Needless to say, a press conference by the PFLO is liable to exaggerate Iranian involvement. Another report by the *People's World*, not exactly friendly to Muscat either, cites the PFLOAG itself as a source of the number of Iranian forces in Oman, stating that "up to 3,000 Iranian troops are fighting in Oman, together with air force and naval units." "Iranian Troops Play Policeman in Oman." *People's World* 37: 5 (1974).

54. Peterson (1977), p. 286.

55. Katz, p. 112.

56. Peterson (1977), p. 286.

57. Safran, N. (1985). *Saudi Arabia: The Ceaseless Quest for Security*. Cambridge, MA: Harvard University Press, p. 138.

58. Peterson (1977), p. 286.

59. Ibid., pp. 289–290.

60. Perkins, K. (1979). "Oman 1975: The Year of Decision." *RUSI* 124: 38–45, p. 38. Indeed, the *Guardian* was reporting, on 18 June 1975, that "Oman rebels fight on," with "PFLO units conducted[ing] daily raids against enemy supply lines and troop movements."

61. The PFLO, predictably, however, did not recognize this defeat, and even in 1977, its leadership continued to claim that the "Omani revolution is not over and has not been defeated." "The Omani Revolution Has Not Been Defeated." *Workers World* 19: 7 (1977).

62. Safran, p. 285.

63. Peterson (1977), p. 288.

64. Rigsbee II, W. L. (1990). "American Foreign Policy toward the Sultanate of Oman: 1977–1987." In *Graduate Education and Research*. Cincinnati, OH: University of Cincinnati, p. 70.

65. Peterson, J. E. (1978). *Oman in the Twentieth Century: Political Foundations of an Emerging State*. London: Croom Helm, p. 193.

66. Zahlan, R. S. (1998). The Making of the Modern Gulf States: Kuwait, Bahrain, Qatar, the United Arab Emirates and Oman. Reading, United Kingdom: Ithaca Press, p. 132.

67. Ibid.

68. Allen and Rigsbee, p. 65.

69. As Skeet rightly asserts, "Nothing could have been accomplished without the attitude, inspiration and leadership of Sultan Qaboos himself." Skeet (1992), p. 51.

70. Ibid.

71. Ibid.

72. Safran, p. 267.

73. Ibid.

74. Kechichian, p. 115.

75. Safran, p. 267.

76. Kechichian, pp. 145–146.

77. Safran, p. 267.

78. Ibid.

79. Ibid., pp. 285–286.

80. Ibid., p. 286.

81. Kechichian, p. 116.

82. Ibid.

83. Ibid.

84. Pradhan, B. (1999). "Indo-Omani Relations: Political, Security and Socio-Cultural Dimensions." In *India and Oman: History, State, Economy and Foreign Policy*. E. A. K. Pasha, ed. New Delhi, India: Gyan Sagar Publications, p. 77.

85. Safran, pp. 285–286.

86. Kechichian, p. 108.

87. Pasha, A. K. (1999). "Aspects of Oman's Foreign Policy." In *India and Oman: History, State, Economy and Foreign Policy*. New Delhi, India: Gyan Sagar Publications, pp. 115–116.

88. Katz, p. 123.

89. Ibid.

90. Bin Huwaidin, p. 203.

91. Ibid., p. 204.

92. Ibid., p. 205.

93. Ibid.

94. Dunn, M. (1992). "Oman: Defending the Strait." *Middle East Insight*. 9: 48–53, p. 48.

95. Ramazani, R. K. (1986). *Revolutionary Iran: Challenge and Response in the Middle East*. Baltimore, MD: Johns Hopkins University Press, p. 122.

96. Duke, J. A. (1987). "Oman, the Gulf and the United States." In *Oman: Economic, Social and Strategic Developments*. B. R. Pridham, ed. London, Croom Helm, p. 179.

97. The Carter Doctrine stated, "An attempt by any outside force to gain control of the Persian Gulf region will be regarded as an assault on the vital interests of the USA, and as such as assault will be repelled by any means necessary, including military force." Skeet (1992), p. 83.

98. Kechichian, p. 101.

99. Ramazani, p. 122.

100. El-Rayyes, R. (1987). "Oman's Role in the Gulf Co-Operation Council and the Region." In *Oman: Economic, Social and Strategic Developments*. B. R. Pridham, ed. London: Croom Helm, p. 198.

101. Ibid.

102. Duke (1987), pp. 186–191.

103. Pasha (1999), p. 111.

104. Gawlik, J. A. (1982). *Persian Gulf Security: The United States and Oman, the Gulf Cooperation Council, and Western Allied Participation*. Department of National Security Affairs, Naval Postgraduate School (Monterrey, CA), p. 49.

105. Ibid.

106. Ibid.

107. Ibid.

108. Not to be outdone, Libya and PFLO also condemned the agreement. Ibid., p. 50.

109. The agreement is very clear. It does not mean the establishment of American bases as that term is generally used. The installations involved will remain absolutely under Omani control, with no American military personnel stationed on them. The agreement does stipulate that the United States may have access to Omani facilities, under specific conditions, if and when that may be necessary, with Omani permission to be granted in each case. Mahrouki, H. (1986). *Oman's Role in the Strategic Balance*. Carlisle Barracks, Army War College (Carlisle Barracks, PA), p. 14.

110. Ministry of Information, Oman. (2001). *The Royal Speeches of H.M. Sultan Qaboos bin Said: 1970–2000*. Muscat, Oman: Ministry of Information.

111. Pasha (1999), p. 111.

112. "Interview with Sultan Qaboos of Oman." *Al-Majallah*, pp. 12–17, 1992. FBIS-MEA-V-82-089, 7 May 1982.

113. Acharya, A. (1989). *U.S. Military Strategy in the Gulf*. London: Routledge, p. 113.

114. Ibid., p. 114.

115. Memorandum: National Security Council: 26 March 1980. Memorandum for: Zbigniew Brzezinski. From: Paul B. Henze: Subject: Oman and the U.S. Relationship.

116. Rigsbee, pp. 70–73.

117. Kechichian, p. 148.

118. Graz (1982). *The Omanis, Sentinels of the Gulf*. London: Longman, p. 175.

119. Owtram, F. C. (2004). *A Modern History of Oman: Formation of the State since 1920*. London: I. B. Tauris, p. 151.

120. Kechichian, p. 101.

121. Peterson, J. E. (1987). Oman's Odyssey: From Imamate to Sultanate. *Oman: Economic, Social and Strategic Developments*. B. R. Pridham, ed. London: Croom Helm, p. 170.

122. Ramazani (1986), p. 13.

123. Ibid., p. 114.

124. Kechichian, p. 104.

125. Graz, L. (1990). *The Turbulent Gulf*. London: Tauris, in association with the Gulf Centre for Strategic Studies, p. 215.

126. Allen, C. H. (1987). *Oman: The Modernization of the Sultanate*. Boulder, CO: Croom Helm, p. 115.

127. Pasha (1999), pp. 113–114

128. Allen and Rigsbee, p. 184.

129. When Iran threatened to close the Strait in mid-1983 and overthrow "retarded" rulers, the Omani ambassador to Kuwait stated that the "strategic Strait of Hormuz is Omani territory and neither Iran nor any other country has the right to interfere in Oman's internal affairs … [We] will not accept this nor allow it to occur." Kechichian, p. 103.

130. Ibid., pp. 10–11.

131. Marschall, pp. 91–92.

132. Ibid., p. 92.

133. Graz (1990), p. 215.

134. Kechichian, p. 105.

135. Ibid.

136. "Muscat's mediation to end the war was not only limited to the parties concerned directly [Iran and Iraq] but was extensively followed with outside powers such as Pakistan and China." Ibid., p. 233.

137. Marschall, p. 103.

138. Peterson (1987), pp. 172–173.

139. Kechichian, p. 93.

140. Graz (1990), p. 214.

CHAPTER 4

1. Allen, C. H., and W. L. Rigsbee (2000). *Oman under Qaboos: From Coup to Constitution, 1970–1996*. London: Frank Cass, pp. 185–186.

2. Kechichian, J. A. (1995). *Oman and the World: The Emergence of an Independent Foreign Policy*. Santa Monica, CA: Rand, pp. 157–158.

3. Ibid., p. 196.

4. Ibid.

5. According to Owtram, during the opening stages of the conflict, "Omani troops were the only GCC force able to communicate effectively with Western forces due to

similarities in equipment and procedures." Owtram, F. C. (2004). *A Modern History of Oman: Formation of the State since 1920*. London: I. B. Tauris, p. 173.

6. Kechichian, pp. 157–158.

7. Ibid., p. 75.

8. Marschall, C. (2003). *Iran's Persian Gulf Policy: From Khomeini to Khatami*. London: Routledge Curzon, p. 153.

9. Ibid.

10. Helms, C. (1989). "Interview with Iraqi Oil Minister." *Middle East Insight* 6, p. 23.

11. Hussain, A. (2000). "Iran-GCC Relations." In *India, Iran and the GCC States: Political Strategy and Foreign Policy*. A. K. Pasha, ed. New Delhi, India: Manas Publications, pp. 180–181.

12. Ibid.

13. Kechichian, p. 157.

14. In particular, it was the U.S. Air Force that benefited the most from the use of pre-positioned supplies at Thumrait, which saved Washington the equivalent of 1,800 C-14 airlift sorties, thus increasing the quickness of the U.S. buildup during Desert Shield. Cordesman, A. H., and Center for Strategic and International Studies (1997). *Bahrain, Oman, Qatar, and the UAE: Challenges of Security*. Boulder, CO: Westview, p. 204.

15. Ibid., p. 205.

16. Gause, F. G. (1994). *Oil Monarchies: Domestic and Security Challenges in the Arab Gulf States*. New York: Council on Foreign Relations Press, p. 130.

17. Allen and Rigsbee.

18. Dunn, M. (1992). "Oman: Defending the Strait." *Middle East Insight* 9: 48–53.

19. Pasha, A. K. (2000). "Iran and the Arab World in the Nineties: Conflict and Cooperation." In *India, Iran and the GCC States: Political Strategy and Foreign Policy*. New Delhi, India: Manas Publications, p. 140.

20. Kechichian, pp. 89–90.

21. Ibid.

22. Interview with Oman's information Minister: *Oman Daily Observer*, 20 November 1991.

23. Kechichian cites various Omani officials expressing dismay at the lack of true progress in security cooperation:

In April 1993, General 'Ali Majid Al-Mamari, the Minister of Palace Office Affairs, articulated Muscat's anxiety at the lack of progress. He regretted the misunderstanding that existed on the proposal and "expressed the hope that others will eventually correct their views." The GCC Assistant Secretary-General for Political Affairs, Saif bin Hashil Al-Maskari, was more forthcoming when he concluded that "implementation of the military aspects of the [Damascus] declaration would be finalized on the basis of separate bilateral agreements between individual states" (Kechichian, p. 90).

24. Ram, H. (1995). "Oman." *In Middle East Contemporary Survey*. Avi Ayalon, ed. Boulder, CO: Westview Press, p. 561.

25. Al-Husayni, H. "Interview with Yusuf Bin-'Alawi, Omani Minister of State for Foreign Affairs." In *Muscat*. FBIS-NES-2003-1220, 5 December 1996, p. 17.

26. Pelletreau, R. H. (1996). "Contemporary Oman and U.S.-Oman Relations." *Middle East Policy* 4: 1–29, p. 20.

27. Ibid.

28. Allen and Rigsbee, p. 187.

29. Gause (1994), p. 190.

30. *Jerusalem Post* (1 July 1993).

31. Gawdat, B. (1999). "Security in the Gulf: The View from Oman." *Security Dialogue* 30: 445–458, p. 453.

32. Jarrah, N. (1994). "Divergent Approaches." *Middle East International* 7: 12–13.

33. Ghanim, A. (2000). "The GCC and Iraq." *Middle East Policy* 7, p. 98.

34. Ibid.

35. Gawdat, p. 453.

36. "Deputy Foreign Minster Interviewed on Gulf Issues." FBIS-NES-95-077, 15 April 1995, p. 10.

37. Dunford, D. (1995). "The US and Oman: An Enduring Partnership." *Middle East Insight* 12: 48–75, p. 63.

38. Al-Husayni, p. 17.

39. Ghanim, p. 99.

40. Sick, G. (1996). "The United States and Iran: Truth and Consequences." *Contention* 5: 59–78, p. 71.

41. Gawdat, p. 454.

42. Joyce, A. (1995). "Interview with Sultan Qaboos bin Sail Al Said." *Middle East Policy* 3: 1–6, p. 4.

43. Sick (1996), p. 61.

44. For a text of Secretary Baker's remarks, see "America's Stake in the Persian Gulf." *Dispatch 1*, 10 September 1990.

45. Hussain, p. 186.

46. Sick (1996), p. 67.

47. Gawdat, p. 454.

48. Allen and Rigsbee.

49. Marschall, p. 158

50. Mattair, T. (1994). "Interview with UN Ambassador Kamak Kharazi of Iran." *Middle East Policy* 3: 125–135, p. 130.

51. Marschall, p. 115.

52. These efforts did include Egypt as well, where Muscat served "as a go between for Cairo and Iran concerning the freeing of Egyptian nationals drafted into the Iraqi army and taken as prisoners of War." Mattair, p. 130.

53. Marschall, p. 114.

54. Kechichian, p. 107

55. Ibid.

56. "Oman: Channel for Oman-Iran Dialogue Opened; Nateq-Nuri to Visit." FBIS-NES-96-223, 19 November 1996.

57. Ibid.

58. Ibid.

59. "Air Force Chief to Visit Tehran; Velayati to Visit Muscat." FBIS-NES-97-069, Monday, 10 March 1997.

60. "Omani Air Force Commander Visits Iran, Discusses Security." FBIS-NES-97-073, Friday, 14 March 1997.

61. Alawi stated "We see these differences between the West and Iran as a situation which might jeopardize the stability in the region." "Oman Frowns at US Iran Policy." *UPI*, Washington, DC, 9 May 1996.

62. Riphenburg, C. J. (1998). *Oman: Political Development in a Changing World*. Westport, CT: Praeger, p. 197.

63. For a short perspective on both sides of the aisle, see the chapters "The Islands Question" and "An Iranian Perspective" in Sick, G., and L. G. Potter (2002). *Security in the Persian Gulf: Origins, Obstacles and the Search for Consensus*. New York: Palgrave.

64. "Qatar: GCC Head on Border Disputes, Other Issues." FBIS-NES-97-002, 6 January 1997.

65. Al-Husayni, p. 17.

66. Marschall, p. 154.

67. Ibid., p. 156.

68. Okruhlik, G. (2003). "Saudi Arabian-Iranian Relations: External Rapprochement and Internal Consolidation." *Middle East Policy*. X: 113–125, p. 114.

69. Ramazani, R. K. (1998). "The Emerging Arab-Iranian Rapprochement: Towards an Integrated U.S. Policy in the Middle East." *Middle East Policy*. 6: 45–62, p. 54.

70. Marschall, p. 157.

71. Lotfian, S. (2002). "Regional Security System in the Persian Gulf." In *Security in the Persian Gulf: Origins, Obstacles, and the Search for Consensus*. G. Sick and L. G. Potter, eds. New York: Palgrave, p. 123.

72. Al-Husayni, p. 17.

73. Pelletreau, p. 22.

74. Allen and Rigsbee, p. 189.

75. Kechichian, pp. 95–96.

76. Pasha, A. K. (1999). "Aspects of Oman's Foreign Policy." In *India and Oman: History, State, Economy and Foreign Policy*. New Delhi, India: Gyan Sagar Publications, p. 118.

77. Kechichian, p. 97.

78. Allen and Rigsbee, p. 189.

79. Kechichian, pp. 98–99.

80. Ibid., p. 255.

81. "Yemeni Foreign Minister Discusses GCC Membership." FBIS-NES-2002-0103, 03 January 2002.

82. Pasha (1999), p. 118.

83. Allen and Rigsbee, p. 190.

84. Al-Husayni, p. 17.

85. Al-Alkim, H. H. (1989). *The Foreign Policy of the United Arab Emirates*. London: Al Saqi Books, p. 175.

86. Quandt, W. B. (1981). *Saudi Arabia in the 1980's: Foreign Policy, Security, and Oil*. Washington, DC: The Brookings Institution, p. 61.

87. Al-Alkim, H. H. (1992). "The Environment of Saudi Foreign Policy." *Arab Journal of Political Science* 7: 39–71.

88. Ibid.

89. Ramazani (1998), p. 51.

90. Gawdat, p. 450.

91. Kechichian, p. 253.

92. Allen and Rigsbee, p. 207.

93. "Omani Envoy Briefs League Chief on Rabin's Visit." FBIS-NES-95-001, 1 January 1995.

It should be noted that not long after Rabin's visit, there were reports circulating that both Oman and Kuwait were already involved in naval exercises with Israel. Both Oman and Kuwait denied that they "would take part in a joint Israeli Arab exercises as reported in Tel Aviv." The Omani defense Minister stated that "this report is without any foundation and has no bearing with reality." ("Kuwait, Oman Deny Naval Exercises with Israel." FBIS-NES-95-034, 20 February 1995.)

94. By April 1995, reports were circulating that Oman had agreed to open an Israeli Liaison Office in Oman, which the Sultanate denied at the time. ("Request to Open Israeli Liaison Office Rejected." FBIS-NES-95-082, 25 April 1995.)

95. Pasha (1999), p. 116.

96. "Oman: Peres Gets 'Red Carpet' Treatment during Visit." FBIS-NES-96-064, 1 April 1996.

97. Ibid.

98. "Omani Official Says Agreement with Israel to Boost Trade." FBIS-NES-96-020, 28 January 1996.

99. Ibid.

100. "Qatar: GCC Head on Border Disputes, Other Issues." FBIS-NES-97-002, 1 January 1997.

101. "GCC Official on Albright Talks, Iran Ties." FBIS-WEU-97-259, 16 September 1997.

102. "Oman: Minister on Regional Problems, Hopes." FBIS-NES-96-237, 5 December 1996.

103. "Israel, Oman: Israel Participates in Two Commercial Exhibits in Oman." FBIS-NES-97-034, 13 February 1997.

104. "Israeli Companies Banned from Oman's Trade Fair." FBIS-NES-97-097, 7 April 1997.

Another report on the banning of Israeli participation stated specifically why the Sultanate froze its relations with Israel, recording that "the freezing of trade relations between the Sultanate of Oman and Israel in light of the latter's decision to build settlement in occupied Jerusalem." ("Oman Rejects Israeli Participation in Computer Fair." FBIS-NES-97-097, 7 April 1997.)

105. "Israel, Oman: Israel Participates in Two Commercial Exhibits in Oman." FBIS-NES-97-034, 13 February 1997.

106. "Qatari Foreign Minister Views Normalization with Israel." FBIS-NES-96-220, 12 November 1996.

107. "Oman: Minister Views Regional Issues, Iraq." FBIS-NES-98-047, 14 Feb 1998.

108. Gawdat, p. 450.

109. "Omani Foreign Minister on Gulf Security." FBIS-NES-1999-1129, 22 November 1999.

110. Kechichian, p. 253.

111. "Oman: Official Will Relay GCC Viewpoint to Tehran." FBIS-NES-96-217, Thursday, 7 November 1996.

112. Hiro, D. (2001). *Neighbors, Not Friends: Iraq and Iran after the Gulf War*. London: Routledge, p. 120.

113. "Saudi Arabia: Saudi Arabia Not to Allow US to Use Territory for Attack." FBIS-NES-98-319, 15 November 1998.

114. Ibid.

115. "Iraq: Gulf States Oppose Military Strike on Iraq." FBIS-NES-98-309, 5 November 1998.

116. "Qatar: 'Text' of Damascus Declaration Statement." FBIS-NES-98-321, 17 November 1998.

117. Ibid.

118. Heisbourg, F. (2003). "A Work in Progress: The Bush Doctrine and Its Consequences." *The Washington Quarterly* 26 (Spring): 75–88, p. 76.

119. Stratfor.com. (2 May 2002). "Oman Statement Blow to U.S. Plans for Iraq." http://www.stratfor.com.

120. *Times of Oman* (2002).

121. "Iraqi Foreign Minister Delivers Saddam's Letter to Sultan of Oman." FBIS-NES-2002-1006, October 6, 2002.

122. Foley, S. (2003). "The Gulf Arabs and the New Iraq: The Most to Gain and the Most to Lose?" *Middle East Review of International Affairs* 7, p. 26.

123. Henderson, S. (2003). *The New Pillar: Conservative Arab Gulf States and U.S. Strategy.* Washington, DC: The Washington Institute for Near East Policy, p. 15.

124. Ibid., p. 69.

125. Foley, p. 30.

126. Gause, F. G. (2003). *The Approaching Turning Point: The Future of U.S. Relations with the Gulf States.* Brookings Institution, Saban Center for Middle East Policy, Washington, DC, p. 23.

127. McMillan, J., and Winner, A. (2003). "Toward a New Regional Security Architecture." *The Washington Quarterly* 26, p. 162.

128. Gause (2003), pp. 23–24.

129. Foley, p. 27.

130. Foley, p. 27.

131. Duke, J. A. (2003). "The U.S.-GCC Relationship; Is a Glass Leaking or a Glass Filling?" In *The Middle East and the United States: A Historical and Political Reassessment.* D. W. Lesch, ed. Boulder, CO: Westview Press, p. 423.

132. Sick, G. (2003). "Iran: Confronting Terrorism." *The Washington Quarterly* 26: 1–16.

133. "Iran, Oman Issue Joint Communique at End of Khatami's Visit." (2004). FBIS-NES-2004-1007.

134. Gvosdev, R. T. N. K. (2004). "Pragmatism in the Midst of Iranian Turmoil." *The Washington Quarterly* 27, p. 39.

135. Ibid., p. 40.

136. Ibid., p. 39.

137. Ibid., p. 47

138. Chubin, S., and R. Litwak (2003). "Debating Iran's Nuclear Aspirations." *The Washington Quarterly* 26: 1–16.

139. Sick (2003).

140. Gvosdev, pp. 47–48.

141. Sick (2003).

142. Ehteshami, A. (2003). "Iran-Iraq Relations after Saddam." *The Washington Quarterly* 26, p. 45.

143. Gvosdev, p. 46.

Bibliography

PRIMARY SOURCES

Unpublished documentary sources, British Foreign Office records/Public Records Office:

FCO8/1	FCO8/1675	FCO8/59
FCO8/1042	FCO8/1676	FCO8/6
FCO8/1072	FCO8/1677	FCO8/60
FCO8/1074	FCO8/1678	FCO8/605
FCO8/1077	FCO8/1679	FCO8/605
FCO8/1080	FCO8/1680	FCO8/62
FCO8/1083	FCO8/1710	FCO8/638
FCO8/1414	FCO8/1776	FCO8/638
FCO8/1422	FCO8/366	FCO8/845
FCO8/1425	FCO8/45	FCO8/849
FCO8/1426	FCO8/568	FCO8/849
FCO8/1427	FCO8/569	FCO8/857
FCO8/1428	FCO8/571	FCO8/964
FCO8/1428	FCO8/572	FO1016/760
FCO8/1667	FCO8/574	FO371/126878
FCO8/1668	FCO8/575	FO371/126879
FCO8/1668	FCO8/576	FO371/126880
FCO8/1668	FCO8/579	FO371/126883
FCO8/1669	FCO8/580	FO371/126884
FCO8/1671	FCO8/581	FO371/126885
FCO8/1672	FCO8/583	PREM11/4923-100752
FCO8/1673	FCO8/585	PREM11/4932-100752
FCO8/1674	FCO8/586	PREM11/4960-100752

(Eisenhower Presidential Library: Ann Whitman collection. U.S. Archives, Department of State.)

SECONDARY SOURCES

Al-Khalij (1988). 4 September.
Christian Science Monitor (1975). 13 February.
"Oman Rebels Fight On." *Guardian* (1975). 6–18.
International Affairs (1969). No. 4: 89.
"Oman: US Advisors Provide Training." *International Bulletin* (1975). 2 (3).
Jerusalem Post (1993). July 1.
"The Sultanate of Oman: Strategic Evolution." *Middle East Insight* (1992). 9: 32–60.
Middle East International (1999). March 26. 14.
Middle East Policy (1996). March. IV.
New York Times (1998). February 21.
New York Times (1998). October 20.
Oman Daily Observer (1991). November 20.
"Iranian Troops Play Policeman in Oman." *People's World* (1974). 37 (8).
"Reiterates Hopes for Averting War in Iraq." *Times of Oman* (2002). February 21.
"The Shah Army Attack Oman Revolution." *Workers World.* (1974). 16 (3): 12.

Abadi, J. (1982). *Britain's Withdrawal from the Middle East, 1947–1971*. Princeton, NJ: Kingston Press.
Acharya, A. (1989). *U.S. Military Strategy in the Gulf.* London: Routledge.
Agius, D. A. (2002). *In the Wake of the Dhow: The Arabian Gulf and Oman.* Reading, United Kingdom: Ithaca Press.
Akehurst, J. (1982). *We Won a War: The Campaign in Oman 1965–1975.* London: Michael Russell Publishing.
Al-Alkim, H. H. (1989). *The Foreign Policy of the United Arab Emirates.* London: Al Saqi Books.
Al-Alkim, H. H. (1992). "The Environment of Saudi Foreign Policy." *Arab Journal of Political Science.* 7: 39–71.
Al-Alkim, H. H. (2002). "The Islands Question." In *Security in the Persian Gulf: Origins, Obstacles and the Search for Consensus.* G. Sick and L. G. Potter, eds. New York: Palgrave, pp. 155–170.
Al-Marayati, A. (1966). "The Question of Oman." *Foreign Affairs Reports* 15: 99–109.
Al-Rawas, I. (2000). *Oman in Early Islamic History.* Reading, United Kingdom: Ithaca Press.
Al-Sayegh, F. (2002). "The UAE and Oman: Opportunities and Challenges in the Twenty-First Century." *Middle East Policy* 9.
Al-Yousuf, A. P. S. (1995). *Oil and the Transformation of Oman, 1970–1995: The Socio-Economic Impact.* London: Stacey International.
Alabdulkarim, A. (1997). *Political Economy and Political Development in the Arabian Peninsula: The Case of the Sultanate of Oman.* Doctoral diss., University of Southern California.
Allan, R. (1957). "Between the Saudis and the Sharks." *Reporter* 1 (17): 22–24.
Allen, C. H. (1982). "The State of Masqat in the Gulf and East Africa, 1785–1892." *International Journal of Middle East Studies* 14.
Allen, C. H. (1987). *Oman: The Modernization of the Sultanate.* Boulder, CO: Croom Helm.
Allen, C. (1991). *Thunder and Lightning—The RAF in the Gulf.* London: HMSO.

Allen, C. H., and W. L. Rigsbee (2000). *Oman under Qaboos: From Coup to Constitution, 1970–1996.* London: Frank Cass.

Allfree, P. S. (1967). *Warlords of Oman.* London: Hale.

Alterman, J. B. (2003). "Not in My Backyard: Iraq's Neighbor's Interests." *The Washington Quarterly* 26.

Amin, S. M. (2000). *Pakistan's Foreign Policy: A Reappraisal.* Oxford, United Kingdom: Oxford University Press.

Appadorai, A., and M. S. Rajan (1985). *India's Foreign Policy and Relations.* New Delhi, India: South Asian Publishers.

Arkless, D. C. (1988). *The Secret War: Dhofar 1971/1972.* London: Kimber.

Arnove, A., Ed. (2000). *Iraq Under Siege: The Deadly Impact of Sanctions and War.* Cambridge, MA: South End Press.

Azzam, A., and K. Seydo (1997). *Ibn Battuta and the Lost Shadow.* London: Hood Hood Books.

Bailey, R. W. (1988). *Records of Oman 1867–1947.* Farnham Common, Archive Editions.

Baldwin, D. (1999). "The Sanctions Debate and the Logic of Choice." *International Security* 24.

Barth, F. (1983). *Sohar: Culture and Society in an Omani Town.* Baltimore: Johns Hopkins University Press.

Bathurst, R. D. (1972). "Maritime Trade and Imamate Government: Two Principal Themes in the History of Oman to 1728." In *The Arabian Peninsula: Society and Politics.* D. Hopwood, ed. Totowa, NJ: Rowman and Littlefield.

Behbehani, H. S. H. (1981). *China's Foreign Policy in the Arab World, 1955–75: Three Case Studies.* London: Kegan Paul International.

Bhacker, M. R. (1994). *Trade and Empire in Muscat and Zanzibar: Roots of British Domination.* London: Routledge and Kegan Paul.

Bhambhri, C. P. (1987). *The Foreign Policy of India.* New Delhi, India: Sterling Publishers.

Bierschenk, T. (1989). "Oil Interests and the Formation of Centralized Government in Oman, 1920–1970." *Orient* 30.

Bin Huwaidin, M. (2002). *China's Relations with Arabia and the Gulf, 1949–1999.* London: Routledge.

Brzezinski, Z. (1997). "Differentiated Containment (Policies toward Iran and Iraq)." *Foreign Affairs* 76 (3): 20–30.

Burdett, A. (1997). *Records of Oman 1961–1965.* Farnham Common, United Kingdom: Archive Edition Ltd.

Burrows, B. (1990). *Footnotes in the Sand: The Gulf in Transition, 1953–1958.* Norwich, United Kingdom: Michael Russell Publishing.

Byman, D. (2001). "Iraq after Saddam." *The Washington Quarterly* 24.

Calabrese, J. (1990). "From Flyswatters to Silkworms: The Evolution of China's Role in West Asia." *Asian Survey* 30: 862–876.

Calabrese, J. (1994). *Revolutionary Horizons: Regional Foreign Policy in Post-Khomeini Iran.* Basingstoke: Macmillan and St Martin's Press.

Carter, J. R. L. (1982). *Tribes in Oman.* London: Peninsular Publishing. Distributed in the United Kingdom and North America by Scorpion Publications.

Chopra, S. (1980). *Studies in India's Foreign Policy.* Amritsar, India: Department of Political Science, Guru Nanak Dev University.

Chubin, S., and R. Litwak (2003). "Debating Iran's Nuclear Aspirations." *The Washington Quarterly* 26: 1–16.

Clayton, P. (1994). *Two Alpha Lima: The First Ten Years of the Trucial Oman Levies and Trucial Oman Scouts, 1950–1960*. London: Janus.

Clements, F. A. (1980). *Oman: The Reborn Land*. London: Longman.

Clements, F. A. (1994). *Oman*. Oxford, United Kingdom: Clio Press.

Committee for the Rights of Oman and the Movement for Colonial Freedom (1965). *The Oman Question and the United Nations*. London: Committee for the Rights of Oman and the Movement for Colonial Freedom.

Cordesman, A. H., and Center for Strategic and International Studies (1997). *Bahrain, Oman, Qatar, and the UAE: Challenges of Security*. Boulder, CO: Westview.

Corser, W. J. L. (1994). *The RAF Masirah Railway*. Pinner, United Kingdom: RAM Productions.

Costa, P. (1991). *Musandam: Architecture and Material Culture of a Little Known Region of Oman*. London: Immel.

Darlow, M., and R. Fawkes (1976). *The Last Corner of Arabia*. London: Namara Publications and Quartet Books.

Duke, J. A. (1987). "Oman, the Gulf and the United States." In *Oman: Economic, Social and Strategic Developments*. B. R. Pridham, ed. London: Croom Helm.

Duke, J. A. (1996). *Oman: Girding and Guarding the Gulf*. J. A. Duke, ed. Washington, DC: US-GCC Corporate Cooperation Committee.

Duke, J. A. (2003). The U.S.-GCC Relationship; Is a Glass Leaking or a Glass Filling? In *The Middle East and the United States: A Historical and Political Reassessment*. D. W. Lesch, ed. Boulder, CO: Westview Press.

Dunford, D. (1995). "The US and Oman: An Enduring Partnership." *Middle East Insight* 12: 48–75.

Dunn, M. (1992). "Oman: Defending the Strait." *Middle East Insight* 9: 48–53.

Dutt, V. P. (1999). *India's Foreign Policy in a Changing World*. New Delhi, India: Vikas Publishing House. UBS Publishers' Distributors.

Dutton, R. (1980). *Arab Village*. London: A. and C. Black.

Eden, A. (1960). *The Memoirs of Sir Anthony Eden, Full Circle*. London: Cassell.

Ederington, B., and M. J. Mazarr (1994). *Turning Point: The Gulf War and U.S. Military Strategy*. Boulder, CO: Westview Press.

Ehteshami, A. (2003). "Iran-Iraq Relations after Saddam." *The Washington Quarterly* 26.

Eickelman, D. F. (1983). "Religious Knowledge in Inner Oman." *Journal of Oman Studies* 6: 163–172.

Eickelman, D. F. (1984). "Kings and People: Oman's State Consultative Council." *Middle East Journal* 38: 51–71.

Eickelman, D. F. (1985). "From Theocracy to Monarchy: Authority and Legitimacy in Inner Oman, 1935–1957." *International Journal of the Middle East Studies* 17: 3–24.

El-Rayyes, R. (1987). Oman's Role in the Gulf Co-Operation Council and the Region. In *Oman: Economic, Social and Strategic Developments*. B. R. Pridham, ed. London: Croom Helm.

El-Solh, R. I. (1999). *The Sultanate of Oman, 1918–1939: External Affairs*. Reading, United Kingdom: Ithaca Press.

El-Solh, R. I. (1999). *The Sultanate of Oman, 1918–1939: Domestic Affairs*. Reading, United Kingdom: Ithaca Press.

El-Solh, R. I. (2000). *The Sultanate of Oman 1914–1918*. Reading, United Kingdom: Ithaca Press.

El-Solh, R. I. (2000). *The Sultanate of Oman, 1918–1939: Administrative Affairs*. Reading, United Kingdom: Ithaca Press.

El-Solh, R. I. (2000). *The Sultanate of Oman 1939–1945*. Reading, United Kingdom: Ithaca Press.

Ellits, H. F. (1988). Foreign Policy Perspectives of the Gulf States. In *Crosscurrents in the Gulf: Arab, Regional and Global Interests*. H. R. Sindelar and J.E. Peterson, eds. London: Routledge.

Esposito, J. L., and R. K. Ramazani (2001). *Iran at the Crossroads*. New York: Palgrave.

Fehmi, A. (1966). *The Question of Oman in the United Nations*. Master's thesis, The American University (Michigan).

Fiennes, R. (1995). *Where Soldiers Fear to Tread*. London: Mandarin.

Foda, E. (1958). "Controversy over Oman." *Egyptian Economic and Political Review* 4.

Foley, S. (2003). "The Gulf Arabs and the New Iraq: The Most to Gain and the Most to Lose?" *Middle East Review of International Affairs* 7.

Gause, F. G. (1994). *Oil Monarchies: Domestic and Security Challenges in the Arab Gulf States*. New York: Council on Foreign Relations Press.

Gause, F. G. (2003). *The Approaching Turning Point: The Future of U.S. Relations with the Gulf States*. Washington, DC: Brookings Institution, Saban Center for Middle East Policy.

Gawdat, B. (1999). "Security in the Gulf: The View from Oman." *Security Dialogue* 30: 445–458.

Gawlik, J. A. (1982). *Persian Gulf Security: The United States and Oman, the Gulf Cooperation Council, and Western Allied Participation*. Master's thesis, Department of National Security Affairs, Naval Postgraduate School.

Ghanim, A. (2000). "The GCC and Iraq." *Middle East Policy* 7.

Graz, L. (1982). *The Omanis, Sentinels of the Gulf*. London: Longman.

Graz, L. (1990). *The Turbulent Gulf*. London: Tauris, in association with the Gulf Centre for Strategic Studies.

Gulf Committee. (1972). *Dhofar: Britain's Colonial War in the Gulf: A Collection of Documents and Articles*. London: Gulf Committee.

Gulf Committee. (1974). *Documents of the National Struggle in Oman and the Arabian Gulf*. London: Gulf Committee.

Gulf Committee and Oman Solidarity Committee. (1975). *Women and the Revolution in Oman*. London.

Gvosdev, R. T. N. K. (2004). "Pragmatism in the Midst of Iranian Turmoil." *The Washington Quarterly* 27.

Gwynne-James, D. (2001). *Letters from Oman: A Snapshot of Feudal Times as Oil Signals Change*. Colchester: Blackwater Books.

Haksar, P. N. (1989). *India's Foreign Policy and its Problems*. New Delhi, India: Patriot Publishers.

Halliday, F. (1974). *Arabia Without Sultans*. Harmondsworth, United Kingdom: Penguin Books.

Halliday, F. (1977). *Mercenaries: "Counterinsurgency" in the Gulf*. Nottingham, United Kingdom: Bertrand Russell Peace Foundation for Spokesman Books.

Halliday, F. (2002). "The Foreign Policy of Yemen." In *The Foreign Policies of Middle East States*. R. Hinnebusch, ed. Boulder, CO: Lynne Rienner.

Hameed, M. A. (1986). *Saudi Arabia, the West, and the Security of the Gulf.* Wolfeboro, NH: Croom Helm.

Harrison, P. W. (1940). *Doctor in Arabia.* New York: Day.

Harvey, A. M. A. P. (1972). "UK Troops Fighting Rebels in Oman." *Manchester Guardian* 11 (8 January).

Hawley, D. (1990). *Oman & Its Renaissance.* London: Stacey International.

Hawley, D. (2003). *Oman.* London: Stacey International.

Hay, R. (1960). "Great Britain's Relations with Yemen and Oman." *Middle Eastern Affairs.* 5: 142–149.

Heisbourg, F. (2003). "A Work in Progress: The Bush Doctrine and Its Consequences." *The Washington Quarterly* 26 (Spring): 75–88.

Heller, K. (1977). "The Omani Revolution Not Defeated." *Workers World* 19 (3): 7.

Helms, C. (1989). "Interview with Iraqi Oil Minister." *Middle East Insight* 6.

Henderson, E. (1993). *This Strange Eventful History: Memoirs of Earlier Days in the UAE and the Sultanate of Oman.* London: Motivate.

Henderson, S. (2003). *The New Pillar: Conservative Arab Gulf States and U.S. Strategy.* Washington DC: The Washington Institute for Near East Policy.

Hill, A., and D. Hill et al. (1977). *The Sultanate of Oman: A Heritage.* London: Longman.

Hinnebusch, N. E. S. R. (2002). The Challenge of Security in the Post-Gulf War Middle East System. In *The Foreign Policies of Middle East States.* A. Ehteshami and R. H., eds. Boulder, CO: Lynne Rienner.

Hiro, D. (2001). *Neighbors, Not Friends: Iraq and Iran after the Gulf War.* London: Routledge.

Hoffman, V. (2004). "The Articulation of Ibadi Identity in Modern Oman and Zanzibar." *The Muslim World* 94: 201–216.

Holden, D. (1966). *Farewell to Arabia.* London: Rediffusion Television.

Hopkins, N. S., and S. E. Ibrahim (1997). *Arab Society: Class, Gender, Power, and Development.* Cairo, Egypt: American University in Cairo Press.

Hopwood, D., ed. (1972). *The Arabian Peninsula: Society and Politics.* Totowa, NJ: Rowman and Littlefield.

Hoskins, A. J. (1988). *A Contract Officer in the Oman.* Tunbridge Wells, United Kingdom: Costello.

Hunter, S. (1990). *Iran and the World: Continuity in a Revolutionary Decade.* Bloomington, IN: Indiana University Press.

Hunter, S. (2003). "Iran's Pragmatic Regional Policy." *Journal of International Affairs* 56.

Hunting Surveys Ltd. (1978). *Oman.* London: Hunting Surveys Ltd.

Hussain, A. (2000). Iran-GCC Relations. In *India, Iran and the GCC States: Political Strategy and Foreign Policy.* A. K. Pasha, ed. New Delhi, India: Manas Publications.

Innes, N. M. (1987). *Minister in Oman: A Personal Narrative.* Cambridge: Oleander.

Jarrah, N. (1994). "Divergent Approaches." *Middle East International* 490: 12–13.

Jeapes, T. (1980). *SAS: Operation Oman.* London: W. Kimber.

Jeapes, T. (2000). *SAS Secret War.* London: HarperCollins.

John Bartholomew and Son. (1977). *Arabian Gulf.* Edinburgh, United Kingdom: John Bartholomew and Son.

Joyce, A. (1995). "Interview with Sultan Qaboos bin Sail Al Said." *Middle East Policy* 3: 1–6.

Joyce, M. (1993). "Britain and the Sultanate of Muscat and Oman and Dependencies, 1958–59." *Diplomacy and Statecraft* 4: 90–99.

Joyce, M. (1995). *The Sultanate of Oman: A Twentieth Century History*. Westport, CT: Praeger.

Kandiah, M. D., and Gillian Staerck. (2000). "Reliable Allies: Anglo-American Relations." In *British Foreign Policy, 1955–64: Contracting Options*. W. Kaiser and G. Staerck, eds. Basingstoke, United Kingdom: MacMillan.

Katz, M. N. (1986). *Russia & Arabia: Soviet Foreign Policy toward the Arabian Peninsula*. Baltimore, MD: Johns Hopkins University Press.

Kaylani, N. (1979). "Politics and Religion in Uman: A Historical Overview." *Middle East Studies* 10: 567–579.

Kechichian, J. A. (2000). The Throne in the Sultanate of Oman. In *Middle East Monarchies: The Challenge of Modernity*. J. Kostiner, ed. Boulder, CO: Lynne Rienner Publishers.

Kechichian, J. A., and Rand Corporation (1995). *Oman and the World: The Emergence of an Independent Foreign Policy*. Santa Monica, CA: Rand.

Kelly, J. B. (1956). "The Buraimi Oasis Dispute." *International Affairs* 32: 318–326.

Kelly, J. B. (1958). "Legal and Historical Basis of the British Position in the Persian Gulf." *Middle Eastern Affairs* 1: 119–140.

Kelly, J. B. (1958). "Sovereignty and Jurisdiction in Eastern Arabia." *International Affairs* 34: 16–24.

Kelly, J. B. (1959). *Sultanate and Imamate in Oman*. Oxford, United Kingdom: University Press.

Kelly, J. B. (1964). *Eastern Arabian Frontiers*. London: Faber.

Kelly, J. B. (1972). "A Prevalence of Furies: Tribes, Politics, and Religion in Oman and Trucial Oman." In *The Arabian Peninsula: Society and Politics*. D. Hopwood, ed. London: Allen and Unwin.

Kelly, J. B. (1980). *Arabia, the Gulf and the West*. New York: Basic Books.

Khalil, M. (1962). *The Arab States and the Arab League: A Documentary Record*. Beirut, Lebanon: Khayats.

Kostiner, J., ed. (2000). *Middle East Monarchies: The Challenge of Modernity*. Boulder, CO: Lynne Rienner Publishers.

Kumar, R. (1962). "British Attitudes toward the Ibadiyya." *Journal of the Indian School of International Studies* 3: 443–450.

Landen, R. G. (1967). *Oman since 1856: Disruptive Modernization in a Traditional Arab Society*. Princeton, NJ: Princeton University Press.

Lewicki, T. (1971). "The Ibadites in Arabia and Africa." *Journal of World History* XIII.

Lotfian, S. (2002). "Regional Security System in the Persian Gulf." In *Security in the Persian Gulf: Origins, Obstacles, and the Search for Consensus*. G. Sick and L. G. Potter, eds. New York: Palgrave.

Maamiry, A. H. (1980). *Oman and Ibadhism*. New Delhi, India: Lancers Publishers.

Macmillan, H. (1973). *At the End of the Day, 1961–1963*. New York: Harper and Row.

Mahrouki, H. (1986). *Oman's Role in the Strategic Balance*. Carlisle Barracks, PA: Carlisle Barracks, Army War College.

Mann, M. (1994). *The Trucial Oman Scouts: The Story of a Bedouin Force*. Norwich, United Kingdom: Michael Russell.

Mann, P. (2000). *India's Foreign Policy in the Post Cold War Era*. New Delhi, India: Harman Publishing House.

Mansur, A. S., and V. Treichel et al. (1999). *Oman beyond the Oil Horizon: Policies toward Sustainable Growth*. Washington, DC: International Monetary Fund.

Marr, P. (2004). *The Modern History of Iraq*. Boulder, CO: Westview Press.

Marschall, C. (2003). *Iran's Persian Gulf Policy: From Khomeini to Khatami*. London: Routledge Curzon.

Mathaf Gallery (1986). *Yesterday in Oman: Tuesday 4th–Friday 14th March, 1986*. London: Mathaf Gallery.

Mattair, T. (1994). "Interview with UN Ambassador Kamak Kharazi of Iran." *Middle East Policy* 3: 125–135.

Maurizi, V. (1984). *History of Seyd Said, Sultan of Muscat*. Cambridge, United Kingdom: Oleander Press.

McMillan, J., and Winner, A. (2003). "Toward a New Regional Security Architecture." *The Washington Quarterly* 26.

Melamid, A. (1956). "The Buraimi Oasis Dispute." *Middle Eastern Affairs* 7: 56–63.

Miller, E. W., and R. M. Miller (1989). *The Third World: A Bibliography*. Monticello, IL: Vance Bibliographies.

Miller, J. (1997). "Creating Modern Oman: An Interview with Sultan Qaboos." *Foreign Affairs* 76: 13–18.

Ministry of Information, Oman. (2001). *The Royal Speeches of H.M. Sultan Qaboos bin Said: 1970–2000*. Muscat, Oman: Ministry of Information.

Mockaitis, T. R. (1995). *British Counterinsurgency in the Post-Imperial Era*. Manchester, United Kingdom: University Press. Distributed exclusively in the United States and Canada by St Martin's Press.

Mordechai, A. (1974). *Oil, Power and Politics: Conflicts in Arabia, the Red Sea and the Gulf*. London: Frank Class.

Morris, J. (1957). *Sultan in Oman*. London: Arrow.

Narayan, B. K. (1979). *Oman and Gulf Security*. New Delhi, India: Lancers Publishers.

Newsinger, J. (1998). "Jebel Akhdar and Dhofar: Footnote to Empire." *Race and Class* 39: 41–59.

Nordan, R. (1963). "The Situation in Oman: A Geopolitical Analysis." *Panta University Journal* 18: 1–17.

Okruhlik, G. (2003). "Saudi Arabian-Iranian Relations: External Rapprochement and Internal Consolidation." *Middle East Policy* X: 113–125.

O'Reilly, M. J. (1998). "Omanibalancing: Oman Confronts an Uncertain Future." *The Middle East Journal* LII: 1–16.

O'Reilly, M. J. (1999). "Oil Monarchies without Oil: Omani & Bahraini Security in a Post-Oil Era." *Middle East Policy* VI: 78–92.

Orlov, Vladimir A., and Alexander Vinnikov, (2005). "The Great Guessing Game: Russia and Iranian Nuclear Issue." *The Washington Quarterly* 49–66

Osborne, C. (1977). *The Gulf States and Oman*. London: Croom Helm.

Owtram, F. C. (2004). *A Modern History of Oman: Formation of the State Since 1920*. London: I. B. Tauris.

Pasha, A. K. (1999). "Aspects of Oman's Foreign Policy." In *India and Oman: History, State, Economy and Foreign Policy*. New Delhi, India: Gyan Sagar Publications.

Pasha, A. K. (2000). "Iran and the Arab World in the Nineties: Conflict and Cooperation." In *India, Iran and the GCC States: Political Strategy and Foreign Policy*. New Delhi, India: Manas Publications.

Pelletreau, R. H. (1996). "Contemporary Oman and U.S.-Oman Relations." *Middle East Policy* IV: 1–29.

Perersen, T. (1992). "Anglo-American Rivalry in the Middle East: The Struggle for the Buraimi Oasis, 1952–1957." *The International History Review* 14: 71–91.

Perkins, K. (1979). "Oman 1975: The Year of Decision." *RUSI* 124: 38–45.

Peterson, J. E. (1976). "Britain and the Oman War: An Arabian Entanglement." *Asian Affairs* 63: 285–298.

Peterson, J. E. (1976). "The Revival of the Ibadi Imamate in Oman and the Threat to Muscat 1913–1920." *Arabian Studies* 3: 165–188.

Peterson, J. E. (Spring 1977). "Guerrilla Warfare and Ideological Confrontation in the Arabian Peninsula: The Rebellion in Dhufar." *World Affairs.* 139: 279–295.

Peterson, J. E. (1978). *Oman in the Twentieth Century: Political Foundations of an Emerging State.* London: Croom Helm.

Peterson, J. E. (1986). *Defending Arabia.* London: Croom Helm.

Peterson, J. E. (1987). "Oman's Odyssey: From Imamate to Sultanate." In *Oman: Economic, Social and Strategic Developments.* B. R. Pridham, ed. London: Croom Helm.

Peterson, J. E. (1988). *The Arab Gulf States: Steps toward Political Participation.* New York: Praeger.

Peterson, J. E. (2004). "Oman: Change and Development." *Middle East Policy* XI: 125–137.

Peyton, W. D. (1983). *Old Oman.* London: Stacey International. Distributed in the United States, and Canada by Humanities Press.

Phillips, W. (1966). *Unknown Oman.* London: Longman.

Phillips, W. (1967). *Oman: A History.* Beirut, Lebanon: Librairie du Liban.

Pillai, K. R. (1997). *Indian Foreign Policy in the 1990's.* New Delhi, India: Radiant Publishers.

Pomeroy, C. A., and Royal Air Force Ornithological Society. (1980). *Report on the RAFOS Masirah Island Expedition, 22nd October–26th November 1979.* St. Mawgan, United Kingdom: Royal Air Force.

Porter, J. D., ed. (1982). *Oman and the Persian Gulf, 1835–1949.* Salisbury, NC: Documentary Publications.

Pradhan, B. (1999). "Indo-Omani Relations: Political, Security and Socio-Cultural Dimensions." In *India and Oman: History, State, Economy and Foreign Policy.* E. A. K. Pasha, ed. New Delhi, India: Gyan Sagar Publications.

Price, D. L., and Institute for the Study of Conflict. (1975). *Oman: Insurgency and Development.* London: Institute for the Study of Conflict.

Pridham, B. R. (1986). "Oman: Change or Continuity." In *Arabia and the Gulf: From Traditional Society to Modern States.* I. R. Netton, ed. London: Croom Helm.

Pridham, B. R. (1987). *Oman: Economic, Social and Strategic Developments.* London: Croom Helm.

Qaboos bin Said. (1991). *The Speeches of H.M. Sultan Qaboos bin Said, 1970–1990.* Muscat, Oman: Ministry of Information.

Quandt, W. B. (1981). *Saudi Arabia in the 1980's: Foreign Policy, Security, and Oil.* Washington, DC: The Brookings Institution.

Ram, H. (1995). "Oman." In *Middle East Contemporary Survey.* Avi Ayalon, ed. Boulder, CO: Westview Press.

Ramazani, R. K. (1972). *The Persian Gulf: Iran's Role.* Charlottesville, VA: University Press of Virginia.

Ramazani, R. K. (1975). *Iran's Foreign Policy, 1941–1973: A Study of Foreign Policy in Modernizing Nations.* Charlottesville, VA: University Press of Virginia.

Ramazani, R. K. (1979). *The Persian Gulf and the Strait of Hormuz*. Alphen aan den Rijn, The Netherlands: Sijthoff & Noordhoff International Publishers.

Ramazani, R. K. (1986). *Revolutionary Iran: Challenge and Response in the Middle East*. Baltimore, MD: Johns Hopkins University Press.

Ramazani, R. K. (1990). *Iran's Revolution: The Search for Consensus*. Bloomington, IN: Indiana University Press in association with the Middle East Institute.

Ramazani, R. K. (1998). "The Emerging Arab-Iranian Rapprochement: Towards an Integrated U.S. Policy in the Middle East." *Middle East Policy* 6: 45–62.

Ramazani, R. K., and J. A. Kechichian (1988). *The Gulf Cooperation Council: Record and Analysis*. Charlottesville, VA: University Press of Virginia.

Rentz, G. (1972). "Wahhabism and Saudi Arabia." In *The Arabian Peninsula: Society And Politics*. D. Hopwood, ed. Totowa, NJ: Rowman and Littlefield.

Rentz, G., and Great Britain Foreign Office Research Department. (1997). *Oman and the South-Eastern Shore of Arabia*. Reading, United Kingdom: Ithaca Press.

Richardson, C. (2001). *Masirah: Tales from a Desert Island*. Edinburgh, United Kingdom: Pentland Press.

Rigsbee II, W. L. (1990). "American Foreign Policy toward the Sultanate of Oman: 1977–1987." In *Graduate Education and Research*. Cincinnati, OH: University of Cincinnati.

Riphenburg, C. J. (1998). *Oman: Political Development in a Changing World*. Westport, CT: Praeger.

Risso, P. (1986). *Oman and Muscat: An Early Modern History*. London: Croom Helm.

Roshandel, J. (2002). "On The Persian Gulf Islands: An Iranian Perspective." In *Security in the Persian Gulf: Origins, Obstacles and the Search for Consensus*. G. Sick and L. G. Potter, ed. New York: Palgrave.

Safran, N. (1985). *Saudi Arabia: The Ceaseless Quest for Security*. Cambridge, MA: Harvard University Press.

Sahwell, A. (1956). "The Buraimi Dispute." *The Islamic Review* 44: 13–17.

Searle, P. (1979). *Dawn over Oman*. London: Allen & Unwin.

Shepherd, A. (1961). *Arabian Adventure*. London: Collins.

Shichor, Y. (1979). *The Middle East in China's Foreign Policy, 1949–1977*. Cambridge, United Kingdom: Cambridge University Press.

Sick, G. (1996). "The United States and Iran: Truth and Consequences." *Contention* 5: 59–78.

Sick, G. (2003). "Iran: Confronting Terrorism." *The Washington Quarterly* 26: 1–16.

Sick, G., and L. G. Potter (1997). *The Persian Gulf at the Millennium: Essays in Politics, Economy, Security, and Religion*. Basingstoke, United Kingdom: Macmillan.

Sick, G., and L. G. Potter (2002). *Security in the Persian Gulf: Origins, Obstacles and the Search for Consensus*. New York: Palgrave.

Sindelar, H. R., J. E. Peterson, et al. (1988). *Crosscurrents in the Gulf: Arab Regional and Global Interests*. London: Routledge.

Skeet, I. (1974). *Muscat and Oman, the End of an Era*. London: Faber.

Skeet, I. (1985). *Oman Before 1970: The End of an Era*. London: Faber and Faber.

Skeet, I. (1992). *Oman: Politics and Development*. Basingstoke, United Kingdom: Macmillan.

Smiley, D. (1960). "Muscat and Oman." *Journal of the Royal United Service Institution* 108: 29–47.

Smiley, D., and P. Kemp (1975). *Arabian Assignment*. London: Leo Cooper.

St. Albans, S. M. A. B. (1980). *Where Time Stood Still: A Portrait of Oman*. London: Quartet Books.

Stouthamer, P., Shell Markets (Middle East) Ltd., et al. (1971). *Sultanate of Oman.* Doha, Qatar: Shell Markets (Middle East) Ltd.

Stratfor.com. (2 May 2002). "Oman Statement Blow to U.S. Plans for Iraq." http://www.stratfor.com.

Thomas, B. (1931). *Alarms and Excursions in Arabia.* London: G. Allen & Unwin Ltd.

Thomas, B. (1938). *Arab Rule under the Al Bu Sa'id Dynasty of Oman, 1741–1937.* London: H. Milford.

Thwaites, P., and S. Sloane (1995). *Muscat Command.* Barnsley, United Kingdom: Pen and Sword Books Ltd.

Timpe, L. G. (1991). *British Foreign Policy toward the Sultanate of Muscat and Oman: 1954–1959.* Doctoral diss., University of Exeter.

Townsend, J. (1977). *Oman: The Making of a Modern State.* London: Croom Helm.

Tripp, C. (2002). "The Foreign Policy of Iraq." In *The Foreign Policies of the Middle East States.* A. Ehteshami and R. Hinnebusch, eds. Boulder, CO: Lynne Rienner.

Vine, P. (1995). *The Heritage of Oman.* London: Immel.

Ward, P. (1987). *Travels in Oman: On the Track of the Early Explorers.* Cambridge, United Kingdom: Oleander Press.

Watson, D. R., and Cambridge Renaissance Oman Expedition. (1990). *Cambridge Renaissance Oman Expedition Report.* Cambridge: Cambridge Renaissance Oman Expedition.

Wellsted, J. R. (1838). *Travels in Arabia.* London: J. Murray.

Wikan, U. (1982). *Behind the Veil in Arabia: Women in Oman.* Baltimore, MD: Johns Hopkins University Press.

Wilkinson, J. C. (1972). "The Origins of the Omani State." In *The Arabian Peninsula: Society and Politics.* D. Hopwood, ed. Totowa, NJ: Rowman and Littlefield.

Wilkinson, J. C. (1977). *Water and Tribal Settlement in Southeast Arabia: A Study of the Aflaaj of Oman.* Oxford, United Kingdom: Clarendon Press.

Wilkinson, J. C. (1987). *The Imamate Tradition of Oman.* Cambridge, United Kingdom: Cambridge University Press.

Wingate, Sir R.E.L. (1959). *Not in the Limelight.* London: Hutchison.

Yodfat, A. (1975). "The USSR and the Rebellion in Dhofar." *South Africa International* 6: 21–27.

Yodfat, A. (1983). *The Soviet Union and the Arabian Peninsula: Soviet Policy towards the Persian Gulf and Arabia.* London: St. Martin's Press.

Yodfat, A. Y. (1984). *The Soviet Union and Revolutionary Iran.* London: Croom Helm.

Zahlan, R. S. (1998). *The Making of the Modern Gulf States: Kuwait, Bahrain, Qatar, the United Arab Emirates and Oman.* Reading, United Kingdom: Ithaca Press.

Index

About the Author

MAJID AL-KHALILI is a lecturer in strategic studies and the modern Middle East in the International Relations Department of Florida International University.